A CULTURAL HISTORY OF
CHILDHOOD AND FAMILY

VOLUME 2

A Cultural History of Childhood and Family

General Editors: Elizabeth Foyster and James Marten

Volume 1

A Cultural History of Childhood and Family in Antiquity
Edited by Mary Harlow and Ray Laurence

Volume 2

A Cultural History of Childhood and Family in the Middle Ages
Edited by Louise J. Wilkinson

Volume 3

A Cultural History of Childhood and Family in the Early Modern Age
Edited by Sandra Cavallo and Silvia Evangelisti

Volume 4

A Cultural History of Childhood and Family in the Age of Enlightenment
Edited by Elizabeth Foyster and James Marten

Volume 5

A Cultural History of Childhood and Family in the Age of Empire
Edited by Colin Heywood

Volume 6

A Cultural History of Childhood and Family in the Modern Age
Edited by Joseph M. Hawes and N. Ray Hiner

A CULTURAL HISTORY OF
CHILDHOOD AND FAMILY

IN THE
MIDDLE AGES

Edited by Louise J. Wilkinson

BLOOMSBURY

LONDON · NEW DELHI · NEW YORK · SYDNEY

Bloomsbury Academic

An imprint of Bloomsbury Publishing Plc

50 Bedford Square	1385 Broadway
London	New York
WC1B 3DP	NY 10018
UK	USA

www.bloomsbury.com

Hardback edition first published in 2010 by Berg Publishers, an imprint of
Bloomsbury Academic
Paperback edition first published by Bloomsbury Academic 2014

British Library Cataloguing-in-Publication Data
A catalogue record for this book is available from the British Library.

ISBN: HB: 978-1-84788-795-5
PB: 978-1-4725-5475-8
HB Set: 978-1-84520-826-4
PB Set: 978-1-4725-5474-1

Library of Congress Cataloging-in-Publication Data
A catalog record for this book is available from the Library of Congress.

Typeset by Apex CoVantage, LLC, Madison, WI, USA
Printed and bound in Great Britain

CONTENTS

     Valerie L. Garver

9   Health and Science   161
     William F. MacLehose

10   World Contexts   179
     Carol Bargeron

     NOTES   197

     BIBLIOGRAPHY   211

     CONTRIBUTORS   233

     INDEX   237

ILLUSTRATIONS

GENERAL EDITORS' PREFACE

The literature on the histories of children and the family has reached a critical mass. The proliferation of encyclopedia, conferences, and professional associations reflects the vitality of these closely related but independent fields. The two subjects are naturally linked; Western conceptions of the family have virtually always included children, and children and youth are irrevocably shaped by their time growing up in families.

A Cultural History of Childhood and Family aims to bring order to these sometimes disparate histories and historiographical traditions with original material written especially for these volumes. More than six dozen editors and authors from five continents and thirteen countries were commissioned to take a comprehensive look at the subject from a Western perspective with more than casual glances at the world beyond. Based on deep readings of the secondary literature and on representative primary sources, each of the chapters is an original work of synthesis and interpretation.

It is our hope that imposing a standard table of contents on a project covering literally thousands of years and hundreds of ethnicities, religious faiths, and communities will help us find otherwise hidden patterns and rich contrasts in the experiences of children and families and in humankind's attitudes about them. There is inevitably a bit of overlap; issues related to children and the family do not form and develop according to convenient beginning and ending dates. But there is also a variety of viewpoints, even on similar topics. Indeed, as general editors we embrace the divergence of interpretations, emphases, and even writing and organizational styles that emerge from these five dozen chapters. Some of the diversity follows naturally from the vastly different conditions facing children and their families in different eras, while in other cases it is inspired by the authors' expertise and personal approaches to the field.

There have always been many childhoods and many families in the West. The purpose of these volumes is not only to look at the constructions of childhood and the family, particularly as they reflect evolving ethnic, gender, religious, national, and class assumptions, but also the lived experiences of children and of the families in which they spend so much of their lives. The symbiotic relationship between child and parent, between brother and sister, and between the individual and the family to which he or she belongs is reflected in the intertwined historical literature on children and families. By studying both, we can learn more about each.

Elizabeth Foyster
Clare College, University of Cambridge

James Marten
Marquette University

Introduction

LOUISE J. WILKINSON

The Middle Ages (800–1400) were rich and vibrant centuries in the history of European culture, society, and intellectual thought. Emerging state powers, the growing influence of the Christian Church, demographic change, and economic expansion and contraction all made an impact upon children and family life. Movements for church reform brought the spiritual and moral concerns of both the clergy and the laity into sharper focus, profoundly shaping attitudes toward gender and sexuality, and how these might be applied to family roles. The growth of trade, the process of urbanization, and the spread of literacy and learning all transformed the upbringings of medieval boys and girls in manifest ways. Yet nor all modern writers readily acknowledge that such a thing as childhood existed in the Middle Ages. In his classic study, *Centuries of Childhood*, the French historian Philippe Ariès offered a stark view of the lives of medieval children. It was his belief that medieval men and women not only looked upon, but also treated, their offspring as miniature adults. There was no understanding of childhood as a separate and special stage of human existence—a state of affairs that rendered medieval families markedly different in outlook from modern families. In Ariès's words,

> In medieval society, the idea of childhood did not exist; this is not to suggest that children were neglected, forsaken, or despised. The idea of childhood is not to be confused with affection for children: it corresponds to an awareness of the particular nature of childhood, that particular

nature which distinguishes the child from the adult, even the young adult. In medieval society, this awareness was lacking.[1]

In reaching his conclusion, Ariès was profoundly influenced by the representation of children in medieval art. Twelfth-century artists were, according to Ariès, unable to portray children as children, but presented their subjects instead as small-scale adults, shorn of any youthful characteristics or expressions. Artists did this not because they possessed insufficient skills, talents, or technical knowledge to render them capable of drawing children, but because they simply did not regard children as children. It was only from the thirteenth century onward that children were depicted in forms that distinguished them from adults. Angels were painted, sculpted, or carved with plump, soft, and womanly countenances to convey their youth. The infant Jesus was increasingly portrayed with delicate features, in warm, playful scenes with his mother, the Virgin Mary, while other members of the Holy Family were pictured as infants with their parents. Yet, even in the thirteenth and fourteenth centuries, there was still no "lay iconography" of childhood—no artistic images of living, earthly children; this would have to wait until the fifteenth and sixteenth centuries.[2]

Ariès uncovered little to support the existence of childhood in other areas of medieval life. In infancy, once babies' swaddling clothes were removed, children's dress mirrored that of their parents, apparently making no concession to youthful age. Games and pastimes, such as playing with a hoop, which were regarded in the modern era as essentially childish in nature, entertained children and adults alike in Western Europe during the Middle Ages.[3] But what lay behind this cultural neglect of childhood? High rates of infant mortality conditioned parents against forming strong bonds of attachment toward their children: infants were "too fragile" and consequently "did not count" until they could participate in adult life.[4] Children, their existence, and their welfare did not occupy a place at the center of the lives of medieval families. They might be raised apart from their parents in other households or apprenticed elsewhere, sent into domestic service from a young age, or educated in schools.[5] For Ariès, sentimentalized notions of childhood and the family were products of the modern world. For Ariès, any attempt to write a cultural history of childhood and the family in the Middle Ages would have been pointless, and the title of this volume an inherent contradiction in terms.

CONSTRUCTING A CASE FOR MEDIEVAL CHILDHOOD

It is now nearly half a century since Ariès wrote his seminal work. During the last fifty years, his thesis has been challenged by a growing number of authors who have questioned both his use of evidence and his conclusions. Scholars such as Danièle Alexandre-Bidon, Albrecht Classen, Sally Crawford, Ronald Finucane, Barbara Hanawalt, Colin Heywood, Didier Lett, Nicholas Orme, Pierre Riché, James Schultz, and Shulamith Shahar have all roundly rejected Ariès's hypothesis as fundamentally flawed: medieval people, from the poorest peasants to the wealthiest nobles, knew what childhood was, and they cared for and cherished their offspring.[6] The important body of research undertaken by these authors has revealed for the first time the richness and variety of sources that illuminate the lives of medieval children and the expectations that surrounded them. In her pioneering study, *Childhood in the Middle Ages*, for example, Shahar drew upon information extracted from chronicles, religious literature (saints' lives, sermons, and pastoral manuals), guild and apprentice-ship records, and a wealth of other legal and administrative documents. The material she collected confidently led her to assert that "a concept of child-hood" did indeed exist at all social levels throughout medieval Europe "and that parents invested both material and emotional resources in their offspring."[7] Shahar criticized Ariès, on the one hand, for failing to recognize the impor-tance of biological considerations, including parental nurture, in shaping the early development of infants, and, on the other hand, for neglecting to make allowance for the wider cultural context in which experiences of childhood were constructed. Legislators and parish priests, as well as the authors of medical texts on babies and children, promoted and disseminated a range of educational theories on early child care and later pediatric development in the medieval West. These reflected, or else were followed or adapted by communi-ties in accordance with, local custom and tradition.

Not all historians, though, have been so ready to acknowledge the impact of contemporary culture upon medieval childhood. The information on child rearing practices, children's activities, and their discovery of the world around them, which Hanawalt gleaned from a study of late medieval English coroners' inquests, left her deeply impressed by the "similarity of child development in the Middle Ages and in modern observations."[8] The children who peopled Hanawalt's survey, like their modern counterparts, displayed a marked propen-sity for accidents that involved play after the age of one. The circumstances in which these happened reflected the toddlers' newfound mobility, their curiosity about their surroundings, and their developing motor skills. For Hanawalt, this indicated "a strong biological basis for child development as opposed to decisive cultural influences;" the nature of child rearing might differ across historical periods, but medieval and modern parents still met "their children's basic biological and psychological needs and thus the early years of maturation were similar."[9]

Admittedly, it remains frustratingly difficult to chart the childhoods of the mass of the European population in the Middle Ages. A literate education remained the preserve of the elite throughout the period under consideration here, and the passage of time has considerably eroded the range of evidence that has survived to the present day. Autobiographical writings in the form of personal diaries, journals, and memoirs, like those that are so useful for studying early modern societies, are either altogether lacking or extremely rare. The quality, as well as the quantity, of the documentary evidence varies considerably across the centuries between 800 and 1400. This situation is due, in part at least, to changing levels of literacy and learning over time, and changing perceptions of the value attached to the written word as a means of preserving memory and as a tool of record. The medieval material that has been preserved in the archives of governments, institutions, and well-to-do families can be fraught with interpretational pitfalls, no matter when or where it was produced. In the case of the children of the English peasantry, it is important to ask how accurate a picture of their daily lives can be re-created by looking at accidental deaths, which were, by their very nature, unusual events. Despite this, the sources for charting medieval childhood are far more plentiful and sophisticated than Ariès realized. So far has scholarly opinion now swung away from that of Ariès that the debate stimulated by his research recently spawned a chapter on "The Medieval Child: An Unknown Phenomenon?" in a collection of essays on popular misconceptions about the Middle Ages.[10] In the words of Orme, a leading English authority on medieval childhood, "it cannot be over-emphasised that there is nothing to be said for Ariès's view of childhood in the middle ages."[11]

TOWARD A CULTURAL HISTORY OF CHILDHOOD AND FAMILY IN THE MIDDLE AGES

The essays in this volume celebrate the ideals and realities of medieval childhood and how they interacted with family life between 800 and 1400 in the West—that is, in the European kingdoms and communities where Christianity held sway and where (Catholic) Church-sponsored Latin learning predominated. The main territories under consideration include the British Isles, France, Germany and its environs, the Low Countries, Italy, and the Iberian Peninsula (modern Portugal and Spain). Reference will also be made to religious and ethnic minority groups, such as Jews, and to the inhabitants of the Muslim-ruled regions of Iberia. Far from supporting notions of medieval indifference toward children, the chapters here recognize that there was a keen awareness among contemporaries that when a child was born it entered upon a distinctive phase of the human life cycle. This phase was noted by the compilers of medical treatises, and acknowledged in canon and secular law, as one that lasted from birth to puberty. It was characterized, on the one hand, by emotional and physical immaturity, and, on the other hand, by physical growth and mental development. Its presence is confirmed by the existence of a widely used vocabulary to describe children and childhood. When a thirteenth-century friar, Bartholomew the Englishman, compiled his encyclopedia, *On the Properties of Things*, he described an order of life which recalled that outlined by an earlier writer, Isidore, bishop of Seville (d. 636). Birth was followed by a period of infancy (*infantia*) until the age of seven and then progressed through childhood (*pueritia*) until the age of fourteen, the beginning of adolescence. In Latin texts, the term *infans*, *puer* (masculine), or *puella* (feminine) might denote a child, while a son and a daughter were designated *filius* and *filia*. Comparable terms existed in the vernacular. In Middle High German, for example, *daz kint* stood for child. The word *child* in modern English derives from the Old English *cild*, *childhood* from *cildhad*, and *childish* from *cildisc*. In Christian monastic literature, children were often associated with the qualities of gentleness, humility, innocence, and vulnerability.

Children occupied a position at the heart of medieval families. After all, in the words of Georges Duby, "Fertile marriage was the bedrock of social order."[12] Despite high rates of mortality among babies and young children—infants accounted for perhaps forty-five percent of all burials excavated at one late Anglo-Saxon cemetery in the English town of Norwich—parents, friends, and neighbors often expressed joy at the safe delivery of a new child.[13] Careful consideration was given to a child's personal name. Biblical and saints' names, which might evoke the protection and divine intervention of a child's heavenly namesake, enjoyed a measure of popularity. Alternatively, the choice of given name might also reflect a child's membership of a particular family group. Spiritual relationships with godparents were also acknowledged. In France, from the eleventh century onward, a noble child's first name often recalled that of a local lord or lady, or the child's connection with a blood relation.

The strength of feeling that medieval parents displayed toward their offspring was mirrored in the romance literature of the period. *Poor Henry*, a German verse novella by Hartmann von Aue, describes a moving scene where a peasant woman begs her young daughter not to commit suicide. Even the stark records of medieval criminal proceedings contain insightful material on family relationships. The relative rarity of reported cases of infanticide dealt with by medieval courts that involved children over the age of one does not necessarily

mean that this was simply an easy crime to conceal. It might be indicative instead of local communities that cared for their offspring. When children died
in suspicious circumstances, their deaths were, after all, commonly attributed
to the mental instability of a murdering parent, a situation that reflected the
dreadful and peculiarly shocking nature of this crime in contemporary eyes.
Although the suspected murders of newborn babies were more commonly
reported than those of older children, German and Italian legal documents reveal that the perpetrators were often mothers who lived in extreme poverty or
who had suffered the social stigma of conceiving children outside wedlock—
that is, women who lived on the margins of society. Medical manuals and
preachers' handbooks went to great lengths to warn parents of the potential
accidents that might befall babies in unstable or poorly constructed cribs, and
of the hazards that awaited crawling infants and toddlers in and around the
home. New parents needed to protect their young from the perils of falling into
ditches, pits, streams, and wells; from burning themselves on household fires;
and from encounters with aggressive animals and poisonous plants. Clerical
authors urged adults to be vigilant for the safety of babies and children, not
disinterested and emotionally detached. English coroners' inquests suggest
not only that parents were reluctant to leave their offspring at home alone, but
also that other members of rural communities might be critical, and openly
disapprove, of those who did so. Medieval parents—especially mothers—were
often the first people to find a dead or badly injured child. Like their modern
counterparts, they were also prepared, without a moment's hesitation, to risk
their own lives to rescue their offspring from a burning building, like Alice, the
wife of John Trivaler, who was overcome with smoke when she reentered her
blazing shop to rescue her trapped son.[14]

While coroners' records yield evidence of parental concern for the well-
being of children, a wealth of stories in religious works demonstrate more
strongly the feelings of tenderness and nostalgia—the sentimentalization—
attached to the idea of childhood in Western Europe during the Middle Ages.
Thousands of miracle stories survive from this period, many preserved in records compiled to support the canonization of individuals. A detailed analysis
of eight European miracle collections, dating from the twelfth to fifteenth centuries, was conducted by Finucane in the 1990s and yielded no fewer than six
hundred stories centered on childbirth or recovery from childhood accidents
and illnesses. Within these narratives, the assistance of the saint in question
had typically been sought through a visit to his or her shrine, by touching relics
associated with that saint, or through the medium of prayer. Even if it is impossible to ignore the moral tone and edifying purpose of such texts, and their

desire to celebrate the saint's holiness, they betray an underlying assumption that parents experienced emotionally charged relationships with their offspring and recognized childhood as a special stage in life. Miracle stories of saintly intervention to secure the safe delivery of mother and child during the travails of childbirth provide surprising detail about the care of newborn infants and how common it was for poor mothers to nurse their own children. One French miracle story vividly recalls the violent grief of a mother named Ersand, who accidentally smothered her baby, Bertula, when she fell into a deep sleep while breast-feeding one night. A distraught Ersand repeatedly attempted to make her dead baby suckle, then put her down and became so hysterical that she had to be physically restrained. After Ersand and the child's grandmother appealed to Saint Edmund, Bertula was miraculously returned to life, whereupon her relieved kin took her gratefully on a pilgrimage to the saint's shrine at Pontigny. Although, in this instance, the maternal bond was particularly strong, similar stories describe the reluctance of fathers to acquiesce to the fates of extremely sick or severely injured children. Indeed, fathers from all walks of life are vividly described praying for the recovery of their sons and daughters, losing their self-control, and succumbing to grief when faced with a stricken child.[15]

MEDIEVAL IDEAS ABOUT THE FAMILY

Many children were raised from birth within a family environment in medieval Europe—that is, within a domestic establishment presided over by their parents or other close kin. Elite children might be sent away to religious houses or receive their education in the homes of other nobles or high-ranking churchmen. At lower social levels, some children and adolescents found employment or learned a craft in urban and rural households. Although there were single men and women in medieval society, marriage was the social norm throughout much of Europe, and it formed the basis for family organization. So influential a concept was the family that "metaphors of family played an important part in representing notions of religious and political solidarity" throughout the period.[16]

A complex framework of ideas fed into perceptions of family structures in the medieval West. Various interlinked and overlapping traditions—those transmitted from the Roman Empire; those of the Germanic peoples who established barbarian successor states within the former imperial territories during the fifth and sixth centuries; and those of the Christian Church, which preserved much Roman heritage—informed notions of what constituted a family. Classical Roman law regarded the family (*familia*) as a group of people or property under the rule of a father figure (*paterfamilias*) or head of household, and not necessarily as a residential unit descended from the father. Patriarchal ideas also permeated the clan or kinship networks of Germanic societies, where the father's right to discipline his offspring was upheld within the earliest law codes and where women typically passed from the control of their fathers into that of their husbands on marriage. Early tribal groups were divided into *Sippen*—clans or kindreds descended from a common forefather—which, in their turn, comprised numerous individual households dominated by the authority that the father enjoyed over his wife, offspring, and slaves.[17] Within and alongside marriage customs in these societies, practices such as concubinage, polygyny, and marriage between kin (incest) persisted, before eventually succumbing to the Christian Church's attempts to govern behavior in line with its views on morality and sexuality.

Christian teaching exerted a profound influence on ideas about the composition of the family, especially as the process of Christian conversion spread among distant peoples and the church clarified its position on what legitimized a sexual union between a man and a woman. By the ninth century, there was a growing, if not yet quite universal, acceptance among royal and aristocratic families of the church's requirements that all Christian marriages should be indissoluble, exogamous (between couples who were not too closely related to one another), and monogamous. Ireland and Iceland, two regions in the most remote corners of Christendom over which the Roman Church came to extend its influence relatively late, were among the exceptions where older customs persisted for longer. Polygyny endured among the north German Swedes into the eleventh century, according to a contemporary author, Adam of Bremen. It was also practiced within parts of the Iberian Peninsula that succumbed to Arab invasion in the early eighth century. Here, elite Muslims lived in sizeable family groups, where the male head enjoyed unquestioned authority over his many wives and their children, and his concubines, who tended to be women of lesser status or slaves, and their offspring.[18]

David Herlihy, a historian who made an extensive study of medieval households, identified two key developments in the early Middle Ages that facilitated the emergence of broadly similar units of domestic organization across all levels of Christian society. First, settlements within the later Roman Empire and early barbarian kingdoms were based upon peasant family farms, where serfs lived and cultivated the land in partnership with their close kin. These replaced and superseded older slave-based forms of agriculture favored by Roman landlords. Second, a growing acceptance of the church's dual insistence upon exogamy and monogamy was vitally important. The observance of exogamy made it easier for men of relatively limited means and influence to find wives, while the practice of monogamy also contributed to the "fairer distribution [of women] across social classes" by limiting the number of brides taken by members of the elite.[19] Non-Christian minority groups, like Jews, adopted the Christian practice of monogamy, even if Judaic law did not expressly prohibit polygyny. Furthermore, although Jewish communities tended to favor endogamy as a means of keeping property within the family, Jews who lived in regions such as Germany were prepared to marry beyond their kin.[20] This all helped to ensure that life within many Christian and Jewish households between 800 and 1400 centered on married couples and their children, be it within a nuclear family (husband, wife, and unmarried children) or extended family (wider kin) setting.

SEXUAL HIERARCHIES WITHIN MEDIEVAL FAMILIES

The structures of medieval families, and contemporary perceptions of the different roles within them, were firmly underpinned by cultural attitudes toward male and female sexuality. As a predominantly Christian society, medieval Europe turned to the Bible and the works of patristic writers for moral guidance, teaching that imposed a strictly regulated sexual hierarchy upon married couples and their offspring. Men, as the descendants of Adam, enjoyed a position of mastery and superiority over their wives. Women, as the heiresses of Eve—who had been made out of the rib of Adam and who had led Adam into temptation, resulting in the couple's expulsion from the Garden of Eden— were regarded by the church as fallible, inferior beings who ought to be subject to strict male control, discipline, and guidance. The literature and sermons that medieval churchmen directed toward their parishioners often echoed the sentiments of Saint Paul, who exhorted wives to submit themselves to their husbands: "For the husband is the head of the wife as Christ is the head of the church."[21] Sensitive to the corrupting influence of human sexuality upon the soul—the act of intercourse threatened its purity, as did the "polluting" influence of Eve's female descendants—Saint Paul laid down that, while virginity was an ideal state in which to live, "marriage was an acceptable second best" as a means of governing sexual activity, governing women, and providing for the procreation of children.[22]

Biological notions of gender difference inherited from the Greco-Roman world gave added weight to Christian sexual stereotypes. Ancient schools of medical thought offered biological explanations for sexual inequality that upheld notions of male mental and physical superiority, and female incapacity and weakness. The ideas of Aristotle, a Greek philosopher who died in or

FIGURE 0.1: *The creation and fall of Adam and Eve.* The Moutier-Grandval Bible, Tours (France), circa 834–843. © The British Library Board (BL Add. MS. 10546, f. 5v).

around 322 B.C.E., and Galen, a Greek physician who was born in or around 129 C.E., were particularly influential, and were adopted and adapted by medical writers throughout the Middle Ages. Aristotelian thought provided scientific evidence for male dominance. In nature, Aristotle observed, the males of different species were typically stronger, more active, and more highly developed than females, who were characterized by passivity. Male superiority was reflected in the human reproductive process. Unlike men, women did not provide seed; they simply provided material for shaping during procreation. It was, therefore, the male semen that was the vital component in the conception of offspring. Galen's ideas also upheld notions of male dominance and female inferiority. His work was based on Hippocratic theory, which divided the world into the four elements of fire (hot and dry), air (hot and wet), earth (cold and dry), and water (cold and wet). Men were hotter and drier, and therefore physically stronger and psychologically more superior, than colder, moister women. The genital organs of the more perfect male developed on the outside of his body when the fetus was in the womb, but those of the less perfect female were inverted and developed on the inside of her body. Unlike Aristotle, Galen held that men and women both produced seed and that sexual pleasure by a woman was necessary for its production. Medieval clerical authors assimilated this learning. Masculinity was believed to embody morality, power, rationality, and strength, while femininity embodied carnality, inconstancy, and both physical and moral weakness. To be a man was to be associated with the spiritual world, which enjoyed dominance over the physical and which, therefore, ought to govern soft and carnal womankind. Isidore of Seville's argument that women should submit to male governance due to their inherent spiritual fickleness enjoyed continued currency with later medieval authors. Excluded from government office and subject to their fathers or husbands, medieval women were expected to focus their lives on their homes and families.[23]

Attitudes toward gender roles within the family did not remain constant and fixed throughout the Middle Ages. Regional customs modified church teaching, just as successive movements for church reform gave extra prominence to particular Christian practices. From the eleventh century onward, for example, reformers attempted to bring the moral and spiritual observances of both clergy and laity more firmly in line with Christian principles to a far greater degree than ever before. The promotion of clerical celibacy as an ideal gave added impetus to the case for women's subordination to men. Before this time, celibacy had been expected only of monks and nuns in religious houses. Henceforth, there was a growing expectation that churchmen be required to renounce all sexual relationships, including those founded on marriage, as a prerequisite for ordination. The canons of the First and Second Lateran Councils (1123 and 1139) starkly forbade clerical marriage and refused to recognize the partners and children of married priests or accord them legal protection. The growing emphasis on celibacy as an ideal sexual state also heightened

awareness of the dangers posed to society by ungoverned and sexually tempt-
ing women. Extramarital sex was considered a sin, no matter the circumstances
in which it took place; sex should take place only within marriage and then
for the procreation of children rather than for personal pleasure. In around
1140, Gratian's *Decretum,* a masterful collection of canon law, reiterated the
case for wifely obedience and subjection. Church courts, which regulated the
moral and spiritual lives of the laity, acknowledged the rights of husbands to
chastise and discipline errant wives. Husbands might already have possessed
an element of practical advantage here, especially among the aristocracy,
where brides were often their husbands' juniors by at least several years. The
age difference between husband and wife—and, in particular, the latter's relative immaturity and inexperience—reinforced patriarchal structures of authority within marriage.[24]

However, developments in religious thought between the eleventh and thirteenth centuries offered wives and daughters more active, less passive, and, indeed, more positive roles. The evolution of an ecclesiastical model, whereby the
church clarified its definition of what constituted a full and legitimate marriage,
and gradually moved to assert its right to oversee such unions, deeply affected
the lives of men, women, and children from all social backgrounds. The application of canon law through preaching and the operation of the ecclesiastical
courts provided vigorous support for the notion that marriage should be based
on the mutual consent of both parties concerned, solemnized by a priest, and
witnessed in public. Although the right to give consent was not necessarily the
same as the right to exercise freedom of choice over the selection of a future
partner, the emphasis on consent potentially made it easier, in theory at least,
for young people to reject matches forced upon them by their parents or other
interested parties. On the reverse side of the coin, marriages conducted in public
made it harder for disaffected husbands to discard or repudiate unwanted wives.
Contracting a valid marriage meant that any resulting offspring would be regarded as legitimate, with full rights to succeed to parental property at law.[25]

The medieval church also encouraged couples to regard marriage as a mutually affectionate partnership, even if it was not necessarily one of equals.
The writers of pastoral manuals, such as Robert Grosseteste (d. 1253), bishop
of Lincoln, celebrated marriage as a source of mutual comfort, companion-
ship, and joy. In underlining the reciprocity of the conjugal debt, Grosseteste
advised couples to make allowance for one another's sexual appetites. Other
authors, such as the early thirteenth-century cleric Thomas of Chobham, sub-
dean of Salisbury, readily acknowledged that wives might exercise a benevolent
influence over their spouses, provided they did not diminish their husbands'

authority. According to Chobham, it was perfectly acceptable for wives to take advantage of their intimate personal relationships with their husbands to persuade their spouses to embrace higher standards of moral behavior. In encouraging their husbands to be generous and merciful to the less fortunate members of society, wives embraced a worthy outlet for womanly compassion.[26]

The Virgin Mary, the immaculate mother of Christ, provided churchmen with an extremely potent example of a woman who acted as a wise counselor and intercessor within a familial context. The Virgin was a tremendously popular figure of religious devotion throughout Western Europe during the Middle Ages, and her iconography evolved to reflect changes in religious thought, a growing interest in Christ's human origins, and a desire among the clergy and the laity to empathize with his experiences. The Virgin's position within the heavenly hierarchy rested upon the uniquely privileged relationship that she enjoyed with Christ as his mother, a relationship that allowed her to mediate with her son and channel his grace on the behalf of humankind. The Virgin was commonly imagined in twelfth- and thirteenth-century painting and sculpture as the queen of heaven and bride of Christ, a humble coruler, and a merciful and forgiving agent of redemption. Yet the elevation of the Virgin Mary's importance within the Holy Family and the widespread appeal of her cult—Cistercian abbeys were dedicated to her, and many religious houses that were not possessed their own Lady Chapels by the later Middle Ages—did not necessarily elevate the position of ordinary, earthly women so that it erased the consequences of Eve's sin. On the one hand, as Penny Schine Gold has argued, a great deal of care was taken in art and literature to convey the Virgin's singularity—how she possessed a unique blend of qualities and virtues that it was impossible for earthly women to match. The Virgin thus represented an impossible ideal, a message most forcefully conveyed by the emergence of the cult of the Immaculate Conception from the mid-eleventh century onward, which maintained that Mary had remained free from the stain of original sin at her own conception.[27] On the other hand, as Henrietta Leyser has pointed out, the image of the Virgin Mary was one that was extremely versatile. Individual churchmen encouraged women to emulate her key attributes and virtues, such as humility, obedience, and intercession, many of which reinforced the submissive role of women within the family.[28] The surviving correspondence between bishops and high medieval queens often betrays an expectation that women royal consorts should imitate the Virgin Mary by acting as informal mediators between their royal husbands and their husbands' subjects. By harnessing a religious ideal, the persuasive wife and mother was thus transformed within the context of her family and recognized as a channel for constructive, rather than

FIGURE 0.2: *The initial O showing the coronation of the Virgin*. Canticles, Hymns, and Passion of Christ, St. Augustine's Abbey, Canterbury, late thirteenth and early four-teenth centuries. With permission of the Master and Fellows of St. John's College, Cam-bridge (St. John's College, Cambridge, MS. K. 21, f. 82v).

destructive, political influence, provided she remained on good terms with her husband and provided he was prepared to listen to her.

FAMILY, SOCIETY, AND PROPERTY

Although Christian thought exerted a far-reaching influence over marriage and household formation in the Middle Ages, economic, political, and social con-cerns also had their part to play in sculpting experiences of childhood and family life. In the wake of the disturbances of the ninth and tenth centuries, the period between 1000 and the mid-fourteenth century witnessed tremendous demographic change. As William Chester Jordan observed, it is likely that the European continent's population more than doubled, rising from thirty-five million to eighty million. The kingdoms, principalities, and communes that now lie within modern France, Belgium, Holland, Germany, Italy, England, Portugal, and Spain saw significant growth. Of course, not all areas of Europe were populated to the same degree or witnessed the same levels of expansion. France's population grew from around five million in 1000 to between fifteen million and nineteen million in the mid-1300s, while that of Iberia possibly rose from seven million to nine million.[29] This invariably impacted upon the regional economies of Europe and thereby influenced the daily occupations and standards of living of their inhabitants. It contributed to the clearance of new lands so that they might be brought under cultivation, the widening of settlement patterns, the creation of new markets and fairs, and the development of more specialized forms of trade and manufacturing. Villages and towns—in the sense of heavily populated communities that supported craftsmen, artisans, and others who provided goods and services for the resident population— multiplied. A strong urban culture already existed in southern Europe, which was a legacy of the Roman Empire. Maritime trade, such as Venetian commerce with Constantinople, which centered on the Mediterranean, provided an important stimulus to urban renewal in northern Italy during the eleventh century. Towns were less numerous in northern Europe, but their numbers rose dramatically here, too. In 1100, for example, there were perhaps one hundred towns in the British Isles, but, by 1300, there were approximately seven hundred in England, fifty or so in Scotland, and eighty in Wales.[30]

Despite urban development and regeneration, the livelihoods of the vast majority of the European population remained based upon the land. Peasants were essentially small-scale cultivators who farmed their own holdings and/or the local lord's fields, depending on whether they were free men or serfs. Serfs were considered to be legally unfree and treated as the lord's chattels, although the nature and extent of their personal obligations toward their lords, in the sense of labor and other services, varied considerably from one place to another. Some twelfth-century serfs were the descendants of former slaves. Although slavery persisted in some parts of southern Europe, the number of slaves fell dramatically in northwestern Europe during the tenth and eleventh centuries, partially as a consequence of the church's opposition to the practice of enslaving Christians. The decline was also a result of the growing popularity of the freeing of existing slaves as a moral and charitable act, and the outcome of the Christianization of the outer fringes of Europe, which inevitably reduced the availability of potential slaves.[31]

The most powerful members of rural society were the lords, the lay and ecclesiastical aristocracies who possessed landed estates and whose wealth and privileges set them apart from those below them in society. The lay nobles of eleventh- and twelfth-century France—known variously as counts, viscounts, and dukes—for instance, accounted for no more than five percent of the total population, and formed military and political elites who fought on horseback. Their families amassed sufficient resources to build fortified residences (castles), purchase costly items, such as jewelry, and found or endow religious houses for the salvation of their souls. The exclusivity of their personal rank— and, more often than not, their distinguished ancestry—was acknowledged by contemporaries.[32] The levels of authority that they wielded over the lives of others varied from region to region, according to their enjoyment of royal favor and, sometimes associated with this, their tenure of governmental office, not to mention their wealth and possession of property.

The relationship between people and their property helped to shape perceptions of the family and of the status of its constituent members throughout the Middle Ages. Some historians, like Constance Bouchard, have persuasively argued that a preference for the descent of property through the male line already existed in the ninth and tenth centuries.[33] The years after 1000, however, witnessed a more marked, or at least a better documented, shift among local and regional elites from cognatic to agnatic kinship networks, whereby patrilineal ties—based on the male line of descent—gradually replaced an older emphasis on bilateral connections. This meant that many women, especially daughters, were apparently marginalized as inheritors of property in order to help preserve male wealth. Women, therefore, lost many earlier claims they had possessed, alongside their brothers, to a reasonable share of the patrimony. The situation that gave rise to a more readily discernible shift toward patrilineage as a basis for kinship structures grew, partially at least, out of a complex set of circumstances, whereby the warrior elite came to depend on their own landed estates for their livelihoods to a greater degree than before and sought to prevent their erosion by abandoning potentially damaging inheritance practices. In England, France, and Germany—societies where land tenure was often tied to a tenant or vassal's tenure of office or performance of military and/or other services to an overlord—"dynastic lineages" tended to prevail, whereby a single, usually male, heir received the lion's share of the patrimony or was recognized as the senior heir by his brothers. In the towns of northern Italy, on the other hand, kindreds came to be based upon "consortial lineages," whereby sons possessed equal claims to the patrimony by holding the property in question in common, thereby adopting a form of kindred organization that suited the commercial joint ventures of Italian merchants.[34]

It is important to acknowledge the enduring diversity, flexibility, and fluidity of medieval inheritance practices in general. "Consortial" and "dynastic" lineages both assigned women a secondary status in relation to their male kin. Yet the prevalence of these customs did not preclude the settlement of property on women for their maintenance when they married. Within the territories closest to the Mediterranean from the thirteenth century onward, the immediate kin of Italian brides-to-be were expected to provide ever-increasing sums of money as dowries, which were seen as essential capital for establishing new households. At the same time, though, the share of her husband's property that a wife might receive in widowhood began to be more strictly limited within communes like Genoa and Florence. Even so, the wealth—moveable or otherwise—that families bestowed upon their daughters and the enduring importance of elite marriage as a means of forging advantageous friendships and transferring rights, helped to ensure, in practice, that unions between couples touched upon the interests of third parties—parents, guardians, and lords. This explains to some extent why, despite the church's insistence upon free consent, arranged marriages, rather than marriages purely based upon love, were the norm. Indeed, Duby has gone so far as to suggest that a second, alternative, "profane" model of marriage existed in the twelfth century alongside the ecclesiastical model. This second model was followed by the royal French dynasty, the Capetians, whose marriages tended to be socially endogamous and whose unions forged alliances with other ruling houses. Royal and aristocratic marriages were too important for couples to be left to decide on their own.[35] There is certainly much to recommend the view that the lay aristocracies of medieval Europe regarded marriage as a vital tool in their diplomatic armory and recognized its potential as a source of wealth, prestige, and future heirs. Yet scholars such as Christopher Brooke, David Herlihy, and Connor McCarthy have questioned elements of Duby's thesis. They have suggested, quite reasonably, that rather than existing as a second model that competed with the church's ideal, the ruling dynasties and aristocracies simply attempted "to bend the Church's rules" to suit their own agendas.[36] In doing so, they embraced a set of attitudes that coexisted alongside the ecclesiastical model and that found legal expression in the form of secular jurisdiction over the accompanying property settlements.

Naturally, each couple's reasons for, and experiences of, marriage and family life in the Middle Ages were unique. As the following chapters in this volume demonstrate, they were invariably shaped by a large number of considerations, including character and personal inclination. Cultural expectations, religious practices, social pressures, and sheer practical necessity sometimes worked to make general trends discernible. After all, it was not just the marriages of the elite that were bound up with the transmission of property and rights. The ability of couples from all walks of life—from the lowliest peasant to the greatest noble—to establish, nurture, and sustain themselves, their children, and their households inevitably rested upon issues such as their access to income and property, and whether they were able to afford a suitable dwelling. By the latter half of the thirteenth century, for example, rising population led to growing competition for land and helped to create a proliferation of small holdings among the peasantry, the produce from which was barely capable of supporting a married couple, let alone their offspring. In fact, it is likely that many rural households in northwestern Europe no longer possessed sufficient lands to sustain themselves by the end of this century. But medieval peasants were not necessarily helpless in the face of changing economic conditions. Some took advantage of localized opportunities to earn a living by wage labor or modified existing agricultural practices by, for example, experimenting with new forms of fertilizer or turning from arable farming to animal husbandry. Nevertheless, manorial rentals and surveys reveal that a significant proportion of rural dwellers—the most poor and most physically weak—faced growing hardship in their daily battle for survival. During the Great Famine and agricultural crisis of 1315 to 1322, when a run of failed harvests and livestock murrains brought arable agriculture and pastoral farming to its knees, as many as ten to fifteen percent of the population of England, northern France, Germany, the Low Countries, Poland, and Scandinavia perished. A further, more dramatic downturn in population levels was caused by the Black Death of 1347 to 1350, during which between one-third and one-half of the population of Europe perished from bubonic and pneumonic plague.

Although, as eyewitness accounts testify, the plague was a horrifying experience for all those who lived through it—families were wiped out or suffered one or more deaths during the pestilence, and many settlements were left deserted—the reduction in population considerably eased the pressure on the land. This situation, combined with a severe labor shortage, helped to improve the general prosperity of the surviving peasantry, who were able to increase the size of their holdings and negotiate more generous wages from lords and other employers faced with a smaller pool of potential workers. These developments inevitably impacted upon family life, influencing marriage patterns and significantly improving the standards of living of many who belonged to the lowest social echelons. The successor epidemics of the late fourteenth century hit the very young particularly hard, reducing the numbers of heirs to succeed to family lands and possibly contributing to an imbalance in sex ratios within local communities; greater numbers of men than women fell victim to the plague. In England, many rural dwellers of both sexes migrated to towns, attracted by the economic opportunities there—a situation that, as Christopher Dyer has plausibly argued, eroded the influence of the family as a social group over the lives of its members.[37]

One immediate psychological consequence of the outbreak of plague was the panic and fear that it instilled. The Italian writer, Giovanni Boccaccio (d. 1375), was struck, in particular, by the way in which the living shunned the sick. In *The Decameron*, he describes how those who could afford to do so voluntarily deserted their families and homes, and sought refuge in the countryside in the hope that the pestilence would not follow them. When the plague was at its height, family loyalties were often forgotten, as parents abandoned children, brothers their brothers, and wives their husbands, to their fates.[38] Boccaccio was just one of a number of contemporaries who regarded the failure of close relationships, the disintegration of notions of familial duty and responsibility, and the erosion of strong personal ties of affection as symptoms of the collapse of morality and social order presaged by the plague's arrival. After all, ideas about childhood and the family were vitally important to medieval men and women, and, as the subsequent chapters in this volume demonstrate, underpinned the social fabric of the medieval West.

CHAPTER ONE

Family Relationships

P.J.P. GOLDBERG

Most children are born and grow up within a familial context, so a broader understanding of family and family relationships is essential to the study of childhood. Although historical scholarship on the family flourishes, this is untrue of the earlier and high medieval eras.[1] In part this is a consequence of the paucity of sources. Historians of family relationships before the modern era must confront some serious methodological problems. Social anthropological approaches, which depend on studying the living, are not possible. Most of our subjects are silent. Before the fifteenth century, letters are rare, autobiographical documents almost non-existent. Lives went unrecorded. Even where noticed, it is in records of administration, taxation, or the law. These say little about family life, even in the abstract. Heretics, higher clergy, the aristocracy, and merchants are all more conspicuously recorded than other ranks of society, but theirs are minority experiences. Women and children are especially invisible. The earlier part of this period is, moreover, substantially less well documented than the latter. These are givens that medievalists work with. The challenge is not so much to find a lot of evidence for particular issues, but to recognize nuggets of evidence that are especially illuminating and to find imaginative ways of approaching this evidence.

HOUSEHOLD AND FAMILY

Family is a problematic term. Modern usage tends to refer either to household, comprising coresident related individuals, or to a broader network of kin.

Medieval culture recognized both these but did not employ a single term. The Latin *familie*, for example, scarcely exists in Middle English. *Familia* implies household dependents but not specifically kin. Modern scholarship—specifically historical demography—has focused on the coresident group and on the average size and composition of the medieval family (meaning household). Only comparatively recently have cultural diversity and change over time come to be recognized. There are, however, many approaches to the study of the family; the historical is but one. Sociological approaches prompt questions about the purpose of the family: the procreation and socialization of children, a place of nurture and recreation, or an economic and work unit. Anthropology emphasizes the ties of kinship that shape how people relate to one another and so has looked beyond the coresident group or household. (This has been especially attractive to early medievalists, who know more about who was related to whom than about who lived with whom.) Art-historical research has drawn attention to the way families are represented visually. Literary scholarship likewise offers the possibility of insights into family as reflected in fictive narratives. Romances, read by both sexes often within a household or familial context, are especially promising; their narratives often highlight and engage with tensions and emotions unnoticed in conventional documentary sources.

Attempts to reconstruct size and composition of medieval households depend on the availability of appropriate sources. We have good evidence from either end of the period but little in between. For the beginning of the Middle Ages, we have some estate surveys known as polyptychs. Perhaps the best known are those of the monasteries of Saint-Germain-des-Prés (near Paris) and Saint Victor (Marseilles) from the early ninth century, though some later ninth-century polyptychs also survive. These seemingly underrecord children and women but still suggest certain possibilities. David Herlihy's analysis of the Saint-Germain-des-Prés polyptych implies households characterized by numbers of coresident siblings as well as simple conjugal households. The comparative paucity of evidence for three-generational households, he argues, suggests children did not bring their spouse to live with them.[2] This may, however, be merely an optical illusion caused by low life expectancy. North Frankish peasant youngsters may, in fact, have grown up alongside aunts, uncles, and cousins, subject to the authority of their father or grandfather.

The polyptych evidence shows a post-Roman world in which people of servile status enjoyed increasing stability, could marry and live within family units, and worked, in effect, their own family parcels of land. Different sources and debates come to the fore for subsequent periods. The evidence tends to relate to kinship ties rather than coresidency and to the experience of royal and aristocratic families; these differences preclude trying to link the two ends of the period. The broad consensus has been that the high Middle Ages saw a shift from a cognatic kinship system—one that valued kin on both sides of the family and women as well as men—to an agnatic or patrilineal system. This would have had particularly negative implications for women. Recent scholarship tends to qualify this view; its applicability to the wider population is, in any case, problematic.[3]

The most impressive demographic source for the late medieval era is the Tuscan *catasto*, or tax survey, of 1427. We also have population listings for parts of Ypres (various dates in the fifteenth century), Rheims (1422), and Nuremberg (1449). The period before 1400 is much less well documented. The English poll taxes (1377, 1379, and 1381) provide valuable data, but children are excluded. Other sources tend to be more anecdotal or problematic. This late evidence nevertheless suggests certain patterns that can be traced backward through time. Western Europe in the late medieval era seems to have been characterized by a variety of household forms. Certain broad regional patterns emerge. Northwestern Europe—northern France, the Low Countries, the Rhineland, England, and perhaps parts of Scandinavia—tended to be characterized by nuclear households, often including servants, particularly in urban contexts. The Tuscan catasto, in contrast, suggests that, despite the frequency of simple conjugal households (parents and children), something akin to a stem-family system prevailed. Emmanuel Le Roy Ladurie's classic study of the heretical Pyrenean community of Montaillou (early fourteenth century) accords with this model.

These two culturally quite distinct systems suggest some significant differences in the dynamics of associated family groups. The stem family—where children may remain at home as long as they remain single, but only one child is permitted to marry and bring his or her spouse to live with them—is concerned to preserve the male blood line and associated family land from generation to generation. It places authority in the male head and values family over individuals. Labor needs are met primarily within the coresident group, but kin relations beyond the household are socially important. Women marrying in to a stem family find themselves subordinate to their mothers-in-law and regarded only as visitors and not full members of the family. As a widow, a woman had no automatic right to remain; she had the right to recover her dowry and could return to her natal family. If she left, however, she could not take her children with her.

The nuclear household, in contrast, required children to leave home—at marriage, if not before—and so make their own way without awaiting an inheritance; parents could not rely on the support of their children in old age because children were likely to have already left home. Labor requirements were not necessarily met by family labor alone. Social networks often looked beyond kin relations. Widows enjoyed dower rights to part of the property shared with their husbands. Jointure, which allowed the widow complete control, was normal by the end of the Middle Ages. It is in this context that later thirteenth- and fourteenth-century English peasants entered into maintenance contracts exchanging land for regular provision of food and clothing. These contracts were sometimes made with kin, such as a daughter and son-in-law; they are also found involving non-kin, even bypassing the direct heir. This is a very different value system from the stem household, where children had a vested interest in supporting their fathers to the moment of death.

It is not known how deep the historical roots of these various family forms are; English sources may suggest that the nuclear family was a late development. Thinking about family forms, moreover, does little to illuminate the dynamics of family life. In predominantly agrarian cultures, most families—children and parents—worked together to make a livelihood. To a degree, tasks were divided along lines of gender and age. Harvesting, whether of grain, grass, or vines, tended to be shared; dairying, weeding, food preparation, brewing, spinning, sewing, and, particularly before the late medieval era, weaving were seen as women's work. Heavier laboring activities such as plowing and mowing with a scythe were generally seen as men's work. Children watched over livestock, collected wood, and ran errands. The home was primarily the locus for eating, sleeping, and domestic production such as weaving or brewing; this is reflected in the spatial arrangements of most houses that comprised a work/living area, a sleeping area, and a cooking area. From the high Middle Ages, these areas frequently evolved into a hall, chamber, and kitchen/services. Some peasant houses sheltered livestock under a common roof. Only in more prosperous urban and aristocratic contexts was the house used for recreational activities. Small spaces and lack of separate rooms allowed most families little privacy. Parents and children slept together in the same room; family members would have been used to seeing one another naked, and married couples would have had sex while their children slept around them. Courtship and other erotic encounters took place outdoors. So did much children's play.

MARRIAGE

Marriage is one aspect of family life that is comparatively well documented. From the beginning of the Middle Ages with the spread of Christianity, the influence of the church appears to have eroded the ability of lords to move or sell servile peasantry regardless of ties of marriage or family. Conversely, the ability of folk, including servile peasantry, to make marriages enjoyed increasing recognition.[4] At the same time, the indissolubility of marriage was more and more upheld. This made it harder for even high-status men to repudiate wives; Pope Nicholas I (858–867) refused to recognize King Lothair II of Lotharingia's attempt to marry again when his queen, Theutberga, failed to give him children. Innocent III similarly stood up to Philip II of France when he repudiated Ingeborg of Denmark. In practice, the church was unable to enforce its teaching before the high medieval era. Even after that, there were married couples who lived apart by consent and others who entered into illicit second unions by moving to where they were unknown. The church did sanction separation in case of a wife's adultery or a husband's excessive cruelty, but this was very difficult to obtain.

The church's teaching also led to a gradual abandonment of the aristocratic practice, exemplified by Lothair and Charlemagne before him, of keeping concubines both to satisfy sexual appetites and to provide heirs should the legitimate line prove lacking. This enhanced the status of wives by marriage, but elite men still kept mistresses. In the slave-owning cultures of the Mediterranean, women slaves regularly served as concubines. In high medieval Iberia, keeping concubines, including slaves, was accepted both culturally and legally; the thirteenth-century law code of Alfonso X of Castile (*Las Siete Partidas*), while noting the church's strictures, regulated what kind of woman could become a *barragana*—she was to be older than twelve, not a virgin, and unrelated to her partner. It also stated which men could keep a concubine—unmarried laity—requiring that the relationship be declared before witnesses.

From the eleventh century, the church acquired real influence on the regulation of marriage through its courts. From the twelfth century, a clear canonical position on what constituted marriage was developed. The centrality of consent, articulated in Gratian's *Decretum* in the mid-twelfth century, was codified in the provisions of the Fourth Lateran Council (1215). This teaching was positioned against arranged marriages, particularly of minors. Children younger than seven years were not to be betrothed at all. A child of seven or older might be betrothed but had to ratify the contract on achieving majority at twelve in the case of girls and fourteen in the case of boys. In fact, because age of consent was linked to classical notions of the age of puberty, girls could be married as young as eleven. Jeanne of Navarre was eleven when she was married to Philip IV of France, though her marriage may not have been immediately consummated.

In framing this canonical teaching, Alexander III and canonists at the papal curia shared certain assumptions of contemporary Roman culture concerning the responsibilities of parents to find partners for their children and of children to obey their parents. The provisions of Lateran IV were not designed to undermine patriarchal authority, only to curb its abuse; parental consent was not written into the canon law, because churchmen assumed that children would marry according to their parents' wishes.

Canon law also insisted that close kin marriage was incestuous and hence disallowed. Initially, marriages within seven degrees of kinship (where a common ancestor can be traced back through seven or fewer steps) were deemed incestuous. This proved unenforceable and allowed noblemen to annul marriages at will by showing that they were related to their wives. Lateran IV reduced this bar to four degrees of kinship. A more narrowly defined bar was placed on marriages between those related through spiritual kinship created by sponsoring children at baptism. Canonical constraints on kin marriage still conflicted with aristocratic preference for marriages designed to consolidate and reinforce existing networks of alliance and to prevent landed interests falling outside familial control. To circumvent this, some aristocrats arranged marriages between related couples but only revealed the relationship after solemnization. By requesting retrospective dispensation from the papal curia, families took advantage of the church's unwillingness to annul established marriages. Thus, in 1332, Maurice de Berkeley and Lady Margery de Vere were allowed to continue their marriage, which had already produced children despite being related within the fourth degree.

The church council of Fréjus (796–797) urged marriage between adults of like age. This was predicated on concerns about child marriage and partners of dissimilar age. Such marriages were regularly found among the aristocracy throughout the period; well-born pubescent girls, in particular, were likely to have had marriages arranged for them to older men. Evidence for marriage ages and practice from the earlier Middle Ages is slight. The early ninth-century polyptych of Saint Victor has been used by Herlihy as "incontrovertible" evidence that, around Marseilles, peasants "were postponing marriage until their late twenties."[5] Others would not share Herlihy's confidence. More certain is the practice among Germanic populations of money (bridewealth) given on marriage to the bride and her father by her husband or his family and of *Morgengabe,* given by the husband to his bride the morning after the consummation of their marriage. These customs imply negotiation between families and a particular interest on the part of fathers in their sons' marriages, but seem to have died out in the high medieval era.

The Tuscan catasto of 1427 demonstrates a pattern of youthful (late teens) and universal marriage for women but more delayed and less frequent marriage for men. This distinctive marriage pattern, which has wider regional resonances, is characterized by a marked age difference between spouses, numbers of men living well into adulthood without apparently marrying, and significant proportions of widows (who tend not to remarry) but few widowers (because widowers regularly do). Two prerequisites, which have important implications for the rearing of daughters, are associated with this so-called Mediterranean pattern: the virginity of the bride until her marriage night, promising chastity within marriage and the bearing of only legitimately conceived offspring, and the payment by the bride's father of dowry. The giving of dowries by fathers to new sons-in-law extended through the social hierarchy. A young woman wanting to marry thus needed a father or some other male protector such as a brother. Dowry symbolized this protection. Without a dowry, a young woman might not marry. The cult of Saint Nicholas reinforced this understanding; he secretly gave three bags of gold to a poor father so that his three daughters might be married and saved from prostitution.

Paternal or fraternal responsibility for the virtue of unmarried daughters or sisters—a responsibility transferred at betrothal to the husband-to-be—encouraged the early betrothal of women within Mediterranean culture. From the age of twelve, Catherine of Siena was made to stay at home and keep her face and neck washed so as to appear attractive to potential husbands; poorer families may have been less able to shelter daughters at home. Anecdotal evidence suggests such girls were vulnerable to sexual abuse or rape. For the citizen elite of the Venetian colony of Ragusa (Dubrovnik), David Rheubottom has shown sons delayed their own marriages—over which they had some control—until after their sisters had all been provided for.[6]

The tendency for virgin brides to be married to somewhat older men and for dowry payments to pass from the wife's family to the husband's was a widespread cultural phenomenon. It may also have had deep historical roots, suggested by analogy with evidence for late Roman marriage patterns. Another possibility that has been argued is that this Mediterranean model is a variety of a general medieval marriage pattern. This is predicated on the paucity (and greater difficulty) of evidence for other regions of Europe. It also supposes that medieval society was universally patriarchal, that daughters across Europe were subject to paternal authority and constraint in respect of their sexuality and their ability to choose marriage partners in a way that was not true of their brothers.

A variant on a medieval marriage pattern has been suggested by Zvi Razi, using manor court roll evidence for peasant society in the English West Midlands in the late thirteenth and fourteenth centuries.[7] He argues for early (i.e., late teens or early twenties) marriage for both sexes. This is a markedly different marriage regime than that documented for Tuscany about a century later. It is also unlike the so-called European (later qualified as northwestern European) regime, characterized by later marriage for both sexes and a significant minority known to have never married, documented for England in the early modern era. The ages and marital status of witnesses in the ecclesiastical court of York from the late fourteenth and early fifteenth centuries tend to reinforce Razi's model for rural peasant society but suggest something more akin to the northwestern model for urban society.[8] Here, continuity of a northwestern marriage pattern seems not to extend back before the fourteenth century, but the peasant model that immediately preceded this was a distinctive regional regime.

The later medieval English aristocracy seems to have followed an aristocratic model, marrying daughters off as young as eleven, though more commonly in the later teens, to men who were somewhat older.[9] Higher aristocratic wards noticed in 1185 were often married when they were about seventeen. Data for other parts of Europe before the later Middle Ages are patchy, anecdotal, and socially biased. These tend to show girls married at various ages between about twelve and the late teens. Ages for men are harder to capture. Evidence for the wider population and of regionally distinctive patterns hardly exists, but parents probably frequently influenced or even arranged marriages, especially for daughters, and the power relationship in marriage was heavily weighted toward the husband. In time, shared responsibilities of raising children and making a livelihood could build lasting and affectionate relationships between spouses, but it tends to be to the aristocracy or in literature that we must look for expression of this. The *Ménagier de Paris,* a late-fourteenth-century French aristocratic instructional treatise, advocates absolute wifely obedience, expects a high degree of competence on the wife's part in managing the household, and ultimately assumes respect and even affection in the marital relationship. Churchmen, who thought of women as generally more devout, urged wives to use the intimacy of the marital bed to instruct their husbands in Christian conduct.

For churchmen, marriage served twin purposes. It provided a legitimate locus of (heterosexual) sexual activity; sex within marriage was preferable to the sin of fornication, and each spouse had to yield to the sexual demands of the other—the so-called marital debt. More importantly, it facilitated procreation. Indeed, in response to the dualistic heretical teachings of Catharism, the church came to adopt a fiercely pronatalist stance on sex; all sexual activity was expected to be penetrative, vaginal, in the missionary position, and free from any contraceptive practice. Clerical disapproval of contraception does not, however, imply a lack of contraceptive practice. Peter Biller, for example, has argued that *coitus interruptus* was relatively commonly known and practiced.[10]

Sex was no doubt an important and expected part of the relationship between couples. High and later medieval medical theory held that, for conception to occur, sex must be pleasurable for both parties. Literature, particularly fabliaux, suggested that women could take pleasure in and have desire for sex as much as men. This may have created expectations that sex should be mutually pleasurable regardless of its impact on conception. Fear of repeated pregnancy, however, may have undermined wives' appetite for sex. The concept of marital debt effectively rendered rape within marriage legally impossible. Adopting *coitus interruptus* or anal sex as contraceptive practices would likewise diminish the woman's pleasure. Some husbands may have used the services of prostitutes in order to enjoy sex without responsibility.

Abortifacients, including remedies to restore menstruation, were known of and no doubt used to limit fertility.[11] These included the herbs pennyroyal and catmint. As with contraceptive practice in the form of herbs and vaginal suppositories, such knowledge probably circulated among women empirics. It is also found in herbals and medical texts. Also documented are attempts to dispose of unwanted children. Exposure, for which there is some pre-Christian Scandinavian evidence, and, more particularly, child abandonment have been much discussed by scholars. Skewed sex ratios in the early polyptychs, for example, have prompted speculation about female infanticide, but there are more benign explanations. Clerical concern about children dying unbaptized ensured that abandonment was noticed but need not imply that it was common. It may have been more of an issue in southern Europe, where extramarital sex and pregnancy were greater taboos; it is in this region that we find the first foundling hospitals at the end of the period. The early medieval, high-status practice of child oblation (whereby children were given to religious houses) has sometimes been treated as a form of child abandonment. In fact, parents used oblates as a way of reinforcing familial bonds with particular monastic foundations and would visit regularly.

CHILDREN

Some couples would have been unable to conceive, but the most common experience of married couples was of parenthood and the regular birth of children over a number of years. Outside of the aristocracy, extended maternal breast-feeding appears the norm, so couples might expect to have conceived and given birth approximately every eighteen months. Margery Kempe (early fifteenth century) had a completed family of fourteen children. A few decades earlier, and in a culture that discouraged women from nursing their own children, Matteo Corsini's first wife bore him twenty children. The numbers of live births would have been lower were conception impeded through contraception or the use of arbortifacients, but repeated pregnancy and childbirth (and, for many, continuous nursing) would have been the normal experience of most adult women.

Not all children survived, but it is impossible to generate death rates or life expectancy. Most parents would have endured the loss of at least some of their children. Mortality was especially acute following the plague pandemic of 1347 to 1350. Several chronicles noted that the late-fourteenth-century epidemics were characterized by high child mortality, and fifteenth-century German personal memoranda suggest very high levels of infant and child mortality. Preplague patterns are harder to reconstruct; cemetery evidence is especially problematic in respect to infants and very young children.

The legacy of Philippe Ariès has polarized debate about medieval child rearing.[12] One camp looks for evidence of parental nurture; the other seeks to show indifference, even neglect. Simple narratives of neglect or nurture are hence preferred to ones that are more complex and nuanced. Little attempt has been made to offer a child-centric perspective on childhood, and insufficient thought has been directed to variation in practice over time, between different cultural regions, and across different levels of society. The aristocracy, in particular, often delegated many aspects of early child care—and hence parenting—to servants. In societies with high birth rates—a consequence of a lack of effective contraception and a culture preference for large families as a guarantee that parents would be supported by their offspring in old age—children would have spent much time socializing with siblings and peers rather than adults. Unfortunately, few sources exist for childhood in this long period. Children did not produce records themselves and rarely had reason to be recorded otherwise. Archaeology is beginning to look for evidence relating to play and to burial culture, but both approaches have a long way to go and still leave much of childhood experience undocumented.

With the coming of Christianity, parents saw their first duty to their children was to have them baptized; the church taught that the unbaptized child could not be buried in holy ground nor be admitted into heaven. The infant Alice de Rouclif, born a few years after the Black Death, was rushed by her nurse to the parish church two miles away to be baptized on the day of her birth. In common with contemporary English naming practice, she was named Alice by one of her two godmothers, herself called Alice. (She also had a god-father, the custom being to have two godparents of the same gender and one of the opposite.) The choice of godparents was determined by a concern to reinforce ties with friends and acquaintances of like or higher social rank, but, in choosing Alice de Beleby as naming godmother, her father Gervase ensured that his daughter carried the same name as her paternal grandmother, just as Gervase had the same name as his paternal grandfather. The name a child was given thus could reflect family tradition and descent, ethnic identity, and, it has been suggested, social rank. In ninth-century Frankia (the region of northwest-ern Europe ruled by Charlemagne), children were regularly given names that borrowed elements from each of the parents' names. On continental Europe, naming children after saints became common by the end of the Middle Ages.

The swaddling of infants, to ensure that their limbs grew straight, seems to have been a universal practice throughout the Middle Ages. Just as birthing practice ideally recreated the womb by allowing the infant to be born into a warm, dark environment, so swaddled babies may have been left indoors close to fires. Barbara Hanawalt's use of English coroners' rolls to study childhood through analysis of accidental deaths is widely influential. Her work follows the "nurturing" agenda, arguing that, from an early age, girls helped their mothers at home while boys followed their fathers outdoors. This mirrors her understanding of work occupying gendered spheres. A reappraisal of the same source suggests, in fact, that younger children—girls and boys—were regularly left to play as much outdoors as in, that (quite young, but especially girl) chil-dren were often given charge of younger siblings, and that it is only with older children that parents may have discouraged daughters from playing outdoors. This looks like benign neglect, but the more important point is that children were socialized through play and learned their gender identities as much by interaction with their peers as their parents.[13]

The evidence from coroners' rolls is culturally and chronologically spe-cific, but there are some parallels for other periods and places. Hagiographic material sometimes reflects a world in which children played unsupervised. An Anglo-Saxon depiction of the life of Saint Patrick, for example, describes the young saint playing games with other boys. Toys impinge little upon the archaeological record for most of this period, though most games were prob-ably played with improvised props and found items. By the end of the period, we notice manufactured toys, such as ceramic spinning tops, lead knights, and cooking vessels. This suggests adult investment in a culture of childhood and implies a concern to inculcate particular gender identities on the part of more affluent parents. Late medieval depictions of the Holy Family of Mary, Joseph, and the young Jesus, where the child plays happily in the home under the watchful eyes of his devoted parents as they pursue work tasks, likewise reflect an ideology of greater involvement with children. Devotional images primarily concerned to project Christ's incarnation and humanity could, however, be positioned against social practice. Italian representations of the Virgin suckling the baby Jesus, for example, critique the well-to-do practice of sending infants away to be nursed.

Wet nurses were widely employed within the household by aristocratic families throughout the Middle Ages; breast-feeding was considered demeaning for a well-born woman and was also understood to inhibit fertility. More affluent families of later medieval Florence sent their infants to rural wet nurses for the first couple of years of life. Wet nurses were also hired to live in the parents' homes in southern French and Castilian towns. This probably represents a regional pattern. In Ragusa, slave women were so employed. These practices are documented, because the hiring of nurses generated records, but they stand in contrast to the almost universal practice of extended maternal breast-feeding that, because unpaid and unremarkable, goes unnoticed. *Las Siete Partidas* required Castilian mothers to nourish their children for the first

Figure 1.1: *Two boys whipping a spinning top*. The Queen Mary Psalter, England, circa 1310–1320. © The British Library Board (BL Royal MS. 2 B. VII, f. 164).

three years. Testimony given in a marriage case from late-fourteenth-century England likewise indicates that peasant women weaned their children once they were three. Analysis of teeth from English cemetery evidence indicates extended breast-feeding. It follows that most children would have formed a particular bond with their mothers, though aristocratic children may have bonded with nurses who sometimes continued to be employed and associated with the family long after the child was weaned.

Many medieval households would have been broken and reconstituted through death and remarriage. Many children would have grown up with older or younger half-siblings. Some would also have had to adapt to a step-mother or stepfather. The folklore tradition of the wicked stepmother is not readily traceable back to the Middle Ages, but children given a new father by the remarriage of their widowed mother had reason to be anxious about their inheritance or the favoritism shown by him to his own children. Some men fathered illegitimate children, and sometimes these were brought into the marital home. Occasionally, children were taken in out of charity. These phenomena have received little scholarly attention.

Most children assisted with household chores and contributed to the household economy, but it would be unwise to attach a minimum age to this. Margaret Exton, glimpsed from a late-thirteenth-century coroner's roll, was six when she went with her two younger sisters to fetch firewood from the yard; was she contributing to the household economy or, as she probably saw it, playing? The same source shows girls of like age given charge of younger siblings. Children are noticed in the fields watching over livestock. They foraged for dry wood, nuts, and berries. Girls must have learned to card, spin, and sew from their mothers, because these were quintessentially female tasks, seen as "natural"—and hence undocumented—by men. Doubtless, peasant daughters also helped their mothers collect eggs, fetched water, and, in time, learned butter and cheese making. In Mediterranean regions, they picked olives. Peasant boys would have been taught various skills by their fathers, but the quintessentially male tasks of mowing and plowing were only acquired once they had gained sufficient height and physical strength. It is likely that girls were more fully absorbed into the household economy from an earlier age than their brothers and that girls were more constrained than boys. This may have been particularly the case once girls approached puberty, especially in southern Europe or in more socially aspirant families.

Children were understood as dependents who owed obedience to their parents just as parents had a duty to nurture. Medieval society tolerated a level of casual violence, and children (and wives) might be beaten by way of punishment.

It is interesting, however, that thirteenth-century friars' sermons urged the need to beat the errant child that it might learn correct behavior; the implication is that many parents were more circumspect about striking their children.[14] Some evidence suggests that boys were treated preferentially to girls, especially in southern Europe, and this may have resulted in higher female child mortality. A more benign picture is suggested by evidence that mothers' responsibility for the socialization of younger children probably included moral and devotional instruction. By the later Middle Ages, and certainly in better-off families, mothers instructed children in reading, the *Ave* and the *Paternoster* being the first reading exercises.

ADOLESCENTS

Just as Ariès argued that there was no "sentiment" of childhood before the early modern era, so he claimed there was no "sentiment" of adolescence. James Schultz has also suggested (using the evidence of Middle High German literature) that society in the period 1050 to 1350 showed no recognition of adolescence manifested in generational conflict or personal crisis and had no vocabulary for adolescence.[15] Although there is much to suggest that childhood was understood to be finite, and we can identify various cultural, religious, and legal rites of passage, the degree to which these were passages to adulthood or an adolescent preadulthood is unclear. Early medieval cemetery evidence, for example, which is not uniform over time or space, tended not to distinguish prepubescent children by gender. Young women, however, were especially valued from puberty in terms of the grave goods in the form of jewelry placed with the body. This reflects cultural values that saw the adolescent girl as marriageable. The postpubescent boy, however, was not given the full attributes of the young warrior until nearer twenty, but he may still have weapons.[16] This may imply that the teenage boys experienced some sort of adolescence, but that girls moved from child to social adult without a liminal adolescent phase.

Puberty enjoyed some recognition as a rite of passage. The early-thirteenth-century *Sachsenspiegel* equated the growth of facial and other bodily hair on boys as a mark of coming of age. Canon law tied age of consent to puberty, glossed as the appearance of pubic hair, though this was fixed at twelve for girls and fourteen for boys. In fact, as previously noted, marriage was often delayed by some years after puberty. The law likewise could only distinguish between the exempt child and the legally responsible non-child. Late Anglo-Saxon law codes did not apply to persons younger than twelve, and Athelstan (924–939) even attempted to protect children younger than age fifteen from the death penalty. Later medieval English common law, however, held that youngsters were responsible for their actions and could be punished as adults once they were of age to distinguish good and evil—that is, from as young as ten; in 1338, a girl of thirteen was burned to death for killing her mistress.

The last example alerts us to the phenomenon of live-in servants, a type of fosterage. In Anglo-Saxon England, some youngsters were fostered as a form of training or secondary socialization. Thus, children of thanes (nobles) were fostered by Alfred in the royal court of Wessex. In the latter part of the period, many young people, especially in northwestern Europe, were employed as servants, living with their employers, but were debarred from marriage. Sometimes servants were related to their employers. Sometimes siblings served in the same household. Apprentices, who were predominantly male and contracted for a number of years, might continue to serve until they were about twenty-one. Here, too, is evidence for generational conflict, though seldom as extreme as the 1338 case. Servants are found in southern Europe, but the institution served a different function, being more of a social safety net than a means of training and socializing young people. Servants there were predominantly female and comprised variously young orphan girls who otherwise lacked a male protector, married women whose husbands could not support them, and older widows who offered their labor in return for security in old age.

Early medieval cemetery evidence suggests a world in which the transition from childhood to adulthood was relatively abrupt. The more complex societies at the end of the period seem to have demanded longer periods of socialization. This is especially true of urban society—the locus of commerce, trade, and manufacture—where there is most evidence for adolescents employed as servants or apprentices. In a discussion of age of inheritance, *Bracton*, a thirteenth-century English law compilation, suggests that different ages apply according to the degree of competence and training needed to fulfill the responsibilities of a knight, a burgess, or a husbandman, respectively. The young burgess had to be able to measure cloth and reckon money, and he would not be able to do this before he was fifteen. A young woman likewise needed to learn how to manage a house, something that she would not be able to accomplish until she was twelve or thirteen. In contrast, a young man had to wait until he was twenty-one before he had gained the skills and discretion needed to fulfill the duties of a knight. *Bracton*'s rationale is ideological—the knight is superior to the burgess, the male to the female—but it probably reflects contemporary social practice. The implication is that, unlike at the beginning of the period, adolescence was extended for high-status boys but was generally abbreviated for girls. By the later Middle Ages, some period of adolescence was probably experienced by all levels of society.

These structural changes over time are qualified by social rank and influenced by cultural geography. The Mediterranean south had deep-rooted cultural traditions that saw the sexual virtue of its womenfolk, guarded by male protection, as central to familial honor. Fathers watched diligently over their daughters but, by betrothing them at a comparatively early age, relinquished this responsibility to sons-in-law. Sons enjoyed more freedom of movement and were permitted some sexual license but remained subject to paternal authority and lived at home—at least at the end of the period—into their twenties. Girls, in effect, had little adolescence; boys had a prolonged adolescence—indeed, they remained in this phase until the deaths of their fathers. In contrast, the nuclear pattern of householding prevailing in northwestern Europe by at least the fourteenth century encouraged children of both sexes to leave the natal home, often in their teens and before they might marry. This custom is reflected in romances, some dating to before the fourteenth century, that have the adolescent setting off from home as a leitmotif. The heroes of Viking sagas likewise often made their first voyage as young as twelve. Migrants to the town were often single teenagers. It was, moreover, into these nuclear households that teenage servants and apprentices were absorbed.

Youngsters occupying positions as servants and living away from home probably enjoyed much de facto freedom, not least in respect to courtship. The same may have been true of children from low-status families whose fathers had little to bequeath and little to gain from their marriages. More well-to-do peasants probably looked to exercise some control, because their children's marriages could consolidate or extend social networks and land. Daughters, in particular, were probably supervised with some care—only girls from lesser families tend to be presented for fornication in English manorial courts of the later thirteenth and fourteenth centuries—and were sometimes bullied into marriages they did not want. In southern Europe, the custom of dowry gave fathers more immediate control over their daughters' marriages.

Many children would have lost one or both parents before they reached maturity. Children without a father tended to be understood as orphaned. Where the child was young, everyday care was left to the mother, but, from the high Middle Ages, feudal and customary law took an interest in guardianship if the child was heir to property. Later, town governments acted in the same manner. Feudal wards were a source of profit for the guardian who administered the ward's lands until of age. They could also marry the ward to their own advantage, sometimes in the case of heiresses to their own son (in effect, gaining lasting control over the

FIGURE 1.2: *A man attempts to embrace a woman at her spinning wheel.* The Smithfield Decretals, France and England, circa 1300–1340. © The British Library Board (BL Royal MS. 10 E. IV, f. 139).

ward's lands). We know much less about provision for other children. Probably, most were taken in by kin; there is evidence both from the high Middle Ages and the Anglo-Saxon era that, in England at least, maternal uncles played a role as carers. Grandparents, when they lived long enough, appear to have taken an interest in grandchildren; there is some evidence for aristocratic grandmothers building particular bonds with granddaughters. Godparents had, in theory, to support the children they sponsored, but the evidence that this extended to taking in orphans is slight. In late medieval Tuscany, orphan girls are found as servants, and older orphaned children elsewhere may similarly have been provided for. There is also slight evidence from the high medieval era and beyond for hospitals to care for orphaned children: York's Saint Leonard's hospital employed sisters to care for orphans and a cow to provide milk.

OLD AGE AND DEATH

Old age, like youth, is not purely a product of chronology. Like gender, it is a cultural construct. Because of the fragility of cemetery data, knowledge of life expectancy is limited. Although some lived to a very advanced age, most did not. Men—women are not reported—appear to have considered themselves old from various ages ranging from about forty upward, but few people knew their exact ages. Old age was thought to be both a strength and a weakness. Where intellectual capacity and experience mattered—as in town government or trade—old men were valued. Where physical strength was needed—as was true of peasant society or the warrior societies of the early Middle Ages—the elderly could, at worst, be seen as a burden. Old women were particularly likely to be marginalized. The support given to the elderly varied between different familial and cultural contexts, yet the return of the dowry or the widow's dower rights could be a source of conflict with children. Families might pressure well-to-do widows to remarry; in this context, some widows took vows of chastity to circumvent these pressures. Some looked for support beyond the family. Aristocratic women sometimes retired to nunneries. Both men and women purchased corodies, a sort of retirement package, from hospitals and other religious houses. In peasant society, old women were allowed to glean after harvest and might do odd jobs for their neighbors. In the later Middle Ages, almshouses sprung up in some regions, but begging was commonplace. In the famine years of the late thirteenth and early fourteenth century, many women succumbed to exposure while seeking alms.

So we come to death. Before the advent of Christianity in the earliest part of the Middle Ages, much can be learned about mortuary culture from the presence of grave goods. These were used to assert, or at least reflect, status, gender, age, and ethnicity. They may tell us as much about the mourners as they do about the deceased; the objects a woman was buried with may not have been used by her in her lifetime and may be determined primarily by the needs of her menfolk, the kin group, and the wider community. Likewise, the burial of a man, or occasionally even a woman, with a spear has been understood to reflect power and social rank, but also age—very young boys and older men tend to be buried with fewer and less gender-specific items. Once Christianity was adopted, grave goods became much less common.

During the first part of the Middle Ages, the church taught that Judgment would come at the end of time. Bodies were aligned east-west with the head in the west to face the Son of God on the Judgment Day, when the dead would be resurrected and sent to heaven or hell according to their merits. This practice continued throughout the period and beyond. Graveyards, attached to parish churches and often centrally located, became the burial places of the entire community. These might be marked by a cross, but individual memorials are not found. From the high medieval era, belief in purgatory changed the emphasis to that of individual judgment and allowed a much larger group of people to contemplate the possibility of (eventual) salvation. This prompted growing concern with preparation for death and how to die well. It also stimulated a need to solicit postmortem prayer from family and friends to reduce time in purgatory—hence, a concern with memorialization. For the more well-to-do, burial in church became possible, and funerary monuments became increasingly common. The chancels of some churches even became de facto mausoleums for local aristocratic families. We find three-dimensional tombs of husbands and wives lying side by side, sometimes with their children around the sides as mourners, the conjugal family immortalized in stone. Cemetery evidence from various dates suggests that people were often buried as part of family groups. Wills sometimes specify where an individual wished to be buried—for example, before a particular altar or part of a church—but sometimes it is specified as alongside a deceased spouse or, more rarely, a parent. Occasionally, we find affective relationships that were not familial; best known is the joint burial at the end of the period of brothers-in-arms Sir William Neville and Sir John Clanvowe.[17]

CONCLUSION

Children were both ubiquitous and numerous in medieval families. Most couples would have given birth to many children, and most children would have passed their early years playing with siblings and being provided for materially within a familial context. What emerges, however, is that how these families were organized varied over time, between different cultural regions of Europe, and between different social strata. In order to reconstruct the history of childhood and children's experiences, we must avoid bland generalities and recognize the diversity of familial experiences that framed childhood. Equally, we must be sensitive to the fact that certain social groups, regions, or periods are comparatively better documented and hence that what we can see may be a very partial picture. We may challenge Philippe Ariès's construction of a medieval childhood that argues for a common medieval perspective, but we should recognize that his pioneering work located children within a familial context and historicized the experience of childhood. This is his lasting legacy.

CHAPTER TWO

Community

JENNIFER C. WARD

Community played a significant role in the lives of children and their families throughout the Middle Ages. The family was all-important in children's lives from birth to adulthood for their upbringing and training and for major decisions on education, work, and marriage, but these matters also involved the community. The community was not, however, a single entity, and parents and children were members of a number of communities in the course of their lives. The most common communities were the places where families lived—whether hamlet, village, or town—from which they took their identity, and the religious community of Christendom, extending over all areas in Europe owing obedience to the Roman Church. Regional and national communities existed but impinged little on the lives of children. Large households, whether of nobles or churchmen, have been categorized as communities in their own right, and nobles and elite merchants can be seen as constituting their own social communities through their common interests and values, which transcended political boundaries.[1] Most families in the West were Christian, and Jews and Muslims comprised minority ethnic and religious communities.

The involvement of the family with these communities became more extensive and elaborate between the ninth and fourteenth centuries. As the whole of Europe became Christianized, and villages and towns grew, close connections emerged between identification with monastery and parish church and the family's place of settlement. Within the town or village by the later Middle Ages, more select communities grew up—notably parish, merchant, and craft guilds—and, in large towns in particular, these enabled people to identify with their neighbors. This development was also due to political and cultural factors. It gradually becomes easier for the historian to trace the work and significance of these communities as literacy became more widespread and recordkeeping increased in church and kingdom. From the thirteenth century onward, a detailed picture of communities can be formed, although some aspects go back to an earlier period.

THE YOUNG CHILD AND THE COMMUNITY

The community was involved with the child from birth. This did not belittle the role of the family, as the child depended on its parents'—notably its mother's—care and training, especially before the teenage years. The Holy Family was seen as the model for the Christian family, with the cult of Saint Joseph growing in the later Middle Ages.[2] Artistic depictions of Mary, Joseph, and Jesus, especially from the twelfth century, bring out parental love for the child, Mary's tenderness and care, and Joseph's role as the family's protector. At the same time, however, the village and urban neighborhood took an interest in the child, and had its own part to play in upbringing. Such communities were small, and a family's affairs were often public knowledge; judging from court records, gossip was rife, usually assumed to be spread by women. There was little privacy in medieval life, inside or outside the home.

Pregnancy and childbirth were regarded as the concern of women, and noblewomen and many townswomen would be cared for by midwives. By the fourteenth century, towns in Germany, France, and the Low Countries appointed municipal midwives who had often served an apprenticeship; Frankfurt-am-Main employed municipal midwives from 1302, and Bruges from 1312.[3] When no midwife was available, neighbors presumably helped the mother and visited her after the child was born. The mother did not return to local life until she had been purified at the service of churching, about two or three weeks after the birth; this marked her public return to her community.

The baby's baptism usually took place within a few days of birth, when the child was taken to church by the godparents. This was the first chance for the local community to see the baby, as is illustrated by two proofs of age of English feudal heirs of 1332.[4] (The proof of age comprised statements by jurors to prove that the heir had reached the age when he or she was entitled to inherit the father's lands.) In the proof of age of John de Lachedon, John de Kyrkeby reported that he and his brother William saw John lifted from the font, while Nicholas Bulloc saw him at the church door in the arms of the priest. Ralph ate

Hille saw him lying in his cradle at home the day after the birth, and William Edelyne heard the birth announced to John's father. John Mauduyt's baptism was witnessed by three of the godparents' servants, and Roger de Berlee saw the child lifted from the font; William de Stourton's wife had a son the next day and became John's wet nurse.

Most mothers were responsible for the child's upbringing during infancy, generally reckoned as the time between birth and the age of seven. This stage of life saw children's greatest contact with their mothers, and, although medieval records are reticent on emotional matters, close relationships developed. This was the case with Guibert de Nogent, who was born in the 1060s and whose autobiography has much to say of his mother.[5] Like many mothers, she took charge of his religious training, teaching him whenever she was not carrying out household tasks; she saw that he had a formal education and was concerned with his physical welfare. Gilbert praised her for her virtue and piety.

Some mothers, however, handed over the care of their babies to others. The use of wet nurses was widespread among royal and noble families as well as wealthier families in town and country. Wet nurses might live with the family; where the baby was sent to the wet nurse's home, it was virtually transferred to a foster family very early in life. Royal and noble families often appointed a mistress to be in charge of the children, although the mother retained ultimate responsibility, and the child may well have developed a closer relationship with its nurses than with its parents.

The community displayed interest and watchfulness over the family. In addition to the treatises on upbringing, which were mainly available to the elite, parish priests advised on child care through the confessional and presumably buried the numerous children who died young. Church courts investigated cases of suspected infanticide and adultery among parents. Socializing with neighbors would have been constant, and cases of defamation were heard in the church courts. Children would have received their earliest social education from playing with local children, sharing simple toys, and hearing rhymes and stories. Young children often played unsupervised, and serious accidents occurred during play that had to be investigated by the coroner.[6]

Strong parallels exist between these early years in a Christian family and the practices of Jewish and Muslim families, which were similarly patriarchal and where the mother was responsible for young children. Although there were contacts between Christian, and Jewish and Muslim families, despite the church's decrees, Jews and Muslims were racially and religiously distinct, and both groups were under pressure from the eleventh century into modern times. For the birth of her child, the Jewish mother was attended by a midwife and other women; the midwife prepared the boy baby for the ceremony of circumcision when the father recognized the child as his son. The mother's lying-in period of about five weeks ended with a special ritual, similar to the Christian churching. The mother breast-fed her child, or the father employed a wet nurse. Boys and girls remained with their mothers throughout infancy. The involvement of the community at this stage of life was limited.[7]

RELIGIOUS TRAINING

The religious element in a child's training was regarded as vitally important by Christians, Jews, and Muslims. Among Christian families, the mother took primary responsibility for her children's religious and moral upbringing throughout their childhood. In 841 to 843, Dhuoda, wife of Bernard of Septimania, wrote her manual for her son, William. She was separated from him and was concerned that he should not only be successful in the world, but also acceptable in God's sight. The manual was designed that he should know and love God and the king as well as his family and fellow nobles. She wanted him to love the church, pray often, and perform good works. With the growth of literacy, more treatises appeared to guide parents. About five hundred years later, the English poem, *How the Goodwife Taught Her Daughter*, stressed attendance at church, almsgiving, and a virtuous life; this poem may have been designed for mistresses to teach teenage servants and apprentices as well as their daughters. The knight of la Tour-Landry imparted detailed religious instruction to his daughters in his treatise on their upbringing. Jean Gerson recorded that he was taught to pray for what he wanted, and his father taught him about Jesus.[8]

Mothers and writers were not the only members of the community delivering religious training. Children probably assimilated religious practices through their parents' and neighbors' example. Local beliefs, whether orthodox, superstitious, or heretical, would be absorbed by the children. The feasts and fasts of the church were reflected in the types of food served at meal times. There were at least two fast days each week when no meat was served, and meat and dairy products were prohibited during the forty days of Lent. As standards of living rose after the Black Death, certain members of the community had specific roles to play. Godparents were expected throughout the Middle Ages to teach the basic tenets of faith, the Lord's Prayer, Hail Mary, and the Creed. The parish priest might run a school for boys wanting to enter the church, and he taught both adults and children through sermons and confession; sermons advising on upbringing were written by Gilbert de Tournai and Humbert de

Romans. Children attending church would assimilate knowledge and values, even if they distracted other worshippers. From the thirteenth century, children in the towns or taken to market by their parents would hear the sermons of the friars. The role of the church is mirrored by the Jewish and Muslim practices of teaching boys in the synagogue or the mosque; the religious education of Jewish boys began at about the age of five because of Christian pressure to convert children. Religion was regarded as fundamental to the well-being of the whole community.[9]

THE COMMUNITY AND ADOLESCENCE

At about the age of seven, the upbringing of boys and girls diverged, reflecting the patterns of their adult lives. In both Christian and Jewish families, boys were trained for their future occupations, while girls remained with their mothers until they married. By the age of seven, children were taught to know the difference between right and wrong. Youth was seen as lasting from the age of seven to the age of twelve or fourteen, the minimum age set by the church for marriage. Adolescence then lasted until the child had reached the age of about twenty.[10] Throughout these periods, community involvement in various forms became more marked than in infancy, because many children were increasingly away from their families.

The peer group continued to be important during youth and adolescence and provided socialization and assimilation into the local community. This was largely achieved through play. Children liked games involving running and chasing; ball games were popular, as were swings, seesaws, and hobbyhorses. It is difficult to identify toys found in excavations, because many objects such as balls, skates, and dice may have belonged to children or adults. Some dice did belong to children, as guessing games were certainly played. Girls had dolls, but many of these were votive objects rather than to be played with. Some objects, like miniature soldiers and domestic utensils, may have foreshadowed future roles.[11]

Some of the play was undoubtedly violent, and young people were not averse to taking risks. In his description of the city of London of about 1175, William fitz Stephen described, among other sports for young men, cockfighting, ball games, mock battles on horseback, archery, javelin throwing, and a form of naval warfare. In winter, when the marsh to the north of the city froze over, games were played on the ice, often resulting in broken arms and legs or heads injured in falls. Injuries occurred in other forms of play; during wedding celebrations at Romney in Kent, John and others were tilting at the quintain, and a child was trampled to death by John's horse and by the spectators. A boy of twelve died during a game of hockey, fatally injured by a boy of ten.[12]

A boy's formal training depended on parental ambitions and on his family's place in the social hierarchy. Most boys stayed with their families and grew up as members of the village community, learning about farming from their fathers and neighbors, and taking on an increasing number of agricultural tasks as they grew older. At the same time, they might be able to earn money for the household; boys were employed as bird scarers at sowing time and collected stones for building projects. They would assimilate from their fathers the role of the head of the household and its consequent obligations of payments of rent, taxes, and tithes; labor services; and attendance and office holding at the lord's court. From the age of twelve in England, they would be enrolled in a tithing, a group of men mutually responsible for their good behavior, and begin to play their part in community life. A boy might have occasion to attend the manor court of the lord if he committed a misdemeanor or if he was able to secure his own land through a grant from his father or through marriage to an heiress or widow; the arrangements would be validated by the court.[13]

Boys destined for a career in the church took on a new social status; they had to be freemen, and they came from peasant, urban, and noble families. They were probably first taught to read by the parish priest before proceeding to a cathedral school or a grammar school; subsequently, in the later Middle Ages, some proceeded to university. During the early Middle Ages, boys entered monasteries as children and received their education there; this necessitated a separation from their families at an early age. Orderic Vitalis wrote of the misery he felt when he was sent to the abbey of Saint-Evroult from his Shropshire home.[14] The practice of oblation ceased in the twelfth century; it became usual for boys to enter as teenagers or in their twenties, so they were able to remain with their families through infancy and youth. However, education and the prospect of a career involving celibacy might well cause divisions in the family and among the boy's friends, who would realize that, in the future, he would enjoy higher status in the universal community of Christendom.

In many ways, the nobility constituted a group distinct from the rest of society. During the early Middle Ages, boys of noble families probably received little formal education; training as warriors was viewed as more important. By the twelfth century, nobles and knights are found as patrons of books, and it became increasingly usual for boys to be taught to read. Henry Bolingbroke made early provision for the education of his children, who were taught either at home or in the households of his father's relations, friends, and officials.[15] Literacy did not preclude training as a knight, which began in adolescence.

Boys were often sent to another household, and this contributed to their social training as members of the noble community. Separation from their natal family meant that they had to be self-reliant at an early age.

Increasingly, with the growth of towns and trade, the sons of merchants and craftsmen needed to be literate, but they also needed occupational training, provided for by apprenticeship during their adolescence. This necessitated leaving home and living with their master and mistress; it might mean leaving their village or town and settling in another community, where they had to build new relationships; many were attracted to the nearest large town, where their parents might have gone to market or done business. They did not necessarily go into the same trade as their fathers. Records date from the fifteenth century but mirror earlier practice. Thus, in 1494 to 1495, John, son of William Bukland of Wellingborough, mercer, was apprenticed to Henry Marler of Coventry, grocer, for the term of eight years; John Griffith of Coventry was apprenticed to John Darlyng of Coventry, capper, for eight years; Thomas, son of Gibben Brettebe, of Nantwich, husbandman, was apprenticed to Richard Brikwode, shearman, for six years.[16] Their apprenticeship brought them into contact with boys and girls of their own age, with the craft guilds, and with the town government, and, at the end of their apprenticeship, they had the option of staying in the town, returning home, or moving elsewhere.

According to the educational treatises, girls were expected to stay with their mothers through youth and adolescence until they married. Mothers were expected to be a formative influence, so that daughters grew up chaste and virtuous, with the skills that would keep them occupied and would be useful in their future household. Spinning and weaving were recommended, and it was taken for granted that girls would learn housekeeping and child care. Girls of the elite were taught music, dancing, and embroidery. Opinion was divided about whether girls should be taught to read, but this skill was increasingly taught in the later Middle Ages as a way to deepen their religious devotion and to fill their time. The image of Saint Anne teaching the Virgin Mary to read and pray was popular in the later Middle Ages.[17]

Communities outside the family were often involved in girls' upbringing. Many girls had a home-based training, but much depended on the expectations of their families and regional social attitudes. Girls entered nunneries as infants in the early Middle Ages, while, later, they were more likely to enter as adolescents—in both cases, leaving their natal families. Nunneries were also used to educate girls and small boys, and they would be supervised as at home. Some urban schools also existed for girls, where they could gain an elementary education.[18]

For the elite, the situation in Italy contrasted with that in northwestern
Europe, with girls being more controlled by the family because of the strong
code of honor, the emphasis on virginal brides, and the early age of marriage.
Moreover, the role of the married woman was more limited than in France,
Germany, and England. According to Alberti's treatise on the family, the husband continued his wife's training in housekeeping, and it is clear that she was
not expected to know her husband's concerns outside the household and was
not to engage in business.[19] In northwestern Europe, elite girls usually married
later, often to husbands of similar age.[20] They had more experience of the world
outside their families; like boys, they were often sent to other households as
part of their education and also made visits with their parents. As wives, they
were expected to run businesses and estates in their husbands' absence; many
continued to do this as widows.

These girls can be seen as going into a form of service with other families.
Like the boys, they often moved into a new community and had to make new
relationships. The ethic of service was widespread and promoted the girls'
social talents, contacts, and self-reliance. The evidence for girls in service is
best for the later Middle Ages, especially after the Black Death, but the practice
probably went back to an earlier period. By the time that most went into service, they would have been accustomed to carrying out household tasks, and
many became general maids, cleaning, cooking, and spinning, and responsible
for poultry and work in the dairy. All these constituted useful preparation
for marriage. The master and mistress took over a parental role, although
natal parents were probably aware of the risk of sexual abuse and rape. Servants were engaged at a young age in southern Europe; at Arles, girls aged
between three and thirteen years worked as servants, and from the age of eight
in Florence and Venice. Teenage girls were employed in England and Germany,
probably in large numbers, judging by the evidence of the English poll tax
returns. Fewer girls than boys were apprenticed, but instances are found in
France, Spain, Germany, and England, mainly in the food and textile trades.
The women's guilds in the silk industry in Paris and Cologne encouraged girl
apprentices, but there are signs in the late Middle Ages that girls' opportunities
in both apprenticeship and service were becoming more limited.[21]

Youth and adolescence for many children marked a break in their lives when
they came into contact with other families and communities. They probably
had more freedom than they would have had at home, and this development
can probably be dated to the growth of towns after about 1100. They were at
an age when they became aware of their sexuality and were exploring social
relationships. Both church and estate records show that boys and girls enjoyed

each other's company and, in some cases, entered clandestine marriages.[22] Even when their parents were involved in the marriage arrangements, the children probably had a considerable say as to whom they wanted to marry. This probably would have been more true of northwestern Europe, with its pattern of later, companionate marriage, than in Italy. Teenagers of the nobility and urban elites were more circumscribed by alliances arranged by their parents, but the social contacts within these groups may well have given them a say as to whom they preferred.

Throughout youth and adolescence, the church provided a framework for religious practice and teaching on behavior, marriage, and morality, as well as

FIGURE 2.1: *The initial* C *showing a clandestine marriage.* Note the presence of a friar rather than a priest. *Omne Bonum*, England, 1360–1375. © The British Library Board (BL Royal MS. 6 E. VI, f. 286v).

for socializing and recreation. The growth in the number of churches by 1200 made it increasingly easy to participate in church life, and children became aware of belonging to a community that transcended boundaries. Before the twelfth century, children who had been baptized were admitted to confession and communion, but the doctrinal and legal changes of the twelfth and thirteenth centuries led to a marked distinction between child and adult, and admission to both sacraments came at about the age of fourteen.

Some children were naturally pious, but all children were taken to church from an early age, despite complaints that they became noisy and restless. Church attendance was expected but not compulsory. Children were also taken to sermons and on pilgrimage to shrines, especially if they were ill or disabled. Through their attendance at mass, they gradually became aware that the service was celebrated for the whole community, living and dead. This social emphasis was vital through to the Reformation. By the time they were communicants, children would participate in the offertory and the sharing of the pax/peace as full members of this community.[23]

The parish church took the child into a very different world from their own homes—a world of lights and color, of paintings of biblical stories, and of images and paintings of saints. Boys and girls were absorbed into the life of the community. Although most parish guilds were for adults, some parishes had guilds for adolescents. In England, a guild of young men existed at Bury Saint Edmunds in 1264, and a guild of young scholars at King's Lynn in 1383. More guilds for young men and for maidens were established in England in the fifteenth century.[24] These guilds participated in processions, as at Saint Margaret's Church in Westminster, and in social activities. Maidens were active in fundraising at Walberswick, Suffolk. On Hock Monday and Tuesday, in the second week after Easter, women were allowed to hold men to ransom, thus overturning the social order.

Men and women were segregated during church services, but there were other opportunities to socialize. Many English parishes held May revels, more of a secular than a religious occasion. Boys were recruited by the church as choristers and servers, while older boys might serve as parish clerk. The appointment of the boy bishop in December represented a temporary overturning of the social order. Children took part in processions, as at Christmas and Easter in the abbey of Saint-Riquier in the early ninth century, and, later, in the Corpus Christi processions in German towns.[25] All over Europe, there were opportunities to watch religious plays and pageants that were mounted for important visitors. Many saints' days were treated as holidays, a time to go out with friends as well as to participate in the religious festival. Throughout their childhood and adolescence, children grew into full membership of the community of the church.

THE COMMUNITY AND BEREAVEMENT

In view of low life expectancy in the medieval world, especially after the Black Death, many children lost one or both parents before they grew up. The questions of inheritance and guardianship were usually a matter for the community, which had the duty of supervising arrangements and of enforcing the law. Such questions did not normally arise over the death of a mother; the usual practice for a man who lost his wife was for him to remarry, and many medieval children belonged to stepfamilies. More serious questions arose on the death of a father. Urban customs varied in the ways they dealt with this eventuality. In Florence, matters were normally decided within the family. The widow might be forced to return to her natal family and abandon her children to her husband's family; if she remained in the marital home, she would be with her children but not entitled to act as guardian. This contrasts with the situation with freemen's families in London, where the mother was usually regarded as a suitable guardian and was expected to remarry. The situation was always supervised by the civic authorities, who kept an eye on the children and investigated cases of neglect; they also controlled a child's apprenticeship and marriage, and ensured that his future property was not wasted. The situation was comparable in Ghent, with the town government exercising general supervision over orphans. Most of the children remained with the surviving parent, who was rarely the legal guardian; the guardian was usually a man chosen from the extended family.[26]

Feudal law saw the dead father's lord as guardian, and he expected to make a profit out of his custody of the heir and his land. Some heirs lived in the lord's household during their minority. By the later Middle Ages, however, it was sometimes possible, as in England, for the heir to remain with his mother, at least during infancy; in the 1290s, Gilbert de Clare remained with his mother until he was about ten years old, when he transferred into the household of Queen Margaret. In Normandy, however, mothers were regarded in law as unsuitable for guardianship.[27]

Among the peasantry, customs varied, as in England, where guardianship was dealt with in the manor courts from the thirteenth century, although some of the customs must have been in place earlier. The father's inheritance might pass to the eldest or the youngest son or might be divided equally among all the sons. In Kent, where partible inheritance existed among gavelkind tenants, the mother or a member of the family usually acted as guardian in a minority, and the heir came of age at fifteen. Elsewhere, among unfree peasants, once the heriot had been paid for the dead father, the mother often became the heir's guardian. At Walsham le Willows, Suffolk, in 1317, after the death of William Typetot, leaving a son, aged six, as his heir, a mare was given to the lord as heriot, and William's widow sought her son's custody; the jurors stated that it was her right and the custom of the manor.[28]

Looking at these arrangements from the child's viewpoint, the greatest continuity was secured where the mother or a close relation acted as guardian, although her remarriage might cause tensions. It was vital for the community to play a part in the arrangements in order to ensure the child's inheritance and future training. The arrangements in Italian families led to instances of personal unhappiness and a double bereavement for the children, but the prevailing attitude in medieval Europe was to encourage self-reliance and discourage displays of emotion and temper. Feudal wards might have found themselves most uprooted, if unable to remain in the household and community where they had been born, but, in any case, they would expect to move to other households in youth and adolescence. The practice in noble families of arranging marriages for their children at an early age was designed to ensure that family plans went ahead, even if the father died.

Where children lost both parents, had no family, or were illegitimate, it was the community that made provision. The problem was most acute in the towns where there was a danger that destitute and abandoned children would die if the community took no action. Hospitals were founded in large numbers from the eleventh century by the church, by guilds, and by individual patrons, and some provided for children. Saint Bartholomew's hospital in London catered for, among other groups, unmarried mothers, and, if the mother died, the child was kept and cared for. The Hôtel-Dieu in Paris cared for the disabled and seriously ill, pregnant women, and abandoned children. In Florence, abandoned children were taken in by the hospitals of Santa Maria della Scala and San Gallo from around 1300. This problem increased in the later Middle Ages, despite the fall in the city's population, and this led to the foundation of the hospital of the Innocenti in the fifteenth century. There were also foundling hospitals in Rome and Venice; Ghent had two small orphanages.[29]

The church, guilds, private individuals, and, in some cases, town authorities were responsible for relieving the poor by means of almsgiving in money and food as well as care in hospitals and almshouses. This was regarded as a religious duty, the poor reciprocating by their prayers for their benefactors. Destitute children may have benefited from casual almsgiving, but documents usually record the types of relief without specifying the groups of poor people whom they hoped to benefit. The parishes in Ghent maintained Holy Ghost Tables, which dispensed food, fuel, and shoes; the wealthiest confraternity in Florence in the fourteenth century, the Orsanmichele, relieved the poor in the famine of 1329;[30] English wills prescribed the rewards for the poor, in money and clothing, for attending funerals and acting as mourners around the bier, and some testators left money for the poor on their estates. In all these cases, children may have been involved.

HORIZONS AND IDENTITY

As a result of the various patterns of education, training, and socialization, children gained different horizons. Most had a sense of place—the town or village where they had been born and spent their early years, and the place where they had trained during adolescence for their adult lives. Many thought in terms of region as well as birthplace. Village children would have gone to local markets from an early age and heard local and national news and rumors. Town children would know of the surrounding villages where their parents had business and social contacts. Migration in the later Middle Ages often took place within an eleven-mile (eighteen-kilometer) radius, indicating the size of region that medieval people knew about.

The horizons of the merchant elite and the nobility took in national and international fields. With their common interests, attitudes, and values, both merchants and nobles can be regarded as communities in their own right, a fact epitomized by their role as separate estates in parliaments and assemblies. Merchant children of the elite would hear stories of their fathers' travels and business and, through apprenticeship, get to know the goods they traded in, where the best markets were, and what these places were like. Having the advantage of books, they may have read and been inspired by the travels of Marco Polo. Trading was risky and dangerous, but, provided that their families did not suffer disaster, there should have been enough wealth to enable them to set up in trade on their own. They would assimilate the aspirations of upward mobility into the gentry or nobility, and political power within their own towns, rated highly by fellow merchants. Merchants constituted a strongly interrelated group.[31] By the later Middle Ages, merchants were marrying into noble families—as, for example, the de la Pole family of Hull, who became earls of Suffolk—and the wealthiest had adopted a noble lifestyle. The great urban confraternities attracted membership from both merchants and nobles and their families over a wide area, such as the Corpus Christi confraternity of York and Holy Trinity at Coventry, giving an added dimension to religious experience and providing increased social contacts.

Being at the top of the social hierarchy under the king, the nobility always enjoyed a special place in society, with a distinct culture; their households can be viewed as communities in their own right, with their own social hierarchy and interests. In the early Middle Ages, the noble and his band of retainers followed a life of fighting, hunting, and feasting, as depicted in the epic poem *Beowulf;* many of the retainers would be adolescents, hoping for rewards and riches. With the growth of chivalry in the eleventh and twelfth centuries, and its increasing elaboration and ritual over the rest of the Middle Ages, the nobility can be viewed as an international brotherhood, adhering to the same values of courage, service, and loyalty, and enjoying the same pursuits of warfare and the tournament. Boys' training was designed to make them chivalrous knights, while girls imbibed the chivalrous ethos in order to play their part of inspiring their knights, notably at tournaments.[32] The emphasis on the knight's quest in romances contributed to this education in chivalry.

On a more mundane level, the nobility were proud of their families and, increasingly, of their lineage. Such pride had to be passed on to the next generation, and it is likely that this was done by informal means. Estate management was vital, and boys needed the administrative skills to supervise effectively the

FIGURE 2.2: *Sir Geoffrey Luttrell, with his wife and members of his household, seated in the center of a long table.* The Luttrell Psalter, England, 1325–1335. © The British Library Board (BL Add. MS. 42130, f. 208).

officials in charge of their estates and to take on public office in the future. In parts of Europe where women took over responsibility for estates in their husbands' absence and as widows, girls needed to gain similar skills. Children may have learned them from their fathers' officials, while gaining some familiarity with the estates themselves. Pride in their lineage was probably gained from stories from parents and servants and from reading the legends of their families, such as the story of the Knight of the Swan of the Bohun family, earls of Hereford and Essex. Parents fostered this pride through their bequests of heirlooms, designed to remain in the family from one generation to the next, as shown in the will of Eleanor de Bohun, duchess of Gloucester, in 1399. Identification with other noble families came through their education in their households, family visits, and membership of the large confraternities. Children also needed to learn how to exercise patronage, and they probably assimilated the actions of their parents in attracting retainers, making gifts to religious houses, giving presents to fellow nobles, and offering hospitality to the locality.[33] The various forms of patronage comprised an essential element in the noble lifestyle that children were expected to maintain in the next generation and to pass on to their heirs.

CONCLUSION

Community is a complex phenomenon in the Middle Ages, taking many different forms. Although the family made the major decisions over upbringing, and the mother was especially important during infancy, communities had a major role to play for both boys and girls, especially during youth and adolescence. Formal training was provided in the community, while community values and traditions were assimilated. In the event of the father's death, guardianship and the child's inheritance were usually regarded as community concerns. As far as the merchant elite and the nobility were concerned, family and community overlapped. Taking the wide variety of meanings of community into consideration, it constituted an essential element in the child's life.

CHAPTER THREE

Economy

PHILLIPP R. SCHOFIELD

Distinguishing between types of domestic economy across Europe and in a time frame of six hundred years, from the beginning of the ninth century to the end of the fourteenth century, presents problems of selection and description. The following discussion will be forced to move between broad generalizations and particular instances, the latter to be employed as much as tests or limits to the general picture as they are to emphasize its typicality. That said, it is reasonable to propose that, across European society in the Middle Ages, the majority of people lived lives that were, in some respect, connected to agrarian activity and that, irrespective of significant cultural—and sometimes material—differences, most lived and died in small, mostly nuclear, households. By contrast, our best and most detailed evidence relates to households that were large and the economies of which were far from typical, even if, in their structure and in their culture, there existed shared features. These vast generalities will underpin a good deal of the following discussion but will not allow us to lose sight of the considerable differences across time and space to which there will be need to make more than passing reference.

Although this chapter has the economy of childhood and family as its focus, the chapter is also geared to a discussion of the relationship between age groups—in other words, not wholly a discussion of the role of children within the family economy but also a consideration of the exchange and economic relationship of parents and their offspring, as infants, juveniles, and young adults. The changing economic relationship between the generations as the members of each age and their role shifts is as or more important to this discussion of the family economy as is the more particular discussion of the importance of childhood per se.

HOUSEHOLD ECONOMIES

The economy of the household, discussed across time and across space, also exhibits the same broad and familiar features as well as the differences of detail. For most of the period and for most of the population of medieval Europe, the economy and overall maintenance of the household was founded upon the labor of its members, including children. Only in the relatively few households that were large and the organization of which was founded on a grander scale—generally, religious or elite households—was the economy of the household most evidently at one remove. This discussion begins with the households of the relatively poor, in town and countryside, to establish a general position before considering some of their variety, this latter to include the relatively wealthy and the particularly discrete household types and their economies.

As noted, most people in medieval Europe spent all or part of their lives in nuclear households in the countryside. Throughout our sources and especially where those sources include per capita listings of household members in the form of cadastres or family lists, it is clear that households were typically fairly small and two-generational. The polyptychs of Saint-Germain-des-Prés from the ninth century, for instance, suggest that forty-two percent of tenants listed on the monastery's estates lived in nuclear, two-generational households. In early-fourteenth-century Macedonia, the households of the dependent peasantry, the *paroikoi,* were predominantly nuclear in structure, the typical structure composed of a married couple and their children. Similarly, in late-fourteenth- and early-fifteenth-century Tuscany, most households were nuclear in structure, though there is also evidence for some retreat of the conjugal nuclear structure in favor of more complex multi-conjugal units. Most people lived and worked in the countryside. Even in the more urbanized parts of Europe, especially high and late medieval Italy, the percentage of those living in towns was relatively slight. In Italy, around 1300, and allowing for some significant regional variation, around twenty to twenty-five percent of Italians (two and a half to three million of a total population of twelve and a half million) lived in towns. Elsewhere the proportions of urban to rural population were significantly lower, as, for example, in Scandinavia, where the urban population was small indeed. Within towns, there was a predominance of nuclear households, often the creation of an immigrant and recently established population, as well as a relatively high proportion of more elaborate household structures and economies established by a wealthy and relatively well-established urban patriciate. This essay will return a little later to consider further the difference between rural and urban household economies in this period. For the moment, it is possible to set out some of the main features of household economies across the period, as well as examining the place of children within them.[1]

It is reasonable to assume, even if it is not always possible to substantiate, that, for most medieval households, the membership of a household was the key determinant of its economy. In a period before industrialization, the possibility that one or two members of a medium-sized to large household would, through their labor alone, generate sufficient resources to sustain the household in its entirety was remote. The modeling of peasant economies for the Middle Ages suggests that the margin between inputs and outputs was quite small and that, in such circumstances, outputs, chiefly in terms of agricultural produce, increased and declined with the size of the family. This is a theory often associated with the peasant household across time, and not only in the Middle Ages, and is, in particular, associated with the work of A. V. Chayanov, whose theory of peasant economy has encouraged some direct and relatively indirect comment on the nature of peasant economies, especially in relation to the market in land in this period. Thus, to follow a relatively early discussion of the land market in medieval England, the involvement of peasant buyers and sellers in such a market was, according to M. M. Postan, occasioned in no small part by "certain abiding features of peasant life," especially the instabilities and inequalities of peasant families.[2] It was therefore the natural increase and decline of individual families and households that encouraged or reduced involvement in extrafamilial economic or quasi-economic activity. While such conceptions of the economic motivation of the peasant family would not be wholly supported by the research of historians working more recently on aspects of the peasant family and economy, the view that the economy of many families was dependent upon their own collective input is accepted. In tenth-century Catalonia, for instance, there is clear indication that natural buyers and sellers existed, with more single men being sellers of land (43.1%) than they were purchasers (27.8%).[3]

We, therefore, conceive of and observe households in the Middle Ages as composed of family members who were employed in work in support of the household and where it also appears reasonably evident that it was the combined product of that endeavor that sustained the household. The relatively few attempts to "model" the economic activity of the medieval household tend to assume a general range of activity that included the input of the majority, but not all, of the members of the household.[4] When evidence for familial labor in support of family and household is considered, instances of a range of economic activity representative of gender- and age-specific activity are revealed, points that will be addressed in the following section. In this respect, some consideration also needs to be given to those who were not expected to contribute to the income of the household (typically for reasons of infirmity) but who were, for reasons as manifold as love, charity, obligation, and investment, afforded opportunities to consume the product of the family and household.

Medieval households were not exclusive economies in which membership was confined only to those who could contribute directly to their and other members' sustenance. There is plentiful evidence both for the support of the elderly within houses and, more obviously, the maintenance of children. Care for the elderly is, for instance, exhibited, in maintenance agreements established between parents and their adult offspring or between siblings in order to ensure the well-being of the infirm party. In the mid-fourteenth century in Anglesey (Wales), to offer one such instance, Gruffydd ap Dafydd gave his goods to his daughter and her husband in return for his maintenance in his old age.[5] There is also clear evidence that children were sustained until such age as they might care for themselves or take on initial forms of employment in support of the domestic economy. We will return to the latter point in the following section, but it is worth noting here that childbirth and the rearing of children, vital to the maintenance of the family and its lineage, undoubtedly placed significant burdens upon the family. Decisions relating to the weaning of children and of wet-nursing reflect the capacity of individual families and households to cope with the additional demands of infancy. In more extreme circumstances, it has been suggested, families abandoned their dependent members. Discussion of infanticide in the Middle Ages has failed to generate a consensus, but there is little doubt that households, if not families, might reject some of their members in the most difficult years. During the Great Famine of the early fourteenth century, the larger lay and ecclesiastical households, according to one English chronicler, reduced the size of their households, dismissing some of their servants and consigning them to possible starvation. In similar ways, a family's capacity to extend its resources to those beyond its membership was undoubtedly and obviously constrained by the limits of its own resources, a point to which this chapter will also return in the discussion of families and their property. As a major precept of the medieval canonical theory of charity, the contention that charity began at home was on reasonably secure ground in a period when most households were poor and lacking in significant expendable surplus.[6]

As noted, the limits of sustainable membership of households and of household economies were not constant, either for individual families or within different social and economic groups. Membership of larger households in the Middle Ages tended to reflect the wealth of those households. It is evident, from estimates and some calculation of peasant households in different parts of Europe and for different periods in the Middle Ages, that wealth was a significant determinant of the size of the biological family. In late-thirteenth- and early-fourteenth-century Halesowen (England), for instance, wealthier families produced five children, and the poorest families produced one. In addition, and perhaps more obviously, the largest and wealthiest households were large not because of the size of the family membership but because of residents who were present because they were "employed"—typically either as paid employees, as some form of retainer, or, in the case of religious households, as monks, nuns, or *conversi*. The largest royal households in the high and late Middle Ages might, for instance, comprise several hundred members, a significant number of whom were servants.[7]

WOMEN'S AND CHILDREN'S LABOR

Within the biological household, both women and children were employed as significant contributors to the household's economy. In fact, women have been identified as "the cornerstone of the family economy."[8] Women's role within the domestic economy has most clearly been associated with the work of wives within rather than beyond the home. Later medieval commentaries illustrate the perceived role of women in this period, as illustrated, for instance, in the late-fifteenth-century English poem, *Ballad of a Tyrannical Husband,* where "the good wife had much to do, and servant she had none,/many small children to look after beside herself alone,/she did more than he could inside her own house."[9] Other evidence supports this sense of wives employed within the home. Court records, including coroners' records, illustrate the proximity of women to the hearth. In medieval England, women were, judging by an analysis of records of accidental death, almost three times as likely as men to die in their homes or in the immediate proximity of the home. Men typically died of accidents, including work-related injuries, further afield. These women's deaths reflect the daily round of work within the household, including deaths associated with the fetching and carrying of water or fuel and injuries arising from laundry work.[10]

FIGURE 3.1: *The toil of Adam and Eve.* A biblical illustration (ca. 1270–1280) inserted
into a fourteenth-century Psalter, England. With permission of the master and fellows
of St. John's College, Cambridge (St. John's College, Cambridge, MS. K. 26, f. 5).

It would not, though, be correct to suggest that women's economic activity in such households was constrained within a domestic sphere. Women were engaged in plentiful activity in support of their families and households that took them beyond the household; a combination of evidence, especially from the later Middle Ages, including material arising from labor legislation and court records in relation to accidental deaths, illustrates the role of women in agrarian activity, for instance. Women and children were employed in important but relatively light agricultural work, such as gleaning. In addition, women were traditionally employed in aspects of pastoral husbandry. Commercial brewing, baking, and other forms of protoindustrial activity also offered employment for married and unmarried women.[11]

At different moments during this period, including relatively brief periods in the later Middle Ages, when a significant fall in the level of the European population reduced the size and availability of the male labor force, women found new employment opportunities beyond both the household and the immediate confines of the domestic economy. At these times, women—more likely unmarried younger women—filled the vacancies more typically occupied by men in heavier agricultural work.[12] Significant also in terms of employment that took women from the immediacy of their own households and families was service within other households. Often associated with the employment of young women and men prior to marriage, service, even where it took place in the household of another, did not necessarily draw women from the economies of their natal households. Research on servants in early modern and modern society has indicated the support that labor and service by those living away from the domestic hearth could offer in terms of, for instance, redistribution of wages and, indeed, the temporary removal of an additional mouth to feed.[13]

In ways that are, in many respects, similar to those observed for women, the employment of children within the family provided more than piecemeal support for the family's economy. Older children in most households undoubtedly supported, and were expected to support, the work and economy of the family and household. This work was divided along gendered lines, with women supported by their daughters and younger siblings and men by their sons and brothers. Thus, girls and younger women involved themselves in work and chores within the household and with elements of child care, supporting their mother in the care of their younger siblings. Boys and young men might be expected to participate in their father's labor, sharing agricultural work and other forms of labor or craft. In the households of elites—and particularly in lay households founded upon landed wealth—women and children fulfilled

FIGURE 3.2: *Reaping and binding sheaves in a harvest field.* The Luttrell Psalter, England, 1325–1335. © The British Library Board (BL Add. MS. 42130, f. 172v).

different roles but ones that contributed to the success and advance of their families and households. Thus, to offer the most obvious instance, heads of households drew upon their women and juvenile members to secure marriage alliances and to maintain lines of succession. In other respects, women might be expected to oversee the running of households, as the histories of women members of the nobility suggest. In the mid-thirteenth century, to offer one example, Margaret de Lacy, countess of Lincoln, widowed at a fairly early age, presided over a significant household and large estates. In more extreme instances, especially those occasioned by the prolonged absence of one or another key member of the household, a gendered division of tasks was often maintained. In thirteenth-century Italy, for example, leading merchants might be absent from their families for years and perhaps even decades; Ricciardo Guidiccioni was absent from his native Lucca and his family for all but short periods over twenty-two years, during which time his wife raised their two children in "an extended fraternal household" overseen by Ricciardo's brother, Guidiccione.[14]

It is almost impossible to disaggregate the contribution of women and children to the familial economy.[15] The role of women, relative to that of men, is typically less easily quantified and, it is seldom easily quantified for men. Where wage labor was the basis of the familial economy, and, for most families for most of the Middle Ages, wage labor was far from being the significant component, then it might be easier to quantify the contribution of the wage earner. Even if it is difficult to gauge accurately the input, it is possible to identify an association between size of household and relative wealth in this period. Larger families were both cause and consequence of relative success; the higher survival rate of infants, for instance, potentially reflected an enhanced availability of resource, while a surplus of resource in land and moveable wealth also presented opportunities for relatively early marriage in the kind of homeostatic marriage formation system associated with the peasantry. In such circumstances, the processes by which, from time to time, larger families employed their members in pressing home their advantage over their neighbors can be identified, as, for instance, in later medieval Halesowen, where the sons of the wealthy villagers bullied and coerced the poorer families of the manor.[16]

In an urban context or where land was not the core component of a rural family's economy, as in the case of the rural landless, then the significance of wage labor or of products sold through some aspect of protoindustry was far greater. In such circumstances, men and women may have contributed to their economies in ways that were directly comparable rather than, as in an agrarian or peasant context, discrete but mutually enhancing. Recent work on the employment and economic role of women in later medieval Porto (Portugal) has indicated the variety of tasks that women might undertake in an urban environment, and, while suggesting that women tended to work as part of the family's "economic cell," their tasks were not confined to the domestic sphere but instead could also draw them into economic dealing beyond the home. Here consideration can also be given to the resources gathered by women and men through such employment as service in anticipation of marriage and household formation, the so-called real wages or proletarian household formation system. Men and women operating within such a system in the later Middle Ages might well have aspired to escape an economy founded upon wages for an economy secured by land or at least to establish their offspring on such a footing; that this would not have been universally the case is evidenced by the labor legislation of the second half of the fourteenth century aimed at reducing excessive wages.[17]

RURAL AND URBAN ECONOMIES

In exploring the differences between types of household formation systems and the nature of economies that operated within them and that helped to establish them, our attention is inevitably drawn to a distinction between the economies of town and countryside. This distinction becomes increasingly evident, especially in those parts of Europe where, in the high and later Middle Ages, an urban economy expanded. Much of the research has been undertaken upon medieval families whose chief resource was land and whose income, either in the form of rent or of direct produce, was generated through landholding and/or land use. In such circumstances, as already noted and as will be discussed further in the final section of this chapter, much else in the familial economy flows from this association, including the employment of its members and the transfer and availability of its resources.

By contrast, the economies of many urban dwellers and their families in the Middle Ages were established differently. It is something of a truism, but one not wholly supported by material from the Middle Ages, that towns were home to those who, in relative terms, operated without the support of family and more distant kin. It is certainly the case that towns attracted those who lacked the support of their families. We tend to think, therefore, of individuals seeking economic opportunity in towns as strangers and operating far from established networks of support. It is for this reason, as more than one commentator has observed, that towns have been identified as the focus for units of support other than the family: guilds and fraternities, hospitals and almshouses, and so on. To quote one instance, and many more could be offered here, peasants in parts of Austria established, by the close of the Middle Ages, parish trusts (*Stiftungen*) in order to support various aspects of social welfare, including the costs of burial.[18]

Towns undoubtedly supported more of a range of economic activity than did villages and smaller settlements in the countryside. The growth and expansion of towns influenced the economies of their hinterlands and also drew some of the urban populace within their orbit. A significant question in terms of the family economy and the role of children in this respect is the degree to which those entering towns and urban economies did so as individuals or chiefly, and in economic terms, as family members. Each can be considered in turn.

The proportion of single men and women entering towns is only occasionally indicated in listings of urban residents. Thus, for instance, the poll taxes from late-fourteenth-century England suggest that a relatively high proportion of town populations included those who were employed in towns as individuals and often within the households of other families as apprentices and servants. The same was also the case in towns in other parts of Europe. The *catasto* of Florence (1427) suggests an influx of women and widows into the town in search of labor and support. Such movement certainly involved the poor more than it did the relatively rich, a feature hardly unexpected in that it was typically only those who lacked familial support who may have sought such opportunities. It is reasonable to suspect, for instance, that the non-inheriting offspring of relatively poor rural dwellers moved from their place of origin in search of employment and new opportunity. It has also been estimated for medieval England and Italy that, in the last decades of the Middle Ages, when this is most evident in our sources, such movement into towns was also marked by an age-specific cohort of those in their late teens and early twenties. For this cohort, towns, including both smaller market towns and the larger towns and cities, provided the potential for wealth accumulation and opportunities for household formation that their own families could not provide. For others, towns, especially in moments of extreme crisis and especially in periods of famine and dearth, offered one last bastion of hope. Narrative accounts of food shortage and its consequence in medieval Europe describe the influx of the needy at such moments, to which the few relatively quantitative sources add further detail. Crisis-driven mobility of this kind speaks to the failure and the endemic vulnerability of many family and household economies in this period, and most particularly in the years of population expansion before the Black Death of the mid-fourteenth century.[19]

Even in such circumstances, however, there was not necessarily an absolute rupture of family ties. As already noted, families left behind by those seeking work might continue to maintain associations, including economic links. Local court records, for instance, indicate (often in no more than a passing reference), that families maintained contact with those of their members who had moved away in search of work, or that they were at least aware of their planned destinations. From time to time, and especially upon the death of tenants, lords sought information on the whereabouts of potential heirs and sometimes discovered that the relatives had left. On occasion, the expectation was that the heir might return to take up the inheritance, and this must have happened sometimes. In such circumstances, as might be assumed and also by employing work on early modern and modern families that addresses the same issue, those living away from the family home might continue to help provide for the family, returning some of their resource to their families in the form of money and kind. If not necessarily a regular contribution, it was an accumulation of capital that might find its way back to the main family hearth. In that sense, though separated from rural or peasant households and families, and operating within a different kind of economy, such individuals were still partly located within the same domestic economy. In other instances, however, it is also as likely that the immigrant family members had struck out into the world in search of entirely new pastures and that their labor and capital accumulation were for their own immediate advantage and the benefit of any new family and household they might establish.[20]

This latter point also reminds us of the familial base of economic dealing, even in an urban context. While the proportion of single men and women was most likely greater in towns, most people lived in families and in households where there was a degree of mutual dependency and support, including support of an economic nature. In that sense, husbands and wives might conduct themselves within the broad spheres of public and private, which have already been identified for the domestic economies of the countryside. The children of urban families might also engage in labor and crafts, supporting their families while, sometimes, resident in the household. Furthermore, there were those relative elites within towns whose economies were often, though not necessarily, founded upon landed wealth and who conducted themselves and operated within a traditional domestic culture. In such circumstances, wealthy urban dwellers engaged in quasi-economic activity consistent with a standard of dealing long associated with landholding elites, cementing their business relationships by marital agreements, maintaining large and complex households, investing capital in landholding, and transferring their assets post mortem by inheritance. The associations of the Ricciardi bankers at Lucca in the late thirteenth century, for instance, were reinforced by kinship and by marital ties. The same was also true of the Guidiccioni at Lucca in the same period, the mercantile business operating from a single household composed of more than one family, including at least eleven men and an unknown number of women and servants. Significantly, mercantile elites in towns, at least in some parts of Europe, were content to reemploy their profits in rural investment rather than in the capital ventures through which they had established their wealth. In England, a process, sometimes described as a "circular tour of rural wealth," saw mercantile capital in the fifteenth century invested in rural estates and a consequent social mobility of merchants whose offspring were elevated into the ranks of the nobility. In such circumstances, it was wealth accumulated by one generation that established the next generation on a wholly different footing.[21]

It is also important to recognize that not all rural contexts operated in ways that were consistent with an economy based in the countryside any more than did every urban context generate what might be considered to be economic dealing of a kind that was particularly "urban." In the countryside, in the high and later Middle Ages, there were, for instance, pockets of industry and protoindustry, such as brewing, mining, and the cloth industry, the characteristics of which were contrary to those most associated with a peasant economy. These protoindustrial economies were often founded upon a high degree of physical mobility and upon a transient population of small families with limited kin bases. Such families might also be associated with a real wages or proletarian household formation system, with relatively late marriage as a consequence and a tendency for the children to leave the natal hearth in search of waged employment or service.[22]

FAMILIES AND THEIR PROPERTY

For a significant majority of individuals in the Middle Ages, rights in property were closely associated with family ties. Medieval families were, in many respects, defined by their property, not least in the capacity of their property to sustain them. Thus, the *terra unius familie,* the land capable of sustaining a single family, was a standard, though far from always maintained, of medieval estates and the allocation of holdings to the tenantry. Those designated as heirs by custom, law, and familial preference and those who did not inherit might expect their futures to be secured by their families. Marriage and the distribution of family property, especially moveable goods, both served to support family members and might operate as alternatives to inheritance.

We can briefly discuss in turn both inheritance and inter vivos (premortem) and postmortem distribution of property to those not designated heirs. Inheritance systems operated in a variety of forms in the Middle Ages. As Goetz has described, there was a developing focus in the early Middle Ages on the immediate family as the most likely heirs in medieval Europe, with a tendency for children to benefit at the expense of more distant kin. Single men were the principal beneficiaries in systems based on primogeniture. At the same time, other inheritance systems operated, including those that favored all surviving male heirs (partibility) and the youngest male heir (ultimogeniture). In certain other contexts—as, for instance, in much of medieval Scandinavia—sons and daughters might both inherit. The consequence of discrete inheritance systems upon family structure and household formation systems is, of course, potentially significant to the extent that it caused individuals to remain close to their natal hearth or to seek opportunity elsewhere. That said, inheritance and non-inheritance were not the only routes to familial support. Non-inheriting children might be established by their families in various ways, including a premortem distribution of land or goods, accommodation within the household of the heir, or as a marriage dowry—the latter, for instance, evident in recent work on dowry in the high Middle Ages.[23]

Martha Howell has also suggested that, in an increasingly commercialized society by the close of the Middle Ages, where marital property was as likely to be founded upon moveable goods as it was upon land, the consequence was to effect a cultural impact upon the nature of the marital relation, redefining it in terms of the relative transience of the economic base of the union and encouraging a greater regard for reciprocity and mutual support.[24] Among other things, the relevance of this thesis is to remind us that households and families in the Middle Ages operated in ways that were not concentrated wholly upon their own domestic economies. Throughout the period, domestic economies interacted, albeit to varying degrees, with market economies. It is not, of course, a simple task to identify all or even most aspects of this interaction. However, land, labor, moveable goods, and capital all found their way to and from the family and household throughout the Middle Ages. For some, such engagement must have been relatively insignificant. The occupants of the *terra unius familie,* for instance, might enjoy a relative degree of isolation from the market in much the same way as the small urban household of the waged labor might be placed in a position of total dependency upon the same.

For the majority of households and families in the Middle Ages it is not possible to establish with any precision patterns of consumption arising from either production within the household or from market engagement. Good evidence survives for dealing in land, labor, and goods, and it is reasonable to assume that these goods were bought and sold as part of the pattern of consumption of families and households. Taxation assessments, wills, litigation over property, and archaeological evidence offer insights into the goods and foodstuffs that circulated in the Middle Ages and allow us to do far more than speculate about general consumption in the period. However, the details and the breakdown of consumption are, in most cases, unavailable, and rather than describe consumption at the level of the family or the individual member of the same, the compulsion is to generalize. That said, wealthier families and their households did generate information that provide details of their consumption patterns, and especially for the later Middle Ages. Thus, for instance, the account books of the more significant lay and ecclesiastical households offer information on income and expenses in relation to foodstuffs, the employment of servants, the costs of maintaining the household, and so on. On occasion, insight into the relatively minor households can be gained, as in the surviving mid-fifteenth-century accounts for two chantry priests in Bridport (England). In such instances, we are frequently impressed by the variety and scale of foodstuffs and the willingness to invest in fairly significant outlays, but also the capacity to adjust consumption according to circumstances, both social and economic.[25]

As has been suggested, the buildings that housed medieval families and their households reflect investment and some evidence for surplus, as do the moveable goods housed within them. High-status households expended considerable proportions of their income on consumption, including investment in luxury goods and fashion. Expensive foodstuffs were a familiar feature of the domestic economy of wealthier households in the Middle Ages, as documentary and archaeological evidence relating to consumption makes clear. Such behavior in terms of consumption, in turn, offers some insight into changing economic conditions and their implications for investment. Thus, for example, early medieval (eighth-century) Italian aristocratic town houses reveal some degree of investment but not, in general terms, one consistent with earlier or later periods and may reflect a period of relative urban crisis.[26]

Distribution of family property was within and beyond families a contentious issue, revealing anxieties over the retention and allocation of resources. Families and their members, especially those responsible for overseeing the distribution of resources within families (essentially the head of the household), were typically expected to meet their obligation to all members of the family. In that sense, family property was frequently perceived as such, and not as the property of the individual. An early-fifteenth-century dispute over property in Florence, for example, includes an exposition on the significance of property and the responsibilities attached thereto, including its appropriate employment for the good of the whole family. In similar vein, some of our earliest views of family property, chiefly land, and its transfer in this period relate to donations to churches by family members. A form of consumption and of an exercise of property right, transfer also resulted in contests over rights of alienation. Disputes between members of the family, often involving more than one generation, were occasioned by these distributions of property, as is evidenced by the ninth-century cartulary of Redon in southeastern Brittany. In Languedoc, in the tenth century, the consent of both married partners and their children was sometimes sought in support of the dispersal of goods to ecclesiastical institutions, with sons and daughters individually identified in charters as agreeing to the donation. In later centuries, the expectation that the spouse, typically the wife, would agree to alienation of property and thereby renounce her dower rights sometimes became a standard of the law of transfer of landed property. Similarly, those with some degree of political or jurisdictional power in this period (governments, lords, local communities) were exercised by the need to contain unfettered distribution of land and of moveable goods; injunctions in relation to alienation, inheritance, rent, and taxation all had implications for the functioning of the economy of the family and of the household.[27]

CONCLUSION

Postan, in a quote employed earlier in this chapter, hinted at the near time-lessness of aspects of the peasant existence, reflecting upon the persistent structures of an economy based upon the family even if, as he recognized, the economy and society of medieval Europe might undergo major changes across the period. Historians would now, though, also locate fundamental changes within the economy of the medieval household and be much less inclined to accept a thesis presenting the rural household as static. The extent to which either individual family members were dependent upon their family's resources or families were self-sustaining (and independent of external markets and other mechanisms for support, such as charitable institutions) varied considerably. That variety also informed choice, which might be limited or extensive, in terms of the allocation of resources, investment in goods and land, the employment of family members, the opportunity for leisure, and so on. In that sense, and as discussion in this chapter has suggested, the variety of causative factors playing upon the economy of the medieval family and the range of potential responses, conditioned as they were by social, cultural, and political contexts, generated discrete experiences even within a context of seemingly general patterns.

CHAPTER FOUR

Geography and the Environment

SOPHIA ADAMS

The daily lives of families in medieval Europe were profoundly affected by their geographical location and the environment. Their material culture and diet were influenced by where and how they lived. Children and adults who lived during the eleventh, twelfth, and thirteenth centuries also experienced significant economic and social change, which impacted heavily upon the world around them. This period saw dramatic demographic growth and an expansion in trade. These were, in turn, accompanied by shifts in the patterns of settlement. Although the greater part of the population continued to farm the land and reside in small rural settlements that might be home to no more than a handful of families, many existing communities grew significantly so that their inhabitants numbered in hundreds and thousands. The livelihoods of those who dwelt both within the older, expanding urban centers and the emergent new towns depended primarily upon commercial activities and manufacturing. By the later Middle Ages, for example, perhaps as many as a quarter of England's population alone pursued non-agricultural occupations—and new forms of building evolved to accommodate these occupations, often within a domestic setting.[1] At the same time, social structures were transformed as the families of the wealthy mercantile elite and skilled craftsmen aspired to rights of self-government and sought to adopt luxurious lifestyles. This was reflected in the quality of their housing, their daily fare, and their clothing, which rivaled those of the lower ranks of the landed aristocracy.

HOUSING

The study of housing in the Middle Ages is constrained by meager physical and documentary evidence in the early part of the period. During the early Middle Ages, most domestic structures were timber built. They are rarely now found standing, and often only negative features survive. Although post holes and foundation trenches may indicate the extent and form of a building, they have limited application to the study of family lives. Examples do survive where anaerobic soil conditions have preserved occupation evidence from the ninth and tenth centuries. Urban excavations in York show a densely populated Viking-age city with numerous tenement dwellings, many occupied by craft workers.[2] However, the limited survival of actual occupation layers and damage by later construction reduce the ability to analyze the settlement in terms of family life. Across Europe, from the twelfth century onward, we find an increase in the number of stone dwellings, resulting in better rates of survival. A few cities, such as Bern (Switzerland), have a wealth of standing buildings from the later Middle Ages. Yet even standing buildings have been altered throughout their lifetime, making it difficult to ascertain exactly what activities were carried out in which rooms. Elsewhere, at times, little more than foundations survive, giving merely a general idea of the plan of the house at or below ground level. It is therefore a problematic task to equate the structural remains of domestic dwellings with the lives of different family members in this period.

The concept of a family home related to a number of different structures in the Middle Ages. It might refer to a single-story peasant dwelling occupied by parents, children, and even grandparents and visitors. Moving up the social scale, a rural landholder's family home might consist of two or more structures occupied by immediate and extended family members as well as household servants or apprentices (depending on the wealth of the owner). Research has been undertaken to estimate the average size of medieval households, based upon the number of people residing in a single dwelling. Figures from before the Black Death (1348–1349) in northern and central England indicate an average household size of four to five individuals.[3] Figures vary from village to village, but the results suggest a pattern of greater wealth of household equating to a greater number of children therein, reflecting the effects of better nutrition, living conditions, and health, which might have increased fertility.

It is difficult to determine how far household size directly correlated with family size. As the chapter on family relationships in this volume has highlighted, nuclear families consisting of parents and their immediate offspring were not necessarily the norm in all parts of medieval Europe. In Genoa, Italy, for example, noble households accommodated extended families who lived together. The unusual survival of notarial archives from the mid-twelfth century onward, combined with standing building evidence, illustrates how aristocratic families occupied their households and shared their time and space. Genoa's exceptional towers were part of the fortifications of aristocratic family enclaves. Adjacent houses around a central square were protected by these fortifications and shared other facilities, including shops, baths, and churches.[4] Like the houses in medieval England, these structures typically contained a central room that functioned like the hall, providing space for eating and entertaining. A separate kitchen located beside or above the hall enabled easy egress of food to the diners. Bedrooms would then be located above and servants quarters above these. Each house was expected to accommodate the immediate family and the families of married sons. The extended family would, therefore, be accommodated with their staff within easy access of one another (if space allowed). The structural remains show that houses in Italy ranged from almost forty-nine feet (fifteen meters) to over two hundred feet (sixty-one meters) wide. Clearly, the latter were better suited to housing an extended family of sons and their offspring. In Portugal and England, the survival of retirement contracts shows that some poorer households accommodated extended families as well. The fortunes of the elderly were very much affected by their status and wealth. Those who held property were sometimes able to arrange a form of pension whereby they bequeathed the property to one of their children with caveats that allowed for their shelter and the provision of food and clothing until death. In some cases, steps were taken to ensure that parents and children were spared the discomfort and inconvenience of residing under the same roof "while they shared the same property" through the construction of separate dwellings.[5]

The number of accidents involving children, as recorded by coroners, offers a rare glimpse of the presence of children in these households. The house and its environs contained many hazards from sharp implements to unstable ladders, from open hearths and constantly hot pots of water to kicking donkeys and biting pigs. Reports describe the burns and other injuries sustained by children. Wells without curbs were particularly hazardous to all ages, and parents suffered the loss of unsupervised children who fell into them.[6] Children were cared for, but with apparently less attention than was needed in such environments. It seems that, in many families, each individual, regardless of age, was responsible for his or her own movement around the space.

STRUCTURAL REMAINS, RURAL
AND URBAN DESIGN

Most pre-twelfth-century houses in Europe were rectangular or sub-rectangular in plan. Variations in form were affected by several factors, including the climate, the physical environment, the availability of building materials (such as stone or Roman bricks for reuse), the social standing and wealth of the owners, and local concepts concerning the negotiation of gender. Ninth-century Roman peasant houses consisted of a single room, while contemporary aristocratic homes were large and elaborate two-story structures set amid storage, stabling, and sometimes bathing facilities. Icelandic houses in the Viking age were single-room, sunken-featured buildings with central hearths and internal work spaces, creating warmth and protection from the elements. These were later replaced by houses more akin in style to those developing elsewhere in Europe: houses with a number of rooms, each for a specific function, from food preparation to sleeping, added on to the basic element of the hall. In rural Britain from around 1200, for example, the basic peasant house was often a two- or three-room dwelling with an unfurnished but well-equipped room for cooking, often with an open hearth, a room for sleeping, and sometimes a separate room for living. The latter was located between the kitchen and the sleeping room, like the hall in typical Wealden hall houses. All family members, from children to grandparents, typically occupied the same living and sleeping space.[7]

Political frontiers and widespread warfare also influenced housing design; defensive considerations and the need to subjugate the surrounding population made fortifications a necessity for wealthy families in areas of disputed control. In England and France during the eleventh and twelfth centuries, for example, nobles constructed castles—initially of earth and timber, then later of stone—typically centered around a donjon or central tower, offering cramped quarters with few windows and raised entrances to deflect missiles and impede the access of hostile forces. The structures of medieval urban houses, whose forms typically evolved in response to requirements specific to their setting, might, on the other hand, be rather different again. Facilities for a hierarchical household were important in large rural houses, but the design of urban houses reflected a more specialized use of space and did not necessarily need to accommodate such a wide range of household staff or activities. Many urban dwellings included shop space and storage facilities appropriate to the types of goods being stored. The families of urban craftsmen often lived and worked in far more cramped conditions than those experienced by many rural dwellers. For the families that occupied shop-fronted properties, work and home life existed side by side. It is possible that children were often present in the shop, thereby reducing the need for extra child care and providing the children with the opportunity to learn the skills of the trade and to help with menial tasks. Builders learned to make efficient use of the limited space available to them in late medieval towns. Urban residences, for example, sometimes incorporated jettied upper floors, which were specifically engineered to allow for upward development and to provide as much space as possible.

PUBLIC AND PRIVATE SPACE

The development of enclosed heating systems and chimneys in the later Middle Ages, in place of earlier open hearths, also influenced the use of space within family homes, increasing the number of rooms into which houses might be divided and offering the potential for greater privacy in wealthy households. It was, for example, no longer necessary for the whole family to sleep together in the same room. The movement toward greater privacy may be observed in the formation of chambers to which the lord and lady might retire, so that less communal living and sleeping occurred in the hall. A desire for greater privacy is also visible through documentary records for urban houses that specify the location of windows and doors in new buildings so that they would not allow a view of private space.[8] Although it is impossible to gauge the full impact of the growing privatization of space upon family and wider household relationships, one suspects that it offered opportunities for greater secrecy, but it might also have broken down the openness and acceptance that came with constant visibility and communal living.

At a structural level, the multiplication of rooms might have allowed for the increased separation of gendered and age-based activities. Specific chambers might, for example, have been assigned deliberately to high-status women within aristocratic households. These were rooms that allowed direct or protected egress to balconies or squints in the castle chapels: areas for women to attend mass without being on display. They were private rooms, located at a distance from public rooms like the hall and with access to secluded outdoor space. The architectural layout of a castle might therefore be viewed as a physical manifestation of contemporary perceptions of the structure of society and of the place of women within it: the higher up in the social hierarchy a person was, the higher up or deeper within the castle her chambers would be.[9] The placing of the chambers of noblewomen away from the public areas of the castle, within protected and inaccessible space, might have reflected contemporary ideas about female virtue and women's limited social roles. Their relationships with their children must have been fraught with tension caused by separation. A lady had separate rooms from her husband, occupied separate space from her children, she may not have nursed her own babies, and her older children were often sent to do service in other households for their own development. The nuclear family living together in a three-room peasant structure would have been an alien existence to many aristocratic families. A young married noblewoman who had yet to bear an heir was expected to maintain her virtue and protect the honor of the household by controlling her movement around the public spaces and regulating those who accessed her chambers. Even so, as the mistress of a domestic establishment, she was still expected, on occasion, to carry out household duties within public spaces and to move beyond its walls in order to visit low-status households and present them with charity.[10]

HOUSEHOLD ROLES, MATERIAL CULTURE, AND THE USE OF SPACE

The designs and structures of houses and households were influenced by cultural ideologies and the negotiation of traditions specific to each region. These might be the result of religious ideals or concerns created by a particular environment. So concepts regarding the protection of women in Muslim houses can be seen to have as much influence on the architecture as the need to keep the internal areas cool in the warm climes of Andalusia. Yet the need to protect one's belongings and resources gave medieval women the opportunity to hold power within their homes.

Keys were associated with women throughout the Middle Ages. In England, they appeared in carvings on women's grave slabs from the eleventh to fourteenth centuries, following an association extending back into the early Anglo-Saxon period, when women were buried with keys suspended from rings at their waists. These keys might have had a symbolic significance, but they were also practical items that at once locked and protected belongings of some kind.[11] Keys appear in settlement contexts from mid-Saxon urban sites (such as Lundenwic) at the same time as competition for space increases; houses are positioned closer to one another, with less external space; and waste disposal becomes a major issue. Growing population pressure might have created a need to control ownership of goods and protect one's own resources. It is logical to bring this evidence together to suggest that women were responsible for controlling access to these protected goods within their homes, thereby placing them in the role of house-keeper or householder. After all, the term *chatelaine,* which might refer to clasps or chains, might equally be applied to the mistress of the household.

Within the setting of the castle, secluded outdoor gardens were perhaps seen as private space for women: a women's domain with all the complex taboos and desires such domains evoked in the Middle Ages.[12] The internal courtyards of the Muslim homes of Andalusia were also partially a design feature that allowed for a protected outdoor space for women. A Muslim home needed to be a private place where the women in the family could be protected in order to maintain "the family's honour."[13] By incorporating a central courtyard into the design, no windows were needed on the outside of the building. Those who entered the house passed through a hall into this open central area rather than directly into the private rooms. With all the chambers looking inward, the family members would have been within hearing of one another and frequently within sight, thereby creating an enclosed household community. In northern Europe, both urban and rural houses often had an enclosed outdoor yard. With many of women's daily activities taking place around the home, it is possible to associate these particular yards with the notion of a protected female domain as well. However, it is probable that they were also occupied and utilized by the men of the household for industrial and craft purposes, perhaps on a seasonal basis, and by children, depending on their age and gender. Notions of dichotomies between male and female, public and private, should be treated with caution. While men had greater status in the public domain, both men and women had the potential to hold property and be legally responsible for their actions (for women, this typically occurred only in the absence of a male head of household).

DIET AND GEOGRAPHY

Within the household, the wife maintained power over its residents through her control of the "storage, serving and consumption of food."[14] The consumption of food occupied a position at the heart of medieval culture. Feasting and drinking accompanied births, agricultural and liturgical festivals, marriages, and deaths. In Christian communities, this began with a baptismal feast and ended with a funerary meal. For the medieval family, food was not only a source of sustenance, but part of the daily negotiations between men and women, between the head of the household and his dependants, and between individuals of higher and lower status within the social hierarchy.[15] It is therefore frustrating that, although the archaeological data allows researchers to make general observations about diet, it is not possible to tell exactly what each family or individual ate. The basic dietary components throughout Europe were cereals accompanied by some form of protein, possibly with homegrown vegetables. Yet the specific detail varied across regions, in accordance with environmental, cultural, economic, and religious concerns. This began to change toward the end of the Middle Ages, when greater long-distance trade and population pressures created a wider market for the distribution of foodstuffs derived from specific environments, as seen in the increase of saltwater fish in inland diets.

Life cycle was, however, an important influence on diet. People were aware that babies and infants possessed different dietary requirements from those of their parents. The authors of didactic literature were firm advocates of breast-feeding, warning mothers against the risk of instilling animal-like behavior in the character of a child nursed on animal rather than mother's milk. This did not, however, deter all from supplementing or replacing breast milk with that of animals, especially in the absence of a mother or suitable wet nurse. In southern Bavaria during the later Middle Ages, for example, infants were fed pap (bread in a base of animal milk or water) for much of their first year of life, while babies in neighboring regions were normally fed mothers' milk. The existence of horns formed into nursing devices lends support to the probability that feeding babies animal milk was a common practice, regardless of whether contemporary writers condoned it.[16] A comparison of the skeletal remains of children who died in Raunds Furnells, Northamptonshire, between 850 and 1100; in Wharram Percy, Yorkshire, between 950 and 1100; and in St. Helen-on-the-Walls, York, between 950 and 1550, which was conducted by Mary Lewis, suggests that children living in rural and urban habitats were equally "exposed to the harmful effects of infected [cows'] milk."[17] This theory is based on the evidence for gastrointestinal, but not pulmonary, tuberculosis in these populations, which would imply the young children consumed contaminated dairy or bovine products from which they contracted the infection. Maternal milk would have been the safer option at this time, before the invention of pasteurization.

The evidence from Lewis's study of children in urban and rural populations has also suggested variations in the age of weaning between the two environments. At Raunds Furnells, weaning occurred at around two years of age, while at Wharram Percy and St. Helen-on-the-Walls, babies were weaned at the age of one.[18] Although the age of weaning appears to have fallen over time, the overlap in periods represented within each cemetery means the variation in weaning age might have had a correlation with urban practices. Raunds Furnells was home to a predominantly rural population with an agricultural subsistence base, while rural Wharram Percy had closer contact with York, and

St. Helen's was an urban parish. Perhaps this reflects a trend in cities toward earlier weaning as a result of fashion or necessity created by the time pressures of an urban existence. Similar evidence from postmedieval Christ Church in Spitalfields, London, indicates that the age of weaning was just six months. Once weaned and eating solid foods, a child's diet would probably have varied only a little from that of adults. Some parents appear to have insisted on a limited diet, devoid of fine and varied foods, while others, particularly those of higher status and those who resided in urban environments, allowed their children more refined foods.[19] Diet in adolescence was affected by the generosity and care of the family with which the child resided. Typically, youths moved into apprenticeships or servant positions at approximately twelve years of age. Meals would be provided by the craftsperson with whom they trained or by the family as part of the payment for service.

The staple diet for adults in the Middle Ages consisted primarily of cereals in both Muslim and Christian communities. These were baked into bread or made into porridge and washed down in northern Europe by ale brewed from the grains. This was supplemented by *companagium*, meaning that which goes with bread, so some form of protein and vegetables. The foundation of monasteries by the Cistercian order in the twelfth century helped to develop the practice of growing fruit trees, particularly in Germanic areas of settlement, although this was resisted until later in the period in Slavic and Scandinavian regions. Milk was typically made into cheese or butter before being consumed; a process carried out by women. Other sources of protein included meat—notably bacon in Christian settlements and lamb in Muslim homes (both Jews and Muslims avoided pork)—eggs, and fish, particularly on Christian fast days. Pigs were popular with Christian communities due to the high and rapid yield of meat over labor in comparison to cattle. They could easily be reared in rural and urban settings, providing a readily accessible local supply of fresh meat.[20]

Although the staple dietary elements seem to have been common across England and continental Europe, regional differences occurred, ranging from the type of grains grown in particular types of soil and climate to the combinations of ingredients used in food preparation (as observed from cookbooks, manorial records, and other documentary sources). In Poland, for example, millet was the favored grain, with all levels of society consuming it in porridge form. In northern Germany, a particular species of oat was grown on coastal farms.[21] Seafood formed a larger part of the diet in coastal regions, with cod being a major dietary component in coastal Norway until the eleventh century. The analysis of stable isotopes in human bones and the actual fish bones recovered from excavations show a major increase in the percentage of salt-water fish in inland diets and a reduction in the quantity of freshwater fish consumed in the eleventh century. Norwegian fishermen increased their yield of cod at this time and profited from the development of a Europeanwide marine fish trade. Remote locations such as the Orkney Islands similarly benefited from a greater market for their dried fish exports. Possible explanations for these changes include the growing influence of Christianity, which incorporated 100 meat-free days within the religious calendar; a movement toward trade that could supply "high bulk, low value, staple goods"; simple changes in taste; and possible damage to freshwater resources by population growth, leading to a heightened demand for saltwater fish.[22] In the northern regions of Europe such as Norway, greater reliance was also placed upon the wild animal resources, though the Saami were known to have domesticated, or at least tamed, reindeer for their milk.[23] Meanwhile, across Europe, rural inhabitants supplemented their diet with wild plants and traded wild berries to urban dwellers.

As a general rule, though, wealth, as well as religious beliefs and geographical location, played an important role in shaping a family's diet. The household accounts of noble families in late medieval England suggest that sources of protein were more readily available and of finer quality at this social level than at that of the peasantry. Their conspicuous consumption of luxury foodstuffs, such as venison and the meat of young animals, in large quantities also offered a visual means of advertising their privileged position within society. At the lower end of the social scale, as Christopher Dyer has shown, manorial accounts documenting the fare of late medieval harvest workers offer useful insights into the diets of English peasants and how they changed over time in response to the workers' demands and fluctuating economic conditions.[24] Harvest workers were paid partly in food and ale, some of which they presumably retained for their households. Barley bread was accompanied by cheese, some preserved fish, and a little salt meat. Aside from ale, milk and water made up the liquid part of the diet. The conclusions drawn from Dyer's research offer a counterbalance to hypotheses that the demographic downturn associated with the Black Death was an important factor in instigating major changes in diet. Dyer suggests instead that the Black Death intensified and accelerated change that had already commenced in the later thirteenth century. From the 1290s onward, for example, on the Norfolk manor of Catton, the quantity of bread was reduced, and more meat formed part of the workers' diet. At the same time, though, the quality of the ingredients used to bake bread improved. Barley became less common and was replaced by wheat and rye, so that, by 1339, wheat and rye accounted for "more than half of the corn used for baking bread."[25] The end of the period saw a peak in dietary improvement.

This brings us to the question of the differences in diet between urban and rural populations. Poor families in both rural and urban communities were certainly vulnerable to starvation during times of dearth; when crops failed and cattle died as a result of disease, little might be left to eat, let alone to send to market. During more prosperous times, though, urban dwellers tended to have access to a more varied diet than their rural counterparts, owing in part to the range of products being sold in these settings and the extent of the hinterland serving each city. Rural communities were more dependent upon that which they were able to produce. The greater prosperity of cities, particularly those where wealthy merchants resided in good trading ports, also meant more of the inhabitants had the means to afford a better quality and greater quantity of products. Therefore, we find more meat being consumed in urban settlements than in rural ones. Also, the percentage of beef in the diet of urban inhabitants was higher than for their rural counterparts.[26] Beef was an expensive meat, because cattle were more costly to rear than sheep or pigs, which matured more quickly. So while the peasants raised the cattle, the city dwellers were better equipped to afford to eat the meat. Fewer animals were reared in the cities, yet it is in cities that we find specialist processing sites, including butchers, tanners, and craftsmen working animal bone. In villages, a range of activities would have been carried out by the same people, so this zoning is not apparent. Rural sites apparently raised animals that were transported live to urban markets before being slaughtered and processed in the cities. This method would have enabled the wealthier citizens to receive the meat fresh. However, legal records highlight problems of access to good fresh meat for poorer families, who were sold very substandard meat by cook shops.

CLOTHING AND CULTURAL ENVIRONMENT

In addition to shelter, food, and drink, clothing was another core necessity of medieval life. Medieval burials have provided archaeologists with valuable information on the apparel of men, women, and children. Metal brooches, jewelry, and bronze spiral ornaments have helped preserve minute fragments of woolen and linen garments, while the position of these metal objects in the graves aids the reconstruction of clothing forms. This is especially true for the richly furnished burials of the Anglo-Saxon period in England. Admittedly, the fashion of clothing for a funeral might represent formal wear rather than daily dress, but it allows us to understand the types and forms of attire available for such occasions. Although the practice of depositing grave goods became less common as the Middle Ages progressed, written records and pictorial sources such as manuscript images and monumental sculptures can also offer useful insights into changes in personal apparel. The culturally embedded meanings of clothing and accessories mean that regional variations occur in design—variations that were also influenced by access to materials, technological knowledge, and craft skills. Trade contacts during this period facilitated technological change across great distances, and the transfer of skills such as knitting. Fashion led by the wealthier members of the populace provided the impetus, especially with the rise of the merchant classes.

Philippe Ariès famously said that children in the Middle Ages were dressed as miniature adults.[27] Anglo-Saxon illustrations in the early Middle Ages and portraits of noble children in the late Middle Ages show them dressed in small versions of adult clothing. However, it is rare to find paintings from this period that show children clothed; most are depicted naked or partially covered. Formally attired children appear dressed in adultlike garb, but, on a daily basis, children might have worn more relaxed clothing suitable for play. The limited examples of children's clothing that survive from the later Middle Ages reflect the style of adult clothing, though perhaps not the latest fashions. This is not to say that some parents did not choose to overdress their children. The Italian sumptuary laws of the fourteenth century blamed the mothers when they criticized the extravagant appearance of children. Children's hats from Tudor England show how colorful and varied designs had become—designs that developed during the preceding centuries.[28] Children's leather shoes were small versions of adults', covering the whole foot and often the ankle in a single piece of leather stitched to a thin sole. Pewter toys, including miniature jugs, ewers, and pitchers, show that children's play must, at times, have mimicked adult lives. Thus, children's material culture reflected adult tastes and styles (this is not surprising, considering most items were manufactured by or under the guidance of adults), but maintained qualities suited to the energetic and haphazard nature of children.

Earlier in the period, and possibly throughout for lower-status families, very young children's dress was probably a more simple affair. When they are depicted clothed in medieval manuscript illustrations, they appear in long, loose gowns, while babies are shown completely wrapped in fabric. The gown was an easy garment for the child to wear, its form perhaps reflecting that of the inner garment of women's clothing. If children had their heads covered, like women, it was by a simple folded head dress, though usually children are portrayed bareheaded.[29]

One fashion peculiar to adults appeared at the end of the period. Known as *poulaines,* these were shoes with excessively pointed toes. Some were tied onto the feet by means of a narrow strap and latchet across the front of the ankle, leaving the upper part of the foot bare, or rather the hose exposed. The fashion was relatively short-lived but, as is the cyclical nature of fashions, returned to popularity again about a century later in the 1480s.[30] For most men, clothing typically consisted of a tunic worn over close-fitting trousers or hose, with a cloak, either short or long depending on his occupation and fashion. Harvest workers, for example, required a short or folded long cloak to allow freedom of movement. Changes in taste also influenced the length of cloaks, as suggested by Emperor Charlemagne's complaints to King Offa that the cloaks being traded from England in the late eighth century were too short and yet cost the same as earlier longer versions.[31] Hose were typically made of cloth; knitted hose did not appear until late in the Middle Ages in Italy and not until the Tudor period in England. The earliest surviving examples found in Switzerland from the seventh century were probably created using knotless netting, which requires great skill in

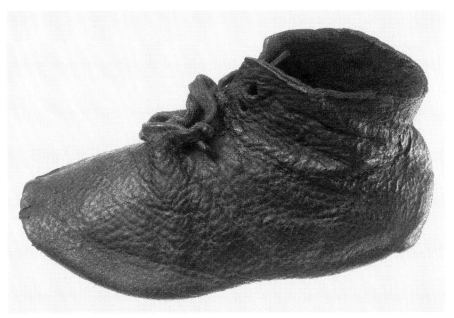

FIGURE 4.1: *A child's leather ankle shoe found in the town ditch, Aldersgate Street, London.* Fourteenth or fifteenth century. © Museum of London (Image Number 001028).

FIGURE 4.2: *A toy knight on horseback, one of the earliest examples of a mass-produced medieval toy*. Late thirteenth to early fourteenth centuries. © Museum of London (Image Number 000482).

using one stick and a hand to create form-fitting garments. Knitting using two, and later more, needles developed from approximately the thirteenth century in Europe, with possible origins in Arabic countries. It became a typically women's occupation in fourteenth-century Italy and Germany, and later spread to the rest of Europe.

Across Europe, fabrics were often made from wool or linen. England prospered from its wool trade. Finer fabrics became more popular with the influence of southern European and Byzantine fashions through trading links. This is perhaps why the majority of early examples of silk cloth in England occur in Viking settlements—for example, a bonnet recovered from York.[32] Clothing manufacture, from homespun fabrics to commercially produced woven items and hand-embroidered garment edges, involved both children and adults at different social levels. Some royal and aristocratic women were commended for their skills in needlework. Queen Edith was credited with embroidering the robes of her husband, Edward the Confessor. It is, however, possible that such women utilized the skills of female household servants, just as their Mediterranean counterparts were keen to employ or own such skilled servants or slaves. English women's needlework was of such international renown that several modern scholars have suggested the Bayeux Tapestry was stitched by English women.[33] This embroidered linen is a valuable source for understanding clothing in England and Normandy during the late eleventh century. The good preservation of the colored woolen threads gives an indication of the range and variability of fabric colors at this time: from terra-cotta to dark blue through yellow and green. It illustrates not only the connection of different garments with people of differing status, but also the manner in which these were worn and manipulated for daily use. In one scene, for example, Harold Godwinson and his followers are shown with their hose removed and tunics hitched up to wade through the shallow waters on the English shore. Few of the English fighting force are shown in armor, supporting theories that all but the wealthy knights of feudal northern Europe could afford protective chain mail and helmets, and would have relied on leather garments at best. The elderly King Edward appears in a long robe, in contrast to the tunics and hose of his contemporaries. His long gown follows the traditional formal dress of English and Norman nobility, which would have been accompanied by a long cloak. The few women who appear in the main narrative panel of the Bayeux Tapestry are all shown in long gowns, with their heads covered, which seems to have been a common mode of dress in the early Middle Ages. Shoes were usually flat, and an open-fronted cloak provided warmth. These gowns appear to have been tunics, essentially long versions of men's clothing, in contrast to the earlier tubular or peplos-style gowns, which were held together at the shoulder by pairs of brooches. While evidence for the earlier peplos-style gown is uncommon later than the seventh century in England, it is visible in eleventh-century Finland with the introduction of Christian-influenced inhumation burials.[34]

Clothing, although a practical artifact for keeping warm, was also important for expressing social position and conveying messages about sexual status. In Finland, for example, only a "sexually mature" woman wore an apron-style garment over the top of her dress.[35] Christian teaching on female modesty, coupled with concerns about female vanity and sexual propriety, probably influenced the fashion for women to cover their hair with either a veil or, in later tenth and eleventh centuries, a hood. There are numerous examples in medieval art and sculpture of women wearing a range of head coverings, some lying over the top of the tunic, some tucked into the neck, and others formed by pulling the cloak up over the hair.[36] Long-sleeved gowns also became more popular during this period, some with wide, open cuffs, others with close-fitting cuffs. These could be gathered at the waist by a girdle or sash and were embellished with embroidery.

The sumptuary laws of the fourteenth century invoked restrictions on clothing based on gender and age. Women, in particular, were targeted, with limits placed on the length of dress trains, the number of buttons on a sleeve, and the expense and quantity of their adornments. Some restrictions, though, applied to both sexes: neither men nor women, for example, were permitted to wear pleated cloth in fourteenth-century Florence. The restrictions of the sumptuary laws were partially designed to sooth moral outrage caused by extravagance but were not intended to eradicate all opulent dress. In fact, Venetians desired their high-status women (women of the doge's family) to dress in bright fabrics, regardless of sober occasions such as mourning. While many legislators deplored immodest clothing, others complained about overly modest outfits. Bartolomeo Marcello in Venice criticized the later medieval fashion for women to cover both head and face.[37]

Sumptuary laws also addressed the status and wealth of the wearer. A woman might therefore be permitted to wear certain fabrics, decorations and designs, depending on how old she was and whether she was of noble, artisan, merchant, or peasant status. Had these laws been strictly observed, it would have been possible to identify a person's specific position within the social hierarchy through their appearance. The aim of such legislation was to reinforce social divisions, preserve social order, and control the spending of each class. The sumptuary law of 1363 in England was so detailed in this regard that a groom or craftsman was only allowed to wear clothing worth up to twenty-six shillings and eight pence, and their wives and daughters were required to limit the cost of their veils. Meanwhile, a yeoman might spend up to forty shillings on his attire.[38] However, despite the elite's efforts to control consumption, the English people generally ignored this legislation. We can see evidence here of the increasing spending power and wealth of the rising mercantile classes, with their flamboyant display and investment in precocious youths (considered to be good salesmen).[39]

CONCLUSION

For families, the Middle Ages were a time of contrasts: contrasts between the living conditions for rich and poor; between the diet and daily existence of rural and urban dwellers; between the quality and expense of clothing dependent on wealth, status, and occupation. Each family was affected by its geographical location and the immediate environment within which it lived. Poor peasant families in England after the Black Death resided in small houses, often with only one child. They might have had other children working away from home, taking advantage of the employment opportunities in towns and cities, and on agricultural estates, created by the massive reduction in the size of the population caused by the Black Death and by successive epidemics of plague. Meanwhile, wealthy Italian nobles lived in protected enclaves, with their extended family and essential amenities, from shops to churches, all on site. Densely populated cities contained greater concentrations of wealthy households with access to a wide hinterland, so overall the diet here was superior to that of rural settlements. However, at a family level, economic status still determined access to a range of quality foodstuffs. While many urban people ate fine foods, many also struggled on the meager morsels they could afford—typically cereals, possibly with some meat from mature animals. Children had a varied existence, again dependent upon the wealth and status of their parents. From the start, their chances of survival were affected by their diet and living conditions. The fortunate ones began life surrounded by feasting. Significant moments in their personal and social development were henceforth punctuated by gatherings of people and food.

CHAPTER FIVE

Education

LOUISE J. WILKINSON

A vast spectrum of educational provision existed in the medieval West, in terms of training children and adolescents for adult life. The nature of that provision was neither consistent nor uniform across Europe—it might be determined by a large number of considerations, including gender, location, religion, social status, and wealth. Christian teaching, for example, combined with medical thought inherited from the ancient world to promote a heavily misogynistic interpretation of the different paths in life open to boys and girls—one where women were deemed inferior and subservient to men. While boys might be educated to fulfill an active role in the world as knights, priests, merchants, artisans, or laborers, girls prepared for their futures as the chaste handmaidens of Christ—nuns and anchoresses—or, more usually, within the domestic sphere as wives and mothers.

Access to education was also, in some respects, determined by when one lived, for the generations who lived during the twelfth and thirteenth centuries experienced a radical transformation in literacy and learning—in how the written word was employed, and in how and where members of the clerical and lay elites were educated in its use.[1] According to Michael Clanchy, this period witnessed a shift "from memory to written record," whereby a largely oral culture of recollection in business and government was replaced by the emergence of a "literate mentality," by a desire to write things down and compile accurate records of day-to-day affairs.[2] This development coincided, and went hand in hand, with an explosion in the number of schools and with the emergence of Europe's earliest universities at Bologna and Paris. "The effects of economic growth [seen in the spread of towns], the proliferation of money exchanges and social diversification," so Jacques Verger argues, "resulted in an increasing demand for competent men of letters."[3] This chapter explores how these developments shaped experiences of childhood and adolescence, and thereby influenced individual and family life. It also takes the discussion of education beyond the formal world of the schools by considering the nature of instruction within royal and noble households, and the value attached to practical, work-based learning at lower social levels, with a view to building upon themes addressed by Jennifer Ward in chapter two.

SCHOOLS AND UNIVERSITIES

The educational experiences of boys and girls followed disparate avenues at an early stage in their lives. While children of both sexes were typically reared within the parental home during early infancy, boys from the rural and urban elites were more likely than their sisters to be sent away to school by the age of seven. The church, the guardian of the word of God and the preserver of knowledge passed down from classical antiquity, was the principle bastion of literacy and learning in medieval Europe. Although members of the parish clergy taught young laymen and clerks as part of their duties, schools, in the sense of places devoted to literate learning or groups of young people studying together, were commonly attached to cathedrals or monasteries in the early Middle Ages—that is, to religious houses that needed to train their recruits in appropriate Christian observance and liturgy. Monasteries, in particular, educated young boys, and nunneries, which were far fewer in number, educated young girls. Many children educated in such institutions—like the Anglo-Norman writer Orderic Vitalis, who was sent to the monastery of Saint-Evroult in his tenth year—were placed in them by their parents in the expectation that they would become monks or nuns (a subject explored more fully in chapter eight). The promotion of organized, formal, church-based learning lay at the heart of the Carolingian renaissance of the late eighth and ninth centuries, and derived considerable momentum from the drive to reform the Frankish church under the emperor Charlemagne and his successors. The General Admonition of 789 stipulated that "schools should be established for teaching boys the psalms, *notas* [writing shorthand, or musical notation], singing, computation, and grammar in every monastery and episcopal residence."[4] The great Frankish monasteries of Fulda, Tours, Metz, and Rheims, to name a few, were famed for the quality of their masters, who taught subjects as diverse as arithmetic, astronomy, music, and philosophy. The religious revival of the tenth century provided a similarly important stimulus to the reinvigoration of learning within the cathedrals and monasteries of Anglo-Saxon England, following a period of decay in the wake of Viking attacks. Figures such as Dunstan, abbot of Glastonbury and later archbishop of Canterbury, and Æthelwold, abbot of Abingdon and bishop of Winchester, regarded education as an indispensable ingredient of monastic life. The work of writers such as Thietmar and Widukind stands as testimony to the intellectual endeavors of the schools of the tenth-century Ottonian kingdom, which flourished under episcopal patronage. Cathedral schools multiplied and thrived in France and Germany during this period at centers such as Cologne, Hildesheim, Liège, Mainz, Ravenna, Rheims, Trier, and Würzburg. The role of the church as a focus for teaching and study in the medieval West received further impetus from the Gregorian reform movement of the late eleventh century, which helped to open up attractive new paths for career progression within the church; priests now needed skills in literacy so that they might teach others the Holy Scripture and be better equipped intellectually to explain that which they taught.[5] The revitalization of church-sponsored learning was addressed at both the Third and Fourth Lateran Councils (1179 and 1215); the former stated that each cathedral should appoint a master to teach poor students and young clerics.[6]

The curriculum offered within cathedral and monastic schools was overtly Christian in nature, focusing on the Bible, its associated texts and commentaries, and the seven liberal arts. The seven liberal arts were the core foundation subjects for the arts and sciences in the Middle Ages. A key part of the classical heritage of the West, they were adapted, with some variation, for study in medieval schools. They included grammar, rhetoric, and dialectic—known as the *trivium*—the three verbal arts or arts of language. Grammar, the study of Latin words and phrases, provided children with the essential base for understanding the Latin language and its literature. Indeed, the centrality of Latin to the Romano-Christian culture preserved by the Western church helped to ensure its continuing supremacy in this context as a written language over the vernacular; the term *literatus* ("lettered") in this period was strictly associated with the ability to read Latin. Rhetoric focused on the ability to engage in persuasive discourse, and dialectic on the ability to investigate truth. The remaining subjects, known as the *quadrivium*—or the four arts of number—embraced geometry, music, astronomy, and arithmetic. With the appearance of universities in cities such as Bologna, Paris, and Oxford in the twelfth and thirteenth centuries, the study of the liberal arts, alongside natural, moral, and metaphysical philosophy, as well as canon law, civil law, medicine, and theology, became concentrated increasingly within the hands of specialist masters. These centers offered older students a more sophisticated and higher level of education than existing schools, either in preparation for careers within the church or within secular government and administration. The universities of Bologna and Paris were particularly influential institutions. Bologna became the chief center for the study of canon and civil law, attracting English, French, and German, as well as Italian students to its schools. Parisian masters were famed for their knowledge of dialectic, as well as canon law and theology.[7]

FIGURE 5.1: *The initial P showing a monk talking to a group of pupils.* The Interpretation of Aristotle's Categories, France, circa 1300. © The British Library Board (BL Burney MS. 275, f. 176v).

The development of formal education in the medieval period was also given a helping hand by the large number of elementary ("reading" or "song") and grammar schools that grew up in the rapidly expanding towns, cities, and ports of Western Europe from the twelfth and thirteenth centuries onward. Although there was a degree of overlap between these and earlier types of school—"song" schools, for instance, typically trained the young choristers of the cathedrals with which they were associated—their emergence undoubtedly improved educational provision for lay children. Indeed, it was a reflection of the enhanced opportunities on offer by the later Middle Ages, so Shulamith Shahar believes, that "in all European towns, the great majority of the children of prosperous burghers attended elementary schools for at least a few years."[8] Within this brave new world of commerce and communal civic government, education was associated with citizenship and success. So keen were the commercially assertive Italians to attract suitable teachers to their cities that they gave them incentives such as exemption from local taxes. Urban schools might be controlled by the local municipal authorities or by an ecclesiastical or lay patron; they might also be private concerns established by enterprising scholars. They were quite often day, rather than boarding, schools, minimizing the potential disruption caused by long-term separation to family relationships.[9]

The education on offer at elementary schools to children between the ages of seven and ten to twelve tended to focus on learning the alphabet and how to read. Pupils also learned basic skills in numeracy and sometimes learned how to write. An understanding of church teachings might be acquired through prayers and hymns. The chief language remained Latin, although the ability to read in the vernacular was also taught from the thirteenth century onward. This body of learning laid the foundations for progression to a grammar—or secondary—school, if the child's parents so wished. Students here were taught Latin grammar, as well as rhetoric and dialectic, and, from time to time, other subjects drawn from the *quadrivium*. Even if there was tremendous variety in individual experiences, boys tended to leave grammar school during their mid- to late teens. Typically drawn from the wealthier ranks of society—the sons of gentlefolk, merchants, artisans, and the wealthier peasant farmers—that is, from those whose families could afford the fees, they often included boys apprenticed to craftsmen, who hoped to acquire skills to assist in their future trades, as well as those intended for careers as civil servants and estate officials. Gender ratios among pupils differed from one school to another. Unlike the predominantly masculine world of cathedral and monastic schools, elementary and, occasionally, grammar schools might admit girls as well as boys. According to the fourteenth-century writer, Giovanni Villani, between eight thousand and ten thousand boys and girls were taught to read and write within Florence's elementary schools. Women teachers were encountered in both this city and Venice. No fewer than forty-one schoolmasters and twenty-one schoolmistresses were also recorded at elementary schools in Paris; some women ran Parisian grammar schools.[10] The presence of such women clearly reveals that it had proven possible for girls to attain a sufficient level of literate education to enable them to teach others. In general, though, the educational attainment of girls trailed behind that of boys, and their upbringings remained focused upon the domestic world of the home, an arena examined later in this chapter. This was true for Jewish as well as Christian girls. The young Jewish women of northern France, England, and Germany were typically educated within the home in a less formal setting than that of their brothers, who might attend local Jewish academies or study halls.

In practice, it remains frustratingly unclear precisely just how many schools came into existence in the medieval West or, indeed, how many children attended school at any one point in time. A limited amount of free schooling did become available in the later Middle Ages, thanks to the generosity of churchmen and private individuals, but this remained the exception rather than the rule. Schools were certainly less common in rural than urban settlements, despite the efforts of one fourteenth-century bishop, Guillaume Durand the Younger of Mende (France), who firmly believed that each village should have a school. The numbers of pupils also varied considerably between different institutions. Some small country schools were probably attended by less than a dozen boys, while the great cathedral schools—like St. Paul's in London—might accommodate more than one hundred pupils at any one time.[11]

When Christian pupils entered the schoolroom, they entered a world ruled by discipline, where regular beatings with the birch were common. Little is known about the physical layout of schoolrooms, but late medieval and early modern images show pupils seated on benches around the central figure of a master; children of different ages were taught together. The school day often began early—sometimes at six o'clock in the morning—and lasted eight or nine hours, excluding time for lunch, easily rivaling the length of an adult's working day. Schoolmasters might be priests, cathedral canons, monks, friars (from the thirteenth century), or clerks in minor religious orders. With the emergence of universities, some of the more prestigious schools expected their teachers to hold the degree of master of arts (i.e., to have completed a course in the arts at university). Not all schoolmasters, however, proved effective either as teachers or disciplinarians. The poor tutoring offered by Hugues of Bray, a schoolmaster in Decize in the French diocese of Nevers in the later Middle

FIGURE 5.2: *A Jewish teacher and pupil.* The Coburg Pentateuch, Coburg (Germany), 1395. © The British Library Board (BL Add. MS. 19776, f. 72v).

Ages, prompted the local inhabitants to compile a petition documenting his many failings. He was criticized, in particular, for allowing his students to play dice and for failing to instill respect in them. His fourteen-year-old students apparently met Hugues's attempts to chastise them for misdemeanors by throwing stones at their hapless master and attacking him with their pens. Such cases perhaps help to explain the concern of civic authorities in some late medieval cities, like Paris, to pass statutes to regulate standards of teaching.[12]

HOME EDUCATION IN ROYAL
AND NOBLE HOUSEHOLDS

The family played a key role in determining the nature of the education received by the children of the nobility of medieval Europe. Although opportunities existed for sons and, occasionally, daughters to be sent away to school, the scions of the ruling dynasties and aristocracies tended to be educated at home, either within their own parental or associated households or, more commonly in England, France, the Holy Roman Empire, and Spain, within the households of other ecclesiastical or lay nobles. This practice was one of long standing. The Anglo-Saxon poem *Beowulf*, for example, recounts how its hero, a great warrior, was raised at his grandfather's court. Admittedly, noble parents tended to play a more supervisory than "hands-on" role in the early upbringing of their children. Soon after birth, children of both sexes were placed in the care of a nurse, whose role it was to nurture and encourage the earliest stages of cognitive development. In his work, *On the Properties of Things,* written between 1230 and 1240, Bartholomew the Englishman, a Franciscan friar, recommended that a nurse ought to sing to her young charges, nourish them, and lavish care and affection on them. She should "raise them and teach them how to talk."[13] Noble girls and boys were often removed from their nurseries at around the age of seven. Boys were placed in the charge of male tutors or governors (usually knights or clerics) and girls under female mistresses (usually well-born women of good reputation and manners) to receive the more formal elements of their education. In 1212, the future King Henry III of England was entrusted by his father, King John, to the charge of Peter des Roches, bishop of Winchester, with whom he remained after his father's death in 1216 until 1221. While under the bishop's tutelage, Henry spent a great deal of time at Wallingford Castle, where he was placed in the day-to-day care of a knight, Philip de Aubigné, from whom he presumably learned to ride and fight. Henry III's younger sister, Eleanor, who was similarly placed initially under the care of des Roches, actually spent much of her youth under the watchful eyes of her governess, Cecilia de Sanford, a woman whom the St. Albans chronicler, Matthew Paris, praised for her nobility and virtuous disposition.[14]

Mothers and fathers might have been physically remote figures at times, but this did not mean that they paid little or no attention to the education, discipline, and welfare of their children. Writing at the beginning of the fifteenth century, Christine de Pisan, the renowned authoress who was the widowed mother of three children, described a mother's duty to oversee the moral and spiritual instruction of her sons and daughters. In *The Treasure of the City of Ladies,* written for Margaret of Burgundy, the wife of the French dauphin, Christine offers an idealized image of the maternal responsibilities of the "wise princess": she takes an active interest in her children's welfare, regularly visiting them and inspecting those in whose care she has placed them; she is also "diligent about their education," ensuring that they learn "first of all to serve God."[15] Similar concerns were expressed in the educational treatises that other royal and noble mothers composed or, more usually, commissioned for their progeny. In 841 to 843, Dhuoda, the wife of Bernard of Septimania, expressed her heartfelt grief at her separation from her son William by compiling a lengthy manual of moral and worldly advice in the form of a Latin letter. Dhuoda urged her son to "recognize that the whole book has been written for you, for the health of your soul and your body."[16] Several centuries later, in the late 1240s, the Dominican scholar Vincent of Beauvais dedicated a special treatise *On the Education and Instruction of Noble Children* to the French queen, Margaret of Provence, possibly to assist the queen in educating her son, Louis, and her daughter, Isabelle. A father's concern for the upbringing of his three daughters during his frequent absences from home lay behind the handbook of advice put together by Geoffroy de la Tour-Landry, a knight from Anjou, with the assistance of two priests and two clerks in 1371 to 1372.[17]

The nature of the education that boys and girls received within the households of the aristocracy diverged sharply. Boys were usually educated in more physically strenuous and intellectually challenging activities, activities that reflected contemporary ideologies of male physical and moral superiority. The aristocracy remained first and foremost a masculine warrior caste throughout the Middle Ages, and its sons were trained in the arts of war. Einhard, the biographer of Charlemagne, for example, described how this ruler "saw to it that when the boys [his sons] had reached the right age they were trained to ride in the Frankish fashion, to fight, and to hunt."[18] Hrabanus Maurus, abbot of Fulda and a courtier of Charlemagne's son, Louis the Pious, recalled a popular Frankish proverb on the training of young boys: "whoever isn't a horseman by adolescence will never be one, or will be one only with difficulty when he is older."[19] Coaching in the more skilled, dangerous, and demanding elements of combat was often delayed until between the ages of twelve and fifteen, when noble boys experienced a period of intensive military training. Away from mock battlefields and hunting grounds, young aristocrats typically received some form of moral instruction and were educated in the courtly manners, etiquette, and idealized virtues associated with their rank: bravery, honor, and largesse. According to the chronicler Lambert d'Ardres, the twelfth-century Flemish nobleman, Arnoul, the son of Baudoin II of Guines, lord of Ardres, embodied many of the qualities that arose from such an education. He was praised during his adolescence in highly flattering terms, not only for his skill in weapons, but also his "integrity," his generosity, his readiness to render service at court and his affable nature. Arnoul was, Lambert tells us, "always gracious and proper in all things."[20] Thus young male aristocrats were effectively trained as future lords and masters—and the manifold public responsibilities that they were expected to assume later in life invariably influenced whether they also received a literate education, a subject to which we shall later return.

Excluded as combatants from the arena of war and regarded in Christian teaching as the inferior sex, noble girls received an education that remained focused on the domestic world of the home and that prepared them for their future lives as wives. This future might come all too quickly, especially when marriages were tied to the transfer of landed estates and the formation of political alliances. When the girl in question was the daughter of a noble or a prince, she might be married off while still a child and under the age of canonical consent (twelve), so that she received the final years of her education in her bridegroom's household. Although girls of the urban elite tended to marry at slightly later ages than their aristocratic counterparts, their domestic education continued as they began to cater for their husbands' daily needs. One elderly bourgeois husband's concern to help his fifteen-year-old wife to understand the religious, moral, and practical skills of housewifery lay behind the book of instruction that the *Ménagier de Paris* wrote in or about 1393.[21]

The moral education of young aristocratic girls was very much concerned with helping them to avoid the worst weaknesses and excesses of their sex. Influenced by the writings of Saint Paul, medieval theologians firmly believed that girls, as heiresses of Eve, should be raised in silence, humility, chastity, and obedience to their parents, masters, and husbands. Displays of temper, excessive talking, and gossiping were frowned upon, and young girls were encouraged to cultivate a character and temperament marked by a tranquil, steady expression, bearing, and appearance. Girls were advised to walk in an upright and dignified manner rather than run around. Certain virtues considered appropriate for boys and men became vices in the hands of girls and women. According to Philip of Novara, a former Lombard crusader and the author of a short treatise on the *Four Ages of Man* (ca. 1265), largesse, for example, was not a desirable quality for a maiden or a wife to cultivate—it might shame the master of the household if his wife was more generous than he and bring financial disaster to the couple if both husband and wife were too generous. Female vanity was another particular concern of the authors of didactic literature. Young girls were advised to avoid makeup and to hold out against the temptation of donning elaborate clothing, thereby resisting the sin of pride and the danger of luring the male sex into temptation. After rehearsing the tale of a knight whose first wife was carried down to hell for owning jewels, rings, "good and gay clothing and furs"—"ten diverse gowns and as many coats"—Geoffroy de la Tour-Landry counseled his daughters that a good wife should dress appropriately to her husband's station and avoid excessive apparel.[22]

As far as practical, feminine accomplishments were concerned, noble girls were not, like their brothers, trained in combat. Music, sewing, spinning, and weaving were considered fitting skills for young women, according to thirteenth- and fourteenth-century conduct literature. Philip of Novara held that young girls from all walks of life ought to learn how to spin and weave—the poor in order to support themselves and the wealthy in order better to understand the lot of others. His advice echoed sentiments expressed by Einhard several centuries earlier, who recounted how Charlemagne "ordered his daughters to learn how to work with wool, how to spin and weave it, so that they might not grow dull from inactivity and [instead might] learn to value work and virtuous activity."[23] The young women of the nobility also often learned how to hunt and hawk, both of which were popular royal and aristocratic pastimes.

THE QUESTION OF LITERACY

There was considerable debate throughout the Middle Ages about whether children of both sexes ought to be taught to read and write. At least one Christian commentator—a student of Peter Abelard—praised Jewish parents who "put as many sons [if not necessarily daughters] as they have to letters, that each may understand God's law."[24] In the princely courts of Christian Europe, boys and girls often learned reading and sometimes writing, and were expected to receive a fairly sophisticated level of academic education. The tone of each court and the nature of its education depended very much upon the interests and aspirations of individual rulers. Charlemagne, a great patron of learning, saw to it that his sons and daughters were educated in the liberal arts. Asser, the biographer of Alfred of Wessex, describes how this Anglo-Saxon king also sought to reinvigorate learning within his kingdom and his court; his sons, Edward and Æthelweard, were schooled alongside their sister, Ælfthryth, within the royal household and in the company of other children recruited from noble and less wealthy backgrounds. They were taught writing and how to read in both Latin and English. At the Ottonian court, the empress Theophanu placed the schooling of her son in the hands of Bernward of Hildesheim so that he might learn letters and manners.[25]

Not all well-born children greeted their studies with enthusiasm. Rosamund McKitterick has suggested that Notker Balbulus's story of Charlemagne's anger on discovering that the sons of his noblemen were lazy and neglectful of their studies "may preserve some sense of most nobles' lack of enthusiasm for learning."[26] In fact, illiteracy was far from uncommon at the level of the nobility before the early twelfth century. With the evolution of the cult of knighthood and the emergence of chivalry in the late eleventh and twelfth centuries, training for knighthood itself became more sophisticated and elaborate than before. It was no longer enough simply for an aspiring warrior aristocrat to be trained in the combat and conduct befitting a knight; a noble boy was expected to acquire some form of literate schooling as well. The hero of the twelfth-century romance, Tristan, for example, learns to read and write, is educated in the liberal arts and law, and becomes conversant with a range of foreign languages and social customs on his travels. Admittedly, this work portrays an idealized picture of the academic education of a knight who is a fictional character. Yet there is plenty of evidence that a growing number of nobles began to acquire, at the very least, a basic understanding of Latin, the principal language of government and administration. Later, in the thirteenth and fourteenth centuries, boys at this social level were often taught to read a growing body of vernacular literature. In the thirteenth century, an English noblewoman, Denise de Montchesny asked Walter de Bibbesworth to produce a treatise in order to teach her children the French necessary for estate management. Yet there also remained those, like William Marshal, earl of Pembroke, the regent of England between 1216 and 1219, who could neither read nor write.[27]

The extent to which noble girls were expected to, and actually did, engage with literate culture has long been hotly debated. Philip of Novara held that there was little point in teaching a young woman to read unless she was destined to become a nun. Yet justification for the literate education of Christian children by their mothers can be found in a letter sent from Jerome to a new mother in 403 C.E., in which he instructed her on how to familiarize her daughter with her letters, teach her how to write with a pen, and learn Holy Scripture, beginning with the Psalter. Jerome's advice on the education of young girls proved to be extremely influential in the Middle Ages; Vincent of Beauvais, for example, drew heavily on Jerome. Throughout the medieval period, the

main way in which most literate noble children learned their ABC was via
the Psalter (book of Psalms), which often functioned as an alphabet book. The
household accounts of Isabeau of Bavaria record the purchase of an "A, b, c, d,
des Psaumes" for her daughter in 1403.[28] Both Vincent of Beauvais and Geoffroy de la Tour-Landry considered reading a valuable accomplishment for young
women and a means of imparting Christian moral values. There were, however,
deep-rooted concerns about the types of books that young girls should read. The
wrong type of book might be dangerous, corrupting the mind of the reader
and distracting her from spiritual concerns. Christine de Pisan accordingly
counseled the "wise princess" to give her daughter books of religious devotion
and contemplation, as well as courtesy texts. "The princess will not tolerate
books containing any vain things, follies or dissipation to be brought before her
daughter."[29] Testamentary evidence confirms the impression that the primary
purpose of reading was to provide spiritual counsel and guidance for Christian
women. Books of piety, such as biblical works and saints' lives, were the most
popular works bequeathed to and by late medieval women in their wills. The
earliest known surviving Book of Hours, a prayer book containing the Hours
of the Cross, the Hours of Saint Louis, or the Hours of the Virgin, a sequence of
prayers addressed to the Virgin Mary, is the de Brailes Hours, which was written for a woman, Susanna, in or around 1240 by William de Brailes, an Oxford
manuscript maker. Books of Hours were the "best-sellers" of the later Middle
Ages, and were frequently commissioned by literate women, as well as men.
Susan Bell has persuasively argued that, in commissioning such works for their
children, mothers "may have exerted a powerful influence" on their contents,
thereby shaping the reading matter, literate culture, and spiritual interests of
the next generation—in a similar fashion to those mothers who commissioned
educational treatises.[30]

Levels of female literacy, like those of male literacy, were not constant
throughout the Middle Ages. As Ceridwen Lloyd-Morgan has observed, even
in heretical sects such as the Cathars of the Languedoc and the English Lol-
lards, where the written word was highly valued as the basis for spiritual
life, "women's literacy, even of the most basic kind, lagged far behind that of
men."[31] Bell's analysis of the evidence for women's book ownership in medieval Europe between 800 and 1500, drawn from sources such as manuscript
dedications, wills, and inventories, identified 242 Catholic women who owned
at least one book in this period. Women's book ownership increased substantially from the thirteenth century onward—Bell found fifteen women who
owned books between 1200 and 1300, fifty-five between 1300 and 1400, and
131 between 1400 and 1500.[32] Bell's figures probably represent no more than

a tiny proportion of the actual numbers of medieval women book owners and have been superseded by the research into testamentary records by Carol Meale and other scholars. Yet there is still much to be said for Bell's view that levels of women's literacy rose during the later Middle Ages. It was, like men's literacy, heavily indebted to developments such as the shift "from memory to written record" as a medium for government and estate administration. Technological advances also had an important part to play, most notably the advent of the enclosed fireplace and chimney flue, the invention of eyeglasses, and the ability to produce reading material—in the form of manuscripts—more cheaply than ever before, all of which made reading a potentially more comfortable and affordable activity in the thirteenth and fourteenth centuries than it had perhaps been for earlier generations.[33]

In discussing literacy in the medieval West, it is important to recognize not only that the ability to read and write did not necessarily coexist during this period, but also that an aristocratic girl's education was usually less formal and less rigorous than that of her brothers. Throughout the Middle Ages, royal and aristocratic women played an important role in commemorating the dead and preserving dynastic memories by passing on oral stories about the past. Yet, although these women often commissioned or acted as oral informants for, and presumably read, histories or saints' lives, they seldom authored such works. Women secular authors—like the Byzantine princess, Anna Comnena, who wrote the *Alexiad,* an account of the reign of her father, the Byzantine emperor Alexius I, and the widowed authoress, Christine de Pisan—were extremely rare. There is, for example, no medieval English author-ess comparable with de Pisan. The names of the handful of women writers in Western Europe that have come down through the centuries are usually of women from convent, rather than courtly, backgrounds. They include figures of remarkable intellect like Hrotsvitha, a canoness at the abbey of Gander-sheim. Hrotsvitha was closely connected with the Ottonian court and pro-duced no fewer than two historical epics, eight verse legends, six plays, and a poem. Another notable woman writer was Hildegard of Bingen, an abbess of noble birth whose authorial legacy included an encyclopedia on medicine and natural science, as well as saints' lives, music, a substantial body of corre-spondence, a morality play, a trilogy of books based upon twenty-six visions, and a range of other works. Yet the educational achievements of religious women such as Hrotsvitha and Hildegard were atypical of their sex. It was rare even for women from privileged backgrounds who were educated in con-vents to be equipped to write and compose texts at the lower academic levels (e.g., hagiography or romances). The patchy nature of female education was also, to some extent, reflected by the lack of Latin learning among laywomen. A familiarity with Latin and an understanding of Latin grammar became less common among women in general after the twelfth century. When the German abbess, Herrad of Hohenberg, supervised the compilation of her *Garden of Delights,* a pedagogical text for young novices at her convent, she thought it appropriate to include German as well as Latin headings. In some late medieval English convents, nuns were unable to read, or at least to understand fully, the contents of their Latin service books and muniments, creating a need for vernacular translations. Women became important patrons of vernacular literature precisely because they were more comfortable reading works in the vernacular. For both men and women of the elite, the need to partake in the physical act of writing was, to some extent, negated by the employment of the clerks in their households who engaged in record keeping and to whom letters and other documents might be dictated. Evidence for women's handwriting is seldom encountered in the British Isles. Lloyd-Morgan's study of Welsh literacy, for example, uncovered no examples of women who acted as scribes in medieval Wales. Women scribes were a little less rare elsewhere in Europe.[34]

WORKPLACE LEARNING

Although the sons and daughters of the aristocracy were often educated within great households, work, or the need to train for work, was an economic necessity for the vast majority of medieval children who dwelt in the towns and the countryside. Demographic change, the commercialization of the medieval economy, and, in particular, the expansion of markets and fairs opened up new opportunities for wage-earning activities and employment in the high and later Middle Ages. Taxation records, such as the English poll tax returns of the late 1370s and early 1380s, reveal that large numbers of adolescents from the lower ranks of urban and rural society left their family homes, either to work for wages or to enter domestic service. Many young boys became apprentices, and their sisters became servants. To acquire professional training in a craft, especially in an economic environment where, from the twelfth century on, specialized guilds began to regulate many aspects of commerce and trade in skilled occupations, a young boy needed to become an apprentice. There was considerable regional variation in the ages at which boys were apprenticed. In some towns, boys were apprenticed at the age of seven, while, in others, they joined their masters' workshops in their early to mid-teens. In Tuscan towns, apprenticeships often began at twelve—much younger than some London trades, which refused apprentices under the age of sixteen. Once an apprentice, a boy would serve his master for a number of years—in some places as few as three, in others as many as fourteen—while he acquired the skills necessary to practice his trade. The length of the apprenticeship generally reflected the demands of the trade, as well as the complexity and nature of the skills and expertise a boy needed to obtain. According to a thirteenth-century *Book of Trades* compiled in Paris by Etienne Boileau, a cook's apprentice needed to serve for two years, and a silversmith's apprentice needed to serve for ten.[35]

As an apprentice, a boy was expected to transfer the obedience and respect that he owed to his father or his guardian to his new master, in return for which the craftsman usually provided him with accommodation, food, training, and, perhaps, clothing. In banking and mercantile occupations, apprenticeship often followed on from, or went together with, attendance at commerce schools, where boys learned practical business skills such as arithmetic and bookkeeping. Some craftsmen saw to it that their skills were passed on to their own children within their own family workshop-households. Apprenticeship was, however, a relatively unusual career path for a girl to follow, especially during times of economic recession, when the guilds closed ranks and might become overtly hostile to the employment of women within their crafts. References to female apprentices are far less common than references to male apprentices in the extant records. Nevertheless, women dominated the highly skilled silk industries of Cologne, London, and Paris. Although the silk workers of Cologne and Paris possessed their own guilds, those of London did not. As Sandy Bardsley has noted, young women were better able to gain access to apprenticeships in trades that were not organized into formal guilds. A study of 208 apprenticeship contracts from Montpellier in France before the Black Death revealed just thirty documents that concerned female apprentices, the majority of whom were apprenticed into traditionally feminized and guild-free occupations, such as textile work.[36]

Some girls from urban families attended elementary or convent schools, but those who did so were usually the daughters of established bankers, merchants, and craftsmen, rather than apprentices. Apprenticeship contracts for girls generally omitted any provision for formal schooling. Many girls from the upper and middle echelons of urban and rural society spent their childhoods, and were often educated, within the parental home, where they received instruction from their mothers in the domestic arts of sewing, weaving, spinning, and embroidery, as well as cleaning, cooking, laundry, and tending livestock. The daughters of craftsmen also often learned, albeit on an informal basis and one seldom recognized by the guilds, the skills pertaining to their fathers' trades or occupations. Domestic service was, however, one of the occupations most accessible to adolescent girls in the late Middle Ages. Having acquired training in household tasks from their mothers, many young girls from poor rural and urban families in northwestern Europe left home to seek employment as servants, nurses, or laundresses in wealthier establishments.

Labor and toil—the "school of hard knocks"—rather than study, characterized the upbringings of most medieval peasants. Peasant children were seldom educated in letters; they received their "education" instead from parents and older siblings in how to perform tasks in and around the family smallholding, while urban children were "educated" in the sense that they might be called upon to perform tasks that contributed to the family business. Barbara Hanawalt's observations on the child rearing practices of the late medieval English peasantry are instructive here. Based on her analysis of 3,118 accidental death inquests drawn from six counties between the late thirteenth and early fifteenth centuries, Hanawalt found that the division of labor, and therefore vocational training, of peasant children was determined by gender from an early age. Between the ages of six and twelve, for example, peasant boys and girls often met with accidents when undertaking tasks that either mirrored those, or offered some form of preparation for performing those, of their adult fathers and mothers. Boys met with fatal accidents when herding geese, fishing, pasturing horses, and holding mock fights, while girls met with accidents when drawing and carrying water, tending fires, cooking, collecting wood, and picking nuts and fruit. By the time that they reached adolescence (between thirteen and nineteen years), fatal accidents involving boys took place in locations while performing hazardous activities that mirrored those of their fathers in the world beyond the family home: plowing fields, driving carts, and harvesting crops. Fatal accidents involving adolescent girls often took place within the confines of the homestead, when they were engaged in hazardous household occupations similar to those of women.[37] The lot of peasant families was a hard one, especially during times of famine and dearth, when children learned alongside their parents the harsh realities of the daily battle for survival.

CONCLUSION

The period between 800 and 1400 witnessed a dramatic, but by no means steady, expansion in literate educational provision, which left a lasting impression upon individual experiences of childhood and adolescence. The rate at which new schools were established varied from region to region and from century to century, as did the nature of the education on offer within medieval classrooms. Girls in fourteenth-century France and Italy, for example, had better access, or at least better-documented access, to institutionalized schooling than young women in England. There is, though, little doubt that the general trend toward the multiplication of schools in the later Middle Ages, and the rising levels of lay literacy facilitated by their emergence, helped to bring a knowledge of letters to a wider cross-section of medieval society than before. Yet one should be cautious of overstating the full significance of these developments; reading and, even more so, writing remained skills enjoyed by a privileged, if growing, minority of the European population (the nobility and the wealthier town and rural dwellers). In the absence of earlier data, David Cressy has suggested that in or around 1500, as many as ninety percent of all men and ninety-nine percent of all women were illiterate in England.[38] For most people, education was largely vocational—practical and work based. Most children reared in rural and urban settings learned, quite literally, on the job. In such circumstances, the family and household—whether a child's natal family or an employer's domestic or craft establishment—was the main forum for instruction in those tasks that would allow him or her to make a living. Knowledge was transmitted from generation to generation by visual demonstration, reinforced by word of mouth and experience.

CHAPTER SIX

Life Cycle

DEBORAH YOUNGS

The West has become accustomed to a paradigm of human progression: modern individuals grow taller and larger, and live longer; the past is filled with short people experiencing very short lives. It cannot be denied that medieval Europe faced the onslaught of famine, warfare, and epidemic disease, and suffered correspondingly high casualties. For Marc Bloch, this resulted in a briefness of life, which meant medieval society "was in fact governed by young men."[1] Scholars living in the period between 800 and 1400 would hardly have demurred from the account of truncated lives, but from an entirely different perspective. They saw themselves living in an aging, decaying world that was heading toward the last days. This theory of regression extended to the human body itself. In the fourteenth century, both the French prelate Gilles le Muisit and the Florentine Giovanni Morelli believed that people did not live as long in the 1300s as they had done a century earlier. Yet the thirteenth century had not been a noticeably golden age either, according to Guiot of Provins, who declared that "the men of the past were handsome and tall. They are now children and dwarves."[2] Reflecting on these opinions, this chapter considers the evidence regarding the medieval life span, the expectancy of life, and medieval attitudes toward the aging process. To what extent was medieval Europe a continent filled with children?

BIRTHS AND DEATHS

The newly married couple in medieval Europe knew that their main purpose in life was to produce children. Women were brought up to see motherhood as their goal: children, in the words of Christine de Pisan, were the greatest "haven, security and ornament" they could have.[3] Some individuals raised very large families indeed. Blanche, wife of James II of Aragon, gave birth to ten children between 1295 and 1310, and she was far from unique among elite women. In Périgueux (southwest France), there was *"une remarquable fécondité"* among the comital families in the late thirteenth and early fourteenth centuries. Similarly, wealthy families in Arras and Limoges boasted an average of nine children, which would have boosted the young cohorts of society.[4]

Unfortunately, virtually all the evidence on medieval fertility and childbirth is anecdotal, with a bias toward the elite. It is impossible to calculate fertility rates or estimate how many couples were prolific, celibate, or sterile. What does survive, however, suggests that Europe's wealthier (especially noble) households had more children than poorer (and non-noble) ones. The reasons may partly lie with the higher meat content of a noble diet, which was iron-rich and may have helped fertility. The elite's regular use of wet nurses should have increased the chances of a quick succession of pregnancies; breast-feeding is known to depress fertility. Of perhaps greater significance was their young age at marriage, which would maximize the fertile period. The canonical age of marriage was twelve, but the timing of the nuptials was determined by various factors, including gender, class, geographical location, and ready finances. Teenage brides were a particular feature of Europe's royalty, aristocracy, and patrician families. The large family of Blanche, queen of Aragon, probably owed much to her marriage at age twelve and the conception of her first child shortly afterward.[5] Wealth, with its promise of power and economic security, also encouraged earlier marriages lower down the social scale. England's richer peasants produced more children than their poorer neighbors.[6]

Large families were not to be found everywhere. Some people simply could not afford to marry, or their fertility was affected by malnourishment. Evidence suggests that smaller numbers of children particularly characterized urban households in late medieval northern Europe. Among London merchants in the period 1288 to 1407, the average number of heirs they left behind never reached two; in the period from 1378 to 1407, it dropped below one.[7] A possible explanation is the later marriages found in northern towns; men married in their mid-twenties with women only slightly younger. Constraints such as the male apprenticeship system and high levels of teenage female employment, particularly as live-in servants, had the potential to delay marriage. Yet the drop in offspring in late-fourteenth-century London points to a more destructive cause. In these plague-torn years, the number of children fell across Europe. In the English village of Halesowen, thirteen percent of tenants had died childless in the early fourteenth century, but, from 1350 to 1400, the figure tripled to thirty-nine percent. During the same period, notable falls in infant numbers occurred in Toulouse and the Lyonnais.[8] It is possible that fertility was suppressed in some way through the demise of partners or the psychological shock of the Black Death. There is, however, no evidence of a decline in fertility rates; rather mini baby booms seem to have occurred after each plague attack.[9]

Instead, the problem lay in the level of mortality. Medieval society experienced what demographers technically call a "high-pressure demographic regime," with high fertility rates matched by high death rates. The Black Death, which hit Europe in 1347 to 1350, came in the wake of numerous other natural and manmade killers: famine, warfare, and increasing outbreaks of diarrhea, dysentery, tuberculosis, and typhus. It is easier to list the problems than to determine what these meant in terms of medieval mortality rates. Without the parish registers and censuses of later periods, medieval demographic historians are forced to make creative and ambitious calculations from a range of unpromising records. It is particularly problematic for earlier periods, which lacked the bureaucratic—and therefore record-generating—developments of the later Middle Ages. Nevertheless, even the fragmentary remains follow a discernible pattern: Western Europe not only suffered high death numbers but experienced great fluctuations in mortality rates, which suggests sensitivity to epidemics and possibly harvest failures. The comparatively rich demographic data for England is revealing. Jens Röhrkasten's reading of wills proved in the court of Hustings, London, produces peaks in 1291, 1300, 1308, 1314, 1328, and the plague years 1361, 1368, 1375, 1382, 1390, and 1395. The plague of 1375, for instance, led to a mortality rate that was nearly twenty-four times the ordinary death rate. Further local studies are required to understand regional variations, but corroborating evidence already supports a peak during the 1310s (a time of famine) in the rural Midlands and among England's wealthy merchant creditors.[10]

Certain individuals were more prone to suffer during these peaks than others. Age was a key variable. Infant mortality at all social levels was high. The current consensus is that between twenty percent and thirty percent of medieval live births ended in death within twelve months. Europe's cemeteries provide some of the most tangible evidence, even though children are commonly underrepresented because their young bones are more likely to be disturbed, dispersed, and to disintegrate. In the cemetery of Notre-Dame of Cherbourg, where the majority of graves date from the ninth and tenth centuries, forty-five percent of the exhumed population was under the age of eighteen, with just over half of this group comprising children younger than four. Higher proportions have been found in Norwegian cemeteries; medieval Scandinavia, as a whole, provides particularly grim reading, with as many as sixty percent of children dying before the age of fifteen.[11]

Throughout the Middle Ages, children's underdeveloped immune systems made them vulnerable to malnutrition, and inadequate hygiene led to gastro-enteritis and diarrheal diseases. It is likely that poor nutrition and parasitic infestation retarded and prolonged the growth of medieval children. Simon Mays estimated that the ten-year-olds who died at medieval Wharram Percy (York-shire) were around eight inches (twenty centimeters) shorter than ten-year-olds in the twentieth century.[12] Children were always prone to epidemics of measles, diphtheria, and whooping cough, but the repeated plague attacks in the late fourteenth century were especially remorseless. Chroniclers across Europe uni-versally claimed that children were the main victims of plague, and historical evidence increasingly supports those claims.[13]

Wealth did not provide immunity to infant mortality, but being in a position to pay for regular nursing attendants may have rendered some advantage over working parents forced to balance labor and child care. This would have been a particular problem in the later fourteenth century, when acute labor short-ages drew more women into the workforce. Any irregular work patterns would have disrupted breast-feeding and general health care. As children grew older, their budding mobility and curiosity, rather than their feeding needs, could prove their downfall. English data show peaks in mortality among three-to six-year-olds, the ages when families began to assign small tasks to the child, in-creasing responsibility and the range of perils. All told, life expectancy at birth was extremely low. Figures derived from the cemeteries of Raunds Furnells (Northamptonshire) and Wharram Percy suggest it was only four years of age. Although this seems incredibly short, it is notably higher than the industrial areas of nineteenth-century England: it was only 1.7 years in Bradford in 1856.[14]

It may have been only one child in two, therefore, who grew to an age where they might have their own offspring. As they reached adulthood, their greater public responsibilities placed their bodies in new dangers. Their ex-pectation of life is difficult to determine, although it was understandably worse in the late fourteenth century than it had been in the thirteenth century. Demographic data for England and the Nordic countries suggest average life expectancy was between twenty and thirty years in the later Middle Ages.[15] But, like all averages, it obscures diversity, and cemeteries show considerable variation across settlements. Urban areas may have generated exceptionally high mortality rates, because their larger, denser, and more migrant popula-tions allowed diseases to spread faster and linger longer. Excavations at the twelfth-century graveyard of St. Nicholas-in-the-Shambles, London, reveal that over three-quarters of those buried had died by the age of thirty-five, and only five percent had reached forty-five years.[16]

Mortality rates and life expectancy among older generations might also differ according to class and gender. Noblemen were less susceptible to famine and continuing plague attacks, but they faced dangers from their prominent political profiles and ventures on the battlefield. Violent deaths of English nobles, for instance, increased markedly during the period of the Hundred Years War.[17] It has been suggested that the military and itinerant lifestyle of aristocratic males might explain why their female relatives lived comparatively longer lives in areas of northern Europe. Karl Leyser's research into the Saxon aristocracy of the tenth and early eleventh centuries produced a "surprising number" of wives and sisters outliving husbands and brothers. Women, however, faced other dangers, and a number of studies have indicated a "supermortality" among women in their twenties. In the late Anglo-Saxon cemetery of Raunds Furnells, twice as many women (forty-four percent) than men (twenty-two percent) died between the ages of seventeen and twenty-five. These ages fall within the optimum period of fertility, and the impact of a large number of pregnancies perhaps made women more vulnerable to disease and infection.[18] Whatever the precise reason, the numbers of women dying at childbearing age would inevitably influence the number of children born and the quality of family life.

None of this bodes well for maturity or for three-generational families. How many parents remained alive to become grandparents is not a question that can be answered with any certainty. We are reliant on a small number of studies on specific communities. Nevertheless, they suggest a picture that was not entirely bleak. Once the hazards of youth were over, a long midlife was a real prospect. In the eleventh and twelfth centuries, the average age of death for Europe's most powerful men (emperors and monarchs) was between fifty and fifty-five years. Similarly, calculations of life expectancy made among working communities in southern England, the Italian City states and urban areas of France in the later Middle Ages indicate that men reaching their twenties could expect another three decades of life—not a bad life expectancy in premodern Europe.[19] Archaeological evidence too shows that certain settlements contained significant numbers of mature people. Calculations based on graves at Wharram Percy indicate that forty percent of people had at least reached their late forties. They may have lived longer, but after this point, the idiosyncratic features a person accumulates in life defies any attempts to determine age satisfactorily.[20] Patchy though the evidence is, therefore, the existence of three-generational families should not be ruled out in certain medieval communities. Nor were older ages unachievable, at least among Europe's most privileged men. Heading a religious community, with its regular meals and careful sanitation, seems to have bestowed long life. Among the forty-three abbots and priors of medieval monastic houses in southern England, more than half were over sixty at death.[21]

What this means is that medieval Europe was home to a range of age groups. The relative proportions varied between settlements, between urban and rural areas, and according to localized plague attacks. Prior to the fourteenth century, age profiles were weighted toward the young; it is likely that many areas had over half of their populations under eighteen.[22] By the end of the Middle Ages, however, older generations had become more prominent in society. The year 1347 marked the beginning of a demographic revolution (lasting to about 1450), during which repeated plague attacks significantly reduced the numbers of young to the point where parts of Europe experienced an aging population. This was the case in Halesowen, where two-thirds of tenants in 1350 were in their twenties and thirties; it was only one-third by 1393.[23] Death alone cannot be blamed, because the opportunities arriving with a reduced population encouraged mobility. Nevertheless, in places like Halesowen, the pool of young and procreating adults had been reduced, and this would have depressed birth rates. In these areas, Marc Bloch's view needs to be revised: children were not growing up in a society dominated by the young but by those in their forties and fifties.[24] The Middle Ages were dominated by the middle aged.

MEDIEVAL VIEWS OF THE LIFE CYCLE

No medieval scholar would have attempted such an analysis of death rates and life expectancy. That does not mean, however, that he (and sometimes she) was not interested in demography or the aging process. By all accounts, medieval society was highly conscious of the passage of time. A vast array of written and visual material commented on the life span, fertility, and the stages of life. The most thorough engagements were ruminations of a theological, philosophical, or scientific kind, drawing overwhelmingly on the inherited concepts and language of antiquity (particularly Hippocrates, Aristotle, and Galen) and the wisdom of Arabic natural philosophy. The great program of synthesis and Latin translation in the eleventh to thirteenth centuries introduced schools and universities to influential works such as the *liber canonis* (canon of medicine) of Avicenna (980–1037), which was translated by Gerard of Cremona in 1127. By the end of the Middle Ages, these ideas became increasingly accessible through vernacular translations.[25]

To medieval philosophers, human life, like nature as a whole, followed a cycle of growth and decay. Adopting classical ideas on the organization of the body, they attributed the length of life to the combination and retention of heat and moisture. At birth, the body had both elements in abundance, necessary for growth to occur. Aging was the natural result of the body's moisture and heat wasting away. For Arabic scientists, life was like an oil lamp, which would eventually burn itself out as the heat consumed the body's moisture. How long that would take depended on an individual's constitution, gender, and lifestyle. For writers influenced by Aristotelian logic, women would die earlier than men because they had comparatively less heat and weaker bodies. Those following the work of Albertus Magnus argued for women's longevity based on their light workload and the purifying power of menstruation. Concomitant theories explained psychological and spiritual development. The twelfth-century scholar William of Conches, for example, correlated the intellectual capacity of the growing person with the relative heat and moisture in the body at different stages of life.[26]

William was following conventional wisdom by dividing life into a series of discrete stages, a theory often termed the "ages of man" (and men were predominantly the focus). The number of stages varied. The dissemination of Aristotle's work ensured support for a three-stage division of childhood, adulthood, and old age, while the seventh-century Latin dictionary of Isidore of Seville, the *Etymologiarum,* was influential in its exposition of six stages.[27] Choice did not mean conflicting interpretations, for what underpinned all theories was the notion of the essential unity and interdependence of the universe. Hence, the stages of human life were directly linked to other numerical schema: a four-stage cycle recalled the four seasons and the four corners of the earth; the seven-stage theory connected to the seven planets and the seven deadly sins. The implications of a single law governing the universe meant that the system of ages was perceived as God given. Every person passed through the stages in a set order, exhibiting qualities deemed natural to each age group. To behave in ways suitable for an age younger or older than one's own was unnatural, a deviation. Demographic changes, even dramatic ones, had a limited impact on such an ahistorical reading of the aging process. High mortality rates did not persuade medieval writers to bring old age earlier or consider young deaths natural. Asser's *Life of King Alfred,* for example, listed the king's surviving children and those "who were snatched away in infancy by an early death." His was not the only text to consider the death of children a "bitter death" (*mors acerba*) and that of young people an unripe death (*mors immatura*). Only the deaths of older people were deemed natural (*mors naturalis*).[28]

Naturally located at the start of the life cycle, childhood was defined by a mixture of dynamism and weakness. Some sensitivity was shown to the dramatic development of the early years. Those describing six or more stages followed Isidore in subdividing the growing-up period into *infantia* (usually to age seven), *pueritia* (until fourteen) and *adolescentia* (up to twenty-eight but possibly to thirty-five). Times of swaddling, weaning, and the first words could also be mapped as the child was described acquiring skills, power, and substance. All amounted to characterizing the first years of life as a "lack." The baby's body was described as unformed and in a state of flux, which meant an inability to walk or talk properly. Vapors from the heated waters hampered infants' reasoning capacities, and they were deemed incapable of making decisions; they were easily angered and easily pleased.[29] Such views were reflected in conventional images showing children in a carefree, playful state, while needing walking frames for support. As a child grew, the cooling of the body allowed instruction to take place and, in adolescence, strength and reproductive capabilities to develop. Until adulthood was achieved, however, the young remained enslaved to an excess of heat and subject to their passions, visible in an infant's tantrums and the fieriness of rebellious youth.

These may have been ideas formed and circulated in the philosophical writings of medieval intellectuals, but they were not divorced from the wider world, where similar conceptions of human development were present in contemporary legal codes. Age, it needs emphasizing, was a means to organize roles and responsibilities in both family and political society. The formulation of canon law introduced a spiritual and social distinction between children and adults, establishing age qualifications for marriage, confession, communion, and the taking of Holy Orders. The separation of children (minors) and adults and the question of when a child should shoulder adult responsibilities featured more heavily in the secular laws of villages, towns, and nations. Codes based on Roman law and south German law paid due attention to the undeveloped and innocent child, albeit with an eye to legitimacy, inheritance, adoption, and criminal culpability. For instance, in the German law code, the *Sachenspiegel,* an underage child was exempt from the death penalty, and any criminal action committed would see the victim compensated by the child's guardian.[30] The choice of age was explained in relation to perceptions of the child's ability, not dissimilar to ages of man theories. The major thirteenth-century law code of Castile, the *Siete Partidas,* stated that seven was the age of betrothal "because then they begin to possess intelligence." Similarly, a child between seven and fourteen was characterized as having "no perfect mental capacity, and, on the other hand, is not entirely lacking in it."[31] Regional customs influenced the legal ages for inheritance and political responsibilities. They might alter with the growing complexity of government and the economy; in England, the age of majority rose over the course of the Middle Ages.[32] What remained constant was that Western European society as a whole carefully guarded and regulated the entrance to social and political adulthood.

SELF-CONSCIOUS CONSTRUCTIONS OF CHILDHOOD

There is no shortage of theoretical and official views on age in the Middle Ages. Far less prevalent are personal reflections on individual childhood experiences. In the modern world, biographies and autobiographies would provide useful material, yet these are rare finds even for the most famous medieval men and women. Where they exist, they are overwhelmingly devoted to high-status groups (mainly the religious), and childhood does not commonly feature. In some cases, the evidence was simply not there. In his *Life of Charlemagne*, Einhard wrote that "it would be foolish for me to write about Charlemagne's birth and childhood, or even about his boyhood, for nothing is set down in writing about this and nobody can be found still alive who claims to have any personal knowledge of these matters."[33] At least Einhard thought such matters would be instructive. It was not always so. The inclusion of life cycle stages was profoundly influenced by the intentions of the work. Entries on childhood were designed to fit a model or schema, not to make specific comment on children themselves. Spiritual autobiographies had clear confessional and didactic purposes. The Dominican, Henry Suso, recounted how his life story was drawn out of him by a nun who wished to know "his beginning and progress" in order to learn from his experience. For this reason, childhood might be ignored or deemed irrelevant. Margarete Ebner did not describe the twenty years before her mystical experiences began, "because I did not take note of myself then."[34] The presence and nature of childhood in medieval sources was also subject to the vagaries of fashion. New artistic directions led to the emergence of convincing images of children only after 1280. Similarly, literary fashions determined that references to children were absent from Middle High German texts before 1100, became popular thanks to the influence of French and Latin texts between 1150 and 1250, before becoming more fragmentary and partial in the fourteenth century.[35]

It is difficult, therefore, to uncover intimate portrayals of childhood in the Middle Ages. More open to analysis is how writers chose to construct the subject's childhood. They bear the influence of ages of man theories. Where the subject is male, childhood is a clearly defined stage of life, and familiar ages symbolize progression. Seven was often used as a key turning point for the young: it was the age that Saint William (d. 812) joined a monastery, and Emperor Charles IV was sent to France, confirmed, given his name, and became betrothed.[36] An interesting departure is found in the lives of female saints, where childhood is less clearly defined, but greater focus is given to the first years in order to demonstrate a girl's early inclination toward holiness. Hence, Birgitta of Sweden's biographer charted her growth in childhood through events that occurred while she was three, seven, ten, and twelve, and Saint Catherine of Siena is described at five, six, seven, and twelve.[37] At these young ages, the family setting has prominence. In hagiographies, parents are regularly involved, experiencing visions or heavenly visitations around the time of the subject's birth. Despite the generic quality of the visions, they at least demonstrate that parents were expected to play key roles as protectors, nurturers, and constraining influences. Eadmer thought he should recall the character of Saint Anselm's parents "so that the reader may know from what root came the qualities which later shone forth in the child." Signs of affection are not uncommon and at times seem to speak to real feelings. Guibert de Nogent's loving portrayal of his mother, written around 1115, described the pains she endured in childbirth, the effect this self-sacrifice had on him, and her guiding hand in his education and spiritual development.[38]

The actions and preoccupations of children were portrayed in standard ways. Childhood is a time of play, dedicated to the pursuit of pleasure and joy, and a sharp contrast to adulthood. Jean Froissart offers one of the best examples in his pseudo-autobiographical *L'Espinette Amoureuse*. His long list of children's games is unique in medieval literature in its tally of entertainments and offers insight into a range of boyish pursuits. The verses associate early childhood with a period of fun—"truly I knew how to enjoy myself." Later childhood is less free-spirited for he "was made to learn Latin" and received beatings at school and at home to curb unruly behavior.[39]

Froissart was not overly negative about childhood, but he still characterized the stage as one of distraction and foolishness. This is more clearly the message of Middle High German texts, which presented childhood as a time of levity, weakness, and helplessness. Where children are praised, it is often because they have begun to adopt adult qualities.[40] Saints' lives pushed this view further, emphasizing the subjects' extraordinariness by separating them from the natural disadvantages of ordinary children. Birgitta of Sweden did not talk until she was three years old, and, on doing so, "she did not speak in the babbling manner of infants, but, contrary to what is natural at such age, she sounded her words perfectly." Likewise, the young Saint Catherine of Siena was admired because there was "nothing childish, nothing girlish" about her behavior, but a "venerable maturity."[41] Such praise exemplifies specific occasions when borrowing qualities from another age group could be appropriate and commendable. Such exchanges only worked one way, however. With silliness and incapacitation so fully attached to children, succumbing to those follies would condemn an adult to accusations of childishness. Medieval writings are full of such warnings, and Guiot of Provins's quotation at the start of this chapter is part of that tradition. To Guiot, all thirteenth-century Europeans should be compared to children in their physical impairments.

To some extent life writings concur with contemporary pedagogical treatises, which proclaimed that whatever was learned in childhood would be borne for the remainder of life.[42] Yet, in many autobiographies and biographies, the connection between childhood and adulthood is underplayed or deliberately broken. This is most explicitly seen in the lives of religious men, where adolescence is a pivotal stage in a person's struggle to lose his childishness and acquire adult spirituality. Youthful exploits are configured as seductive and therefore a temptation. Saint Aelred of Rievaulx described in his *De Spirituali Amicitia* the time when "still a boy (*puer*) at school" he had been attracted by "the bad habits to which that age usually inclines."[43] Where religious writings saw a "conversion crisis," secular writings characterized the putting aside of childish things as the mark of becoming a man. Abbot Suger's account of Louis the Fat described how the twelve-year-old Louis became a man when "he could no longer endure hunting and the amusements of boys at a stage of life when most tend to be playful." Facing an attack from William II of England, the pressure "took away his idleness, opened his eyes to good sense, destroyed his leisure and aroused a sense of duty."[44]

It is difficult to avoid the conclusion that the dominant discourse in these life writings saw childhood as mercifully brief. Nevertheless, it was not the only message to filter through, and child-centered feelings are detectable. Innocence was celebrated as a positive quality of childhood, and acting child-like was considered endearing in certain cases. The young William Marshal delighted onlookers with the childish innocence of his words when he was faced with three life-threatening situations. He saw the world as a giant playpen; his instruments of torture as mere toys. "What a swing!" he said of the catapult intended to kill him. While an obvious allusion to infantile naïveté and misunderstanding, the lack of guile that separates William from the cruel adult world is commended here. King Stephen was much taken with him—"*trop set beles enfances dire*"—that he spared William's life.[45] Even the baby's body, unappreciated by ages of man literature, could be a joy to behold. Bishop Hugh of Lincoln (1140–1200) was entranced by the movements and chuckles of a six-month-old he held in his arms. That his biographer was puzzled by it and tried to explain it away ("what ... made so important a person pay such attention to so small a being") indicates the strong filters acting against such sentiments being committed to parchment.[46]

Finally, not everyone agreed with adult-centered learning. Guibert de No-gent regretted that the regimented education he received prevented him from living the carefree, indulgent, and unruly life of other youths that was "natural to that age." In criticizing his tutor, he opposed those who treated youth "like old men who are completely serious." Similarly instructive is Guibert's rather sheepish comment that he was driven to work by a "child's eagerness" rather than religious desire. In highlighting the dedication of children, he provides an alternative view to the idle, easily distracted youngster.[47]

LIFE CYCLE RITUALS

As medieval life writings illustrated, the journey of life was not simply marked by a succession of age stages but was punctuated with milestones of individual development. While some were naturally person specific and privately recorded, the main biological and social changes were celebrated by established public rituals, now termed rites of passage. In the Middle Ages, they included rituals such as baptism, which were mandatory for all Christian children and would happen only once in a lifetime. Others, like marriage or childbirth, might occur on multiple occasions. In the Christian West, these rituals were subject to regional variations, with distinct local customs particularly evident in marriage ceremonies. The growing influence of the church and Christian symbolism during the high Middle Ages, however, ensured some degree of uniformity. The rituals also shared characteristics first identified by Arnold Van Gennep in his groundbreaking work on rites of passage.[48] In his three-fold scheme, a person is separated from one stage and experiences a transitional or liminal period before becoming fully incorporated into the next life stage and a new identity. This model cannot be applied too rigidly to medieval society, but it draws attention to three important purposes of these rites: to purify, to smooth over transition, and to declare publicly the new state of being.

These intentions are most clearly seen in the first act of life, childbirth, where Christianity added a further negative dimension to the child's form. Not only was the newborn full of excess heat, but his or her imperfect body was infected with the taint of original sin, a potential polluter of sacred spaces.

Simultaneously, birth made the mother ritually unclean, preventing her from entering the church, and separating her from normal life (she had to abstain from sexual relations). For children, the process of cleansing came through the sacrament of baptism. It was intended to wash away the original sin and place the child in a state of grace; it was a rebirth. The importance of this ritual can be seen in the speed with which it was undertaken soon after birth and the concession that, in emergencies, it could be performed by a layperson. This was a highly regimented ritual, which began at the church door, indicating that the child was on the threshold of Christian society. Only once the priest had exorcised the child was entrance into the church allowed. The procession, symbolizing the transition from sin to grace, moved toward the altar, where the godparents made a profession of faith on behalf of the child, who was now a fully fledged member of the Christian community. A parallel ceremony took place at the churching of the mother. The mother, veiled, was brought to the church door, where she offered her child's baptism robe, a gift, and a lighted candle. By blessing the candle, a priest purified the woman's body, which allowed entry into the church. Inside, as the woman prostrated herself in front of the altar, masses were sung to mark her ritual readmission to the Christian Church and the wider community.[49]

Further rituals of progression and purification clustered around the threshold between childhood and adulthood. There was no single rite to acquiring majority; it differed according to gender and social status. The most widespread entry to adulthood was marriage, which transformed the social standing of both men and women. It also legitimized sexual relations, preventing sin at a time when the church and elite families looked suspiciously at young single people, especially women. It was the danger that saw Saint Catherine of Siena kept at home when she reached the marriageable age of twelve.[50] Among aristocratic males, knighthood propelled the youth toward majority and admission into a war band. Symbolic purification—through the use of water and the color white—was central to the ceremony. According to Geoffroi de Charny, on the eve of the ceremony, the potential knights would confess, repent of their sins, and enter a bath to be cleansed of their impurities. The following day, they were dressed in white clothes tied with a white belt, symbolizing chastity, over which they placed a red cloak, denoting their pledge to shed their blood to defend the church.[51]

These rituals bestowed a new identity on the individual and created a new family. It was through baptism that the child received his or her name and was formally acknowledged by godparents, the new spiritual guardians of the reborn child. Marriage entirely changed a woman's legal identity and formed

FIGURE 6.1: *The baptism of Isabella, daughter of King Charles V of France. Chroniques de France ou de Saint-Denis,* late fourteenth century. © The British Library Board (BL Royal MS. 20 C. VII, f. 190v).

new social and spiritual alliances, widening the kinship network. We may include here the brotherhood of fighting men, of tithing groups, and monastic communities. The process of integration was marked at a communal level, often with a feast, and spiritually through the inclusive ceremony of the mass. These rituals may have been based on negative attitudes toward the sinfulness of life, but they were also joyous, thanksgiving occasions that celebrated a person's progress through the life cycle. Queen Philippa of England's suit of squirrel fur was intended to turn many an eye at her churching, which followed the birth of Edward of Woodstock in 1330.[52]

Similar processes are found in the final rite of passage, death. The Middle Ages witnessed an elaboration of death rituals linked to the development of the idea of purgatory and the desire for a "good death." They began on the threshold of death with the administration of the last rites, separating the dying from the living. Once death had occurred, the body was cleansed and wrapped in a white sheet. The procession to the church marked the journey from one life stage to the next, while the funeral acknowledged the soul's integration into the community of the dead. Most of the ceremony was reassuringly familiar, but the rituals also symbolized the deceased in ways that highlighted his or her individual family, status, gender, and indeed age.

High infant mortality rates meant that funerals of children were common. Parental distress is incalculable on such occasions, and we know too little about individual funerals, but there is evidence that the European ceremonial response was scaled down for children. In Spain, confraternities carried half as many candles at the funeral of someone younger than fourteen as they did for an adult guild member. In England, the peals of bell-ringers lasted longer for the adult than for the child.[53] A differentiation was also marked in burial observances. Unbaptized children were treated like suicides, heretics, or excommunicates and placed on the periphery of the graveyard, beyond sacred ground; a physical limbo to match their spiritual one. Baptized children were spared this treatment, but, in certain instances, they were not accorded the same respect in the ground as the adult dead. The lack of children in Anglo-Saxon cemeteries may point to the disposal of bodies by some other means, such as in water. This practice faded away in later centuries, but, in times of crisis, children appear to be the first victims of disorder. In the thousand or so burials of East Smithfield (London), from 1348 to 1350, individual graves were more likely to comprise adults, whereas the mass burial pits contained higher numbers of infants and children.[54]

Funerals and burials reflected hierarchy, and children were not as socially and politically important as adults. That is not to say they were forgotten.

FIGURE 6.2: *Blanche of France (d. 1243), a young daughter of King Louis IX, detail of the tomb.* Basilique Saint-Denis, France. © Clement Guillaume/The Bridgeman Art Library.

Apart from the Black Death years, there is much evidence to show that infants were buried with care. At higher status levels, they might even be memorialized; children were appearing on Europe's monuments by the thirteenth century. A fine example is the gravestone at the church of Rüdenhausen (Germany), which marked the death, in 1325, of Friedrich von Castell at the age of five. The image is of an archetypal young boy, playing with birds and dogs.[55] Children also appeared with their parents and increasingly so in the later fourteenth century. Why this should be the case is debatable. The link with high infant mortality during the Black Death has been suggested but remains unproven. Overall, the intentions appear less focused on the children themselves than with their symbolic demonstration of family strength; they celebrated "paternal power and maternal fertility." For Paul Binski, this places the children in "the same realm of family attributes as pets." Sophie Oosterwijk, on the other hand, is more willing to accept that personal sentiment and fond memories lay behind the memorials.[56] At least it can be said that a monument acknowledged the death of an infant and explicitly incorporated him or her into the ancestral line and family memory.

CONCLUSION

As would be expected of a six-hundred-year period, Europe changed dramatically in every direction. In 1400, life was more governed, more literate, more urban, and more aware of the costs of epidemic disease than it had been in 800. The period witnessed extraordinary population growth and decline, during which mortality rates fluctuated considerably. There was no steady decline in life expectancy, as late medieval writers believed; it varied across communities, time, and space. Infancy remained the most dangerous time of the life cycle, and localized plague attacks of the later fourteenth century hit the young disproportionately. Against this background, representations of children developed and changed. From the twelfth century onward, children had a more prominent presence in literature and memorials, and a more realistic one in artwork. Significantly, however, none was the product of a shift in attitudes toward childhood itself, and there was considerable continuity in the symbols and practices used to mark childhood and other life cycle stages. From legal codes to wall paintings, childhood was recognized as a distinct stage in life that was defined in opposition to adulthood. Infants were at the bottom of the life cycle; they were legally minors; their lack of public prominence was reflected in rites of passage; and memories of childhood were not seen as essential to life stories. One progressed to adulthood, regressed to childhood. The persistence owed much to the continual influence of classical models and the spread of Roman and Germanic law codes. It also owed much to the fact that the overwhelming majority of opinions on childhood during the Middle Ages were written by adult men. Until that changed, the recorded cultural history of childhood would remain a field peopled by adults, not by children themselves.

CHAPTER SEVEN

The State

RICHARD HUSCROFT

The subject of this chapter is the way in which the state interacted and dealt with families and children in Europe between about 800 and 1400. Most historical writing about the European Middle Ages accepts that state power increased during this period. However, such a development was neither linear nor consistent across Europe. In some areas, notably the kingdom of England, there was a steady, but by no means rapid or uninterrupted, growth in centralized state power from the ninth century onward. Things were different in mainland Europe, however. In 800, much of the continent was dominated by the Frankish empire of Charlemagne, but little over a hundred years later, this loosely bound collection of territories and tribes had collapsed. In the East, the foundations of what was to become the Holy Roman Empire were being laid; in the West, the seeds of what eventually grew into the kingdom of France had been planted. Within these lands before the twelfth century, meanwhile, although there were kings, their practical authority was limited and political power was exercised locally. In Iberia, small Christian kingdoms struggled for survival against each other and their Muslim neighbors who occupied most of the peninsula until toward the end of this period, and, in Italy, political control was disputed between Muslims, Byzantines, Lombards, and Franks. These states, such as they were, were unstable, the meaningfully coercive powers of their rulers were circumscribed, and their long-term futures were far from secure.

In the second half of this period, by contrast, between about 1100 and 1400, the political map of Western Europe assumed the appearance it was, in broad terms, to keep until the eighteenth and nineteenth centuries. The demographic and economic changes underlying these political developments are complex and beyond the scope of this chapter. However, their consequences were momentous. Single rulers, usually but not always kings, expanded the amount of territory they controlled, either directly or through others on their behalf, and the number of people who accepted the authority of these rulers and followed their orders increased significantly. The rulers' ability to demand and collect taxes, dispense justice, raise armies, and, in general terms, get their will done also grew. Inevitably, this meant that the degree of control exercised by single, centralized authorities over the people within the territories they controlled increased steadily and significantly during what is often called the high Middle Ages. However, the growth of secular power over families and children during this period should not be overstated. Rulers were concerned only to a limited extent with the stability or cohesiveness of the family unit. Standards of parenting, education, and child welfare were usually of interest only in so far as they contributed to tax yields and good order, and, as this period went on, these areas and more general issues of behavior and morality were left increasingly in the hands of another "state," the Western church under the authority of the papacy. During this period, the authority of the church came gradually to be universally recognized across Western Europe. Its largely unchallenged power cut across national frontiers to affect the lives of priests, monks, and nuns but also those of laymen, -women, and children of all social ranks. Basic notions of what constituted a valid marriage, a legitimate birth, and the age of legal maturity (matters of genuine social and political significance) came increasingly to be dictated by ecclesiastical rather than secular authorities; provision for the poor and orphaned, schools, and hospitals were managed by the church. No analysis of developments in the nature or structure of the medieval family would be complete without a consideration of how the rules and practices of the church affected relationships between husbands and wives, and between them and their children, and of how sometimes those rules and practices clashed with the ambitions and priorities of secular rulers.

JURISDICTION OVER MARRIAGE

Marriage was the basis of family life. Throughout the period under consideration here, marriage had little to do with mutual attraction between individuals, let alone love. These might be there at the beginning of a marriage, or they might come in time. But they were neither required nor expected, and, a famously passionate example such as the marriage of Abelard and Heloise notwithstanding, marriage was first and foremost a way of bringing families together for political or dynastic reasons and, usually, a way of acquiring, transferring, or protecting property, principally land. Appropriately enough, therefore, until about the ninth century, jurisdiction over marriage belonged exclusively to the secular authorities. But accepted norms of what constituted a valid marriage varied across Europe.[1] In those areas settled by Germanic invaders from about 500 onward, several kinds of marriage were regarded as equally valid. Some, but by no means all, might involve the transfer of property, and there was no bar to multiple partnerships, especially among the powerful and rich, before 1200. Meanwhile, in those parts of Europe where the Roman inheritance was strongest, principally around the Mediterranean, a clearer distinction was maintained between legal marriage on the one hand and concubinage on the other. The latter tended to be a temporary partnership between a man and woman of, respectively, higher and lower rank or status, and no property rights were involved. It also tended to be a form of union preferred by younger men prior to a permanent marriage, which required an agreement between families, an endowment of the married couple by the bride's family, and (increasingly) the consent of the bride and groom. It was also regarded, if only in rather idealized theory, as a monogamous relationship between consenting equals based on affection and respect. Gradually over this period, and with the support of the ecclesiastical authorities, it was this form of marriage that came to be regarded as the ideal union across Western Europe.

In Carolingian Europe, however, marriage was still a purely civil matter, a contract between families, and the church was involved little in its organization and administration. Of course, the church had its opinions and doctrines on marriage. The Bible had much to say on the subject, but its message was far from clear. Solomon's 700 wives were problematic for a church that stressed the values of monogamy, for example, and the "perfect" marriage of Mary and Joseph presented difficulties, too. Saint Matthew's Gospel records how Jesus was conceived by a virgin and that Joseph "knew [Mary] not till she had brought forth her first-born son."[2] However, many medieval Christians thought that Mary remained a virgin all her life and that the "sons" born to her and Joseph were actually cousins of Jesus, not his brothers. The official position of the church held that virginity, as exemplified by Mary, remained the ideal state to which all Christians, men and women, should aspire. Marriage was reluctantly accepted as very much a second best, a necessary evil required for the production of children and as a cure for lust. According to Saint Paul, "It is good for a man not to touch a woman. Nevertheless, to avoid fornication, let every man have his own wife, and let every woman have her own husband."[3] And, around the start of the fifth century, it was Saint Augustine's view in *The Excellence of Marriage* that, "by being confined to the lawful bond sensuality might not wander around ugly and degenerate." That is to say, men and women should marry, or they would do much worse.[4]

It was not until the eleventh and twelfth centuries that the church's teachings on marriage and other family matters began to carry much more than moral force. Penances for sins arising out of a range of sexual relationships might be set, but it is impossible to know how far such punishments were imposed and enforced. As early as the late seventh century, for example, the *Penitential of Theodore* (Theodore of Tarsus was archbishop of Canterbury from 668 to 690), set out a range of penances that could be imposed by English confessors for fornication and marital irregularities of various kinds.[5] Ecclesiastical authorities might also hope to influence the tone and content of ostensibly secular legislation. King Cnut's injunctions against adultery and his injunction that a Christian man "shall have no more wives than one" smack of a king attempting to enact Christian doctrine. However, his laws also accept the reality of a less-than-ideal world and address the consequences of such matters as concubinage, forced marriage, incest, and rape. One law in particular (II Cnut 53) orders the mutilation of a woman guilty of adultery, a much harsher penalty than that imposed in seventh-century Kent (Æthelberht 31), when a woman's adulterous partner had to pay the appropriate wergild and the expenses incurred by the wronged husband in acquiring another wife.[6]

Nevertheless, a shift was on the way, and, remarkably, it involved the surrender by Europe's secular powers to the church of all jurisdiction over marriage and other "spiritual matters." Reasons for this are hard to discern, but it has been suggested that, by the eleventh century, lay and ecclesiastical elites across Europe both had much to gain from this development. Church authorities, in particular the papacy, were keen to define and extend their influence over the Christian world. In the first instance, this meant controlling the clergy with bans on abuses such as clerical concubinage and simony. However, it also meant the assertion of church control over matters that hitherto had been regarded as the preserve of secular authorities: marriage, adultery, divorce, and more all came to be regarded as exclusively spiritual concerns that could only be dealt with by spiritual judges. The twelfth-century manual of English legal practice known as *Glanvill* is quite explicit in this respect: in a dispute about whether a marriage was legally valid, "then the plea shall not proceed in the court of the lord king; and the archbishop or bishop of the place shall be ordered ... to enquire about the marriage, and to inform the lord king or his justices about his judgment in the matter."[7]

As for the secular aristocracy during the tenth and eleventh centuries, its acceptance of these changes went hand in hand with another shift—the gradual replacement of clan by lineage as the basic structure of high-status family organization. The reasons for this development are complex, and neither its suddenness nor its completeness should be overstated. But, so one argument goes, eleventh-century Europe was a violent place where warfare was endemic, and families needed to consolidate and solidify to protect themselves against neighbors and rivals for local control.[8] One way of doing this was to try and ensure that lands passed smoothly from one generation of the same family to the next, and this, in turn, required a succession of clearly identifiable heirs. The church's job, the *quid pro quo* indeed, for the laity's surrender of control over spiritual matters, was to act as a neutral arbitrator in disputes over marriages, divorces, legitimacy, wills, and the like and to give the stamp of divine approval to the dynastic arrangements of the Western Christian aristocracy. From this point on, and at least until the Reformation, the idea that the church had primary responsibility for dealing with such questions was undisputed.

Such changes meant that definitions of important concepts concerning marriage had to be clearer. Because even though a preferred type of marriage did emerge in Western Europe during this period, its use did not become uniform; local customs differed, and rituals and practices were loose and informal. It seems to have been generally accepted that consent was an essential precondition for a legal marriage. But the consent did not always need to come from the parties to the marriage themselves; their parents, or those with parental authority over them, could give consent on their behalf, and, in early medieval society, marriage usually took the form of a contract between the bridegroom's and the bride's kindred with little, if any, reference to the wishes of the betrothed couple. As time went on, however, the bride's consent was increasingly seen as important. An English document, probably from the first half of the eleventh century, known as *Concerning the Betrothal of a Woman*, stresses that a woman should only be betrothed to a man if "it so pleases her and her kinsmen."[9] Moreover, it was unclear whether consummation was required before a marriage could be regarded as fully valid. But given that the main purpose of marriage was the production of legitimate children, it is likely that coitus counted as much as consensus in the early medieval period.

Clarification of such matters was provided by the church in a flurry of legislative activity during the twelfth and thirteenth centuries.[10] Through a series of papal decretals issued between 1250 and 1300, it was settled that a valid marriage was made by words of present consent (*verba de praesenti*). Thus, if a man said to a woman, "I promise to take you to wife in the future," the couple was engaged but not married; whereas if he said, "I promise to take you to wife here and now," the marriage immediately took effect. Ages of consent in matrimonial matters were more clearly defined, too, although uncertainty remained. According to some, girls and boys were both deemed capable of consenting to marriage at seven, but consummation could not take place before a girl was twelve and a boy was fourteen. Others held that twelve and fourteen, usually considered the ages at which girls and boys respectively reached puberty, were the ages of discretion. Many marriages took place before the partners were this old, however, and well before any reasonable notion of consent could be applied. Europe's ruling elite, in particular, used its children to form alliances and confirm pacts, and the boys and girls involved can have had little idea of what was happening. In 1158, when four years old, Henry, the eldest son of King Henry II of England, was betrothed to Margaret, the six-month-old daughter of Louis VII of France and Constanza of Castile. The marriage was ratified in October 1160 and rushed through in November by Henry II, who wished to acquire control over the Norman Vexin, Margaret's dowry. As time went on, however, disquiet increased about very young children being formally married. According to Gratian's *Decretum,* "Those who give boys to girls in their cradles achieve nothing unless each of the children consents when it comes to the age of discretion, even if father and mother have willed and arranged the marriage." And, in the 1190s, Bishop Hugh of Lincoln forbade "any priest or devout Christian" from attending a proposed wedding between "a certain youth" and an heiress "who was not yet four years old." The rush to marry was prompted by the concerns of the bridegroom's elder brother "that something might prevent his [brother's] acquisition of her inheritance."[11] The place and timing of a marriage were peripheral concerns, however, and any failure to observe desirable niceties was not fatal to the essential legality of a union based on the freely given consent of the man and woman (or boy and girl) who were becoming husband and wife. Moreover, consent could not be given for the couple or on their behalf, and neither witnesses, a church ceremony, nor consummation were legally required for a fully binding marriage—although all of these might have been sensible just to be on the safe side.

The logical consequence of these developments was that individuals of any social rank became free to marry as they wished. This inevitably gave rise to friction between the lay and ecclesiastical spheres. The idea that a man or a woman could marry whoever they wanted without the consent of a lord, parents, or other family members conflicted with the unavoidable reality that third parties had economic and proprietary rights in such marriages. Since unions involving their tenants and dependants involved the creation of alliances between

FIGURE 7.1: *A marriage ceremony.* Note the presence of a priest and witnesses. *Liber Sextus Decretalium* of Boniface VIII, with gloss of Johannes Monachus, England, circa 1335–1350. With permission of the master and fellows of St. John's College, Cambridge (St. John's College, Cambridge, MS. A. 4(II), f. 67v).

families, the transfer of property, and the descent of inheritances, no lord could afford to ignore them or allow them to proceed without his involvement. Even the marriage of a peasant carried implications for the lord of the land because it might take away valuable labor from his fields. By the twelfth century, therefore, lords across Europe had an acknowledged right to control the marriages of a tenant's heiresses, underage male heirs, and widows. *Glanvill* was again clear about the situation in England and made no concession to ecclesiastical rules on the freedom to marry: "no woman who is heir to land may be married without the direction or consent of the lord." And it is even more obvious in the later thirteenth-century English legal manual known as *Bracton:*

> When the heir is within age [i.e., a minor] and unmarried and in the
> wardship of the lord ..., whether the heir is male or female the marriage

will belong in full right to the chief lord in whose wardship he is; he may
give the heir in marriage when and where he wishes ... indeed he may
give him in marriage not only once but several times, as often as he is
within age and without a wife.[12]

And further down the English social scale, the payment of a sum of money
to one's lord (known as merchet), in return for his permission to marry, was
a recognized badge of unfree status by the early thirteenth century. Even the
church had difficulty observing its own rules on the freedom to marry when
these clashed with its own economic rights. Pope Adrian IV (1154–1159)
declared that a marriage between slaves was valid if the parties consented.[13]
However, churchmen acting in their capacity as the holders of land still insisted
on extracting merchet into the fourteenth century. When, in 1319, some unfree
tenants of the abbot of Bury St. Edmunds claimed that they were not obliged
to pay merchet to the abbot because they held some of their land freely, they
received short shrift in the manor court.

   Whatever the official position of the church was by 1200, therefore, in
practice most men and women, rich and poor alike, were unable to marry
without the permission of a superior lord. Marriages that took place without
such approval were not illegal, but the social conditions of the day made entering into them imprudent and almost certainly expensive. If one of the English
king's barons married without their royal lord's consent, a fine was almost
certain to follow. Under Henry II, the average fine in such case was seventy-five
pounds, or about five years' income for a knight.[14]

MAN AND WIFE IN LAW

The dominant partner in most medieval marriages was the husband. There
were good reasons for this, according to the church. After all, women (Eve)
were created out of the substance of man (Adam's rib), so they must be subject
to men and dependent on them. Saint Paul said much about the relationship
between husbands and wives, but, in essence, husbands should love their
wives, and wives should fear their husbands.[15] With such authority in mind,
the theologians and canon lawyers of the Middle Ages reasoned that husbands
were entitled to chastise their wives physically if they were disobedient or
remiss, and secular laws reinforced this.[16] The *paterfamilias* was responsible
for the behavior of the members of his family; his wife and daughters, therefore, were not required to be members of a tithing in England, for example.
And the husband/father was expected to discipline his female relations in all

matters short of felony, where the lay courts took over. The justifiable extent of such physical punishment was more difficult to determine, however, and, by the mid-thirteenth century, it had become fairly well established in canon and secular law that a husband could not simply treat his wife as he liked and that, if he exceeded his legitimate disciplinary powers, there were potentially serious consequences. The cruelty of a violent husband slowly became accepted as grounds for legal separation, if not divorce.[17] Even rulers knew of the dangers of spousal violence, and some attempted to safeguard their children against it. In 1199, for example, when a marriage was arranged between King Alfonso IX of Leon and Berengaria, the daughter of King Alfonso VIII of Castile, a prenuptial agreement stipulated that the entire marriage gift would be forfeited in the event of abuse during the marriage.[18]

Available to English women was the principle that, if a wife feared violence "exceeding a reasonable chastisement," her husband could be bound to keep the peace by a royal court.[19] He would be punished if he killed or maimed her, although not necessarily in the same way as any wife who killed her husband in late-fourteenth-century England. After the passing of the Statute of Treason in 1352, the killing of a husband by his wife was deemed treasonous, and the guilty woman could be burned, like other women traitors. There certainly seems to have been a particular stigma attached to incidents of spousal violence and less tolerance of it than of other forms of homicide in society at large. In late medieval England, for example, it has been shown that a husband who killed his wife or a wife who killed her husband were more likely to be hanged or burned than other murderers.[20]

DIVORCE AND ANNULMENT

More conflict developed during this period between the secular and ecclesiastical authorities over questions of marital separation. The church was reluctant to endorse the idea that marriages might come to an end; wives, husbands, and other interested parties might have their own good, earthly reasons for wanting to sever a union. For much of the earlier Middle Ages, however, there was little obvious problem in this regard. Husbands behaved as their Roman predecessors had done and felt relatively free to discard one wife and take another. Indeed, such practices continued throughout the medieval period. Most famously, in their unremitting pursuit of male heirs, the Capetian kings of France regularly replaced their wives. Robert the Pious (996–1031) had two marriages annulled, and every French king from Philip I (1060–1108) to Philip II (1180–1223) was divorced at least once. Two things changed as the centuries went by, however. First, as in the area of lawful marriage, the church came to exercise greater influence over such matters. And, second, as this development proceeded, the bases for a legal separation were clearly defined.

The church, once it had accepted the necessity of marriage, stressed the values of monogamy as an ongoing restraint on carnal impulses: "It is better to marry than to burn," Saint Paul had said. And there was also clear scriptural and secular authority for the indissolubility of marriages. According to Saint Mark, husband and wife were "one flesh," joined together by God, which man could not "put asunder." And in the same vein a thousand years later, one of King Cnut's laws (I Cnut 7.3) declared that a Christian man "shall have no more wives than one, and that shall be his wedded wife, and he who seeks to observe God's law aright and to save his soul from hell-fire shall remain with the one as long as she lives."[21] It was the position of the church until relatively modern times, therefore, that divorce was prohibited. But even here there was ample room for doubt. In Saint Matthew's Gospel, a man was condemned as an adulterer if he took a second wife after leaving his first, unless, that is, he had put away the first wife "for fornication." In other words, there appeared to be circumstances in which a man could legitimately remarry while a previous wife was still alive. In broad terms, however, where a marriage had been validly contracted, it was officially indissoluble. Having said that, dissolution could happen in the case of partners who, like Abelard and Heloise, both entered religious houses, and remarriage might be allowed if a spouse had been taken into captivity or enslaved. But such occurrences were rare, and much more often, some form of legal separation would take place. As noted, this could be on the grounds of spousal cruelty, but the difficulty here was that the man and woman in question remained married even if they lived apart, and—in theory at least—the husband could continue to demand sexual intercourse with his estranged partner.

Marriages were much more likely to be annulled rather than dissolved. In other words, they were treated as never having existed, even if the partners had thought they were married and had had children. Annulments were usually justified on one of two bases: non-consummation or consanguinity. Even though, by 1200, consent was seen as the essential prerequisite of a valid marriage, the view that an unconsummated marriage was somehow incomplete retained a powerful hold throughout the Middle Ages. Archbishop Theodore's *Penitential* had acknowledged a wife's right to repudiate her husband on the grounds of impotence, but, for the ecclesiastical authorities, such an idea always remained troubling.[22] Sex, even in marriage, was to be avoided, unless it was engaged in joylessly and then only for the production of children. Moreover, the idea that the marriage of Mary and Joseph could have been annulled because, as many thought, it had remained unconsummated, seemed outrageous. Nevertheless, the twelfth-century papacy, in the person of Pope Alexander III (1159–1181), was compelled reluctantly to accept that non-consummation, and in particular impotence, provided sufficient reason to nullify a marriage. More often, though, and especially at the highest levels of European society, annulments were sought on the grounds of consanguinity; that is, because the partners were related within the so-called prohibited degrees. As early as the fifth century, the church had emphasized its abhorrence of incest by forbidding cousins to marry. According to Bede, writing in Northumbria in the eighth century, Pope Gregory the Great (590–604) had stipulated that marriages between third and fourth cousins were prohibited. But by the eleventh century, this ban had been extended to marriages within the sixth and even seventh degrees of kinship. Such restrictions made life very difficult for the aristocracy of Western Europe. They tended to marry by arrangement and endogamously, from within the ranks of their social equals. Indeed, when Magna Carta stated in 1215 that "heirs shall be married without disparagement," this working principle was explicitly restated.[23] It was therefore almost impossible for an aristocrat to avoid marrying a cousin of some kind. When, at the end of the eleventh century, King Philip I of France abandoned his first wife and married the wife of the count of Anjou, he was condemned as much for committing incest (he and Bertrada of Anjou were distantly related) as adultery.[24] This was probably less of a problem for the lower ranks of medieval society, where exogamous marriage, from outside a particular clan or group, seems to have been more prevalent. Nevertheless, such extreme restrictions on an individual's choice of marriage partner had the potential seriously to inconvenience all members of medieval society. At the Fourth Lateran Council in 1215, therefore, it was announced that only marriages within the fourth degree of consanguinity were invalid.

The complexity of the rules on consanguinity might make them easier to ignore or avoid, of course. It seems highly unlikely that every marriage followed an exhaustive inquiry into the relationship between the parties. However, the rules could prove useful to the aristocracy, too. The marriage of Louis VII of France to Eleanor of Aquitaine was annulled in 1152 on the grounds that they were third cousins. In reality, although Louis was a pious man who might have had sincere concerns about such things, a more pressing reason for the annulment was the failure of the marriage to provide a male heir. Louis's son, Philip II, based his rejection of his second wife, Ingeborg of Denmark, in part on the argument that they were fourth cousins, and Philip's contemporary and

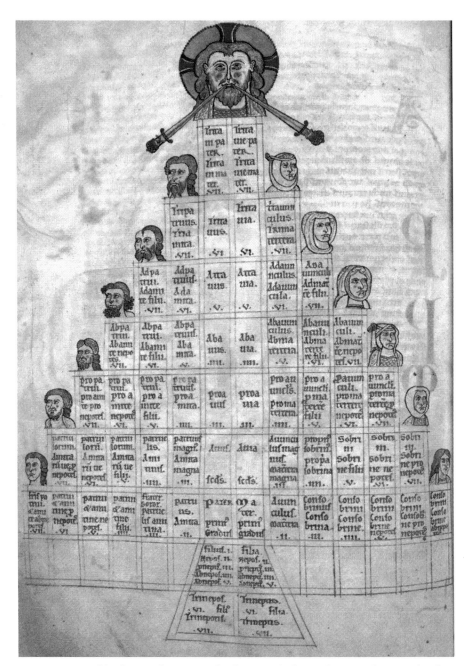

FIGURE 7.2: *A table (f. 60v) illustrating the degrees of relationship in order to make clear the prohibitions on marriage within one's own family.* Isidore of Seville's *Etymologiae*, Wigmore Priory, Herefordshire, late twelfth century. With permission of the master and fellows of St. John's College, Cambridge (St. John's College, Cambridge, MS. H. 11, f. 60v).

rival, King John of England, used the same excuse (a relationship in the third degree) to have his marriage to Isabella of Gloucester annulled in 1199. In fact, Philip seems simply to have disliked Ingeborg, while John, who had certainly known about his kinship with Isabella before their marriage, had just found another woman whom he preferred. For those with the resources and determination to do so, therefore, consanguinity could be used "as a ploy to secure the effects of divorce." The rules were "at once a marvelous excuse for cynics and a sad burden on tender consciences."[25]

PARENTS AND CHILDREN IN THE LAW

Evidence is scarce and sometimes difficult to interpret, but it seems that most medieval children were brought up by two parents and in company with two or three siblings. The associated ideas, once widely held, that premodern households were multigenerational and that extended families lived together under the same roof is no longer as popular as it once was among historians. Members of the wider family, godparents ("spiritual kin"), servants, neighbors and many others might play some role in caring for a child, but primary responsibility for a child's upbringing usually rested with his or her mother and father, and there was little by way of official guidance or stipulation to dictate how they should carry out their duties. The state, in other words, left most medieval families to their own devices, and issues surrounding the birth, nursing, and education of children remained a private, domestic preserve. Even baptism, which was almost universally recognized as a necessity for all Christian children, was not required by law.

A minority of children, of course, were not brought up in conventional nuclear families. The sons and daughters of royalty or the high aristocracy were often placed in households of their own, containing their own servants and companions; or they might be brought up in the household of a wealthy relative. Other children might be sent to religious houses to begin careers in the church. The monk and historian Orderic Vitalis famously described his tearful departure from his family in Shropshire at the age of ten to be raised as a monk in the Norman monastery of Saint-Evroult.[26] In such cases, everyday responsibility for the care of the children in question would pass to those in charge of the households, monasteries, or nunneries in question. Once again, though, the care they provided was largely unregulated, as was that given by a stepmother or stepfather to a child who had lost a parent or to one who had been sent to be cared for by other relatives. At other times, the death of a father might mean that his children were raised by a foster parent or guardian.

There were certain expectations placed on such individuals: that they would not abuse their position and frivolously waste the land of the young heir in their care, for example.[27]

Somewhat different considerations applied to illegitimate children. There were many of these—the children of prostitutes, servants, and other unmarried women—who were looked on with disfavor by society and who were subject to various legal restrictions. In medieval England, for example, secular law held that the son of unmarried parents could not inherit, even if his mother and father subsequently became husband and wife. This principle ran directly counter to canon law, which held that a marriage legitimized those children born before it had taken place.[28] If, in the English system, it was unclear whether a child had been born before the parents' marriage, this question was resolved by an ecclesiastical court, which then informed the lay court of its finding. The two jurisdictions were therefore supposed to cooperate on this important matter, but this did not always happen. In 1236, the English bishops refused to accept the idea that canon law in this area could be overridden by secular law, and they asked the king and his magnates to accept that subsequent marriage legitimized children born out of wedlock and entitled them to succeed like other heirs. However "all the earls and barons answered with one voice that they were not willing to change the laws of England that were used and approved."[29]

In most cases, it seems fair to assume that children were looked after by one, if not both, of their birth parents for most of their childhood years. If they were not, there were probably particular reasons for this. Some aristocratic children were raised apart from their parents, for example, in part because of the latter's peripatetic lifestyle: high-status men and women tended to move around between their estates, leaving little time for close family relationships to develop. Lower down the social scale, accident or poverty might be the determining factor. Some parents could not afford to feed all their children; women might become pregnant out of wedlock with an illegitimate child. These situations could lead to parents giving up, abandoning, or even killing their unwanted children. And then there were orphans, deprived of the care of parents, wider family, or godparents. Orphans were generally regarded as being under the protection of the church. In a general sense, too, lay rulers and lords were expected to protect them. And gradually over time, urban authorities assumed special obligations toward them. What such obligations meant in practice is less easy to determine. In the City of London in the later Middle Ages, an orphan was defined as a child who had lost a parent, usually the father, who was a "freeman" of the city. About a third of the adult male population of London were freemen by 1400, and, on such a citizen's death, the municipal authorities took responsibility for ensuring that his children were adequately cared for and housed.[30]

The orphaned children of those London residents who did not rank as citizens were not so fortunate. Most obvious among the sources of support for them, and for those who had simply been abandoned, were the religious houses, which would give alms, and the hospitals, which had begun to appear across Europe toward the end of the eleventh century and could be found in most major towns by the middle of the thirteenth. These institutions, which had usually been founded by some kind of ecclesiastical body, did not tend to provide medical care, but they did provide permanent or temporary food and lodging for those with longer-term disabilities. They were havens for the elderly, the infirm, and the disabled; poor or unmarried pregnant women; and, in some cases, abandoned children (the offspring of parents who could not afford another mouth to feed, perhaps, or even the illegitimate children of the better-off) and orphans younger than a certain age. In Florence, for example, the hospital of San Gallo, which was established in the thirteenth century, took in abandoned children as well as the ill and disabled; more than one Italian hospital was founded to prevent infanticide.[31] In London, too, the hospitals of Saint Bartholomew, Saint Thomas, and Saint Mary without Bishopsgate provided such services by the thirteenth century, and, in 1421, one of the charitable bequests in the will of Richard Whittington, merchant and former mayor of London and later figure of legend, stipulated that eight beds should be endowed at Saint Thomas's Hospital for unmarried mothers. It also stated that the identities of these women should remain secret so that their chances of marrying might not be damaged.[32]

Monasteries, convents, and hospitals relied on the generosity of individuals like Whittington and on exemptions from taxation allowed them by the state and the church. They were not publicly run or publicly funded organizations, however, and, in the absence of such care, there was little, if any, formal welfare provision available for those men, women, and children who had fallen on hard times. Their wider families might be in a position to help, and private charity and almsgiving played a role, too. The state, however, stood back from assuming particular responsibility for the daily care of the poor and the destitute until the sixteenth century.

Where children and parents did survive and live together, however, there is no reason to think that sons and daughters were less loved or cherished by their fathers and mothers than they are today. The idea that medieval parents were generally indifferent toward their children, largely because infant mortality rates were so much higher, no longer has much support. Katherine, the disabled and mute daughter of King Henry III of England, died at the age of three and a half in 1257. The contemporary chronicler Matthew Paris described how her mother, Eleanor of Provence, grieved so much at Katherine's death that she became ill herself and could not be comforted.[33] One story about a royal family may not be representative of attitudes more generally, of course; but although infant mortality rates were high, there is no reason to doubt that the death of a child was an occasion for grief and sorrow, not just a passively accepted fact of everyday life. Nevertheless, if medieval parents felt as strongly about their children as modern ones do, there were differences in how society expected or allowed those parents to behave toward their sons and daughters. The validity of the ultimately biblical maxim "spare the rod and spoil the child" was generally accepted, and the notion that children would only flourish if punished, physically or otherwise, for any wrongdoing was widespread.[34] Such punishment would appear extreme to modern eyes. In fourteenth-century London, for example, a five-year-old boy was struck by his neighbor when he was in her house and picked up something that she did not want him to have. He died as a result of the blow, but a jury decided that this was legitimate disciplinary conduct and that the killing was not unlawful.[35]

THE END OF CHILDHOOD IN LAW

Ecclesiastical and secular authorities had much to say about when childhood officially came to an end. This was clearly an important issue, because an adult, unlike a child, bore a range of political, fiscal, and military responsibilities toward society in general. Unfortunately, there was little clarity about when a boy or girl became a man or a woman. This would depend on a number of factors, including the age, status, wealth, and gender of the individual in question. According to one twelfth-century English authority, for example, the son of a knight came of age at twenty-one, the son and heir of a sokeman at fifteen, and the son of a burgess "when he can count money carefully, measure cloth and generally do his father's business."[36] Within territories and across Europe, in other words, there was no single age of majority for boys and girls. However, the transition to puberty was generally regarded as a decisive time. According to the church, boys reached puberty at fourteen and girls at twelve. At that point, they could take communion, give confession, make monastic vows, pay ecclesiastical dues, and receive extreme unction. As has been stated, these were also the ages at which boys and girls were deemed capable of consummating a marriage.

For the secular authorities, however, a boy was regularly considered to have become a responsible member of society well before his fourteenth birthday. In eleventh-century England, King Cnut provided that all free men should become members of a tithing at twelve, and, by the twelfth century, every twelve-year-old boy was obliged to join a tithing and take an oath to keep the peace.[37] This rule echoed that provision of the Council of Rouen in 1096 which, according to Orderic Vitalis, held that men were capable of giving oaths at the age of twelve.[38] As for criminal responsibility, rules were similarly in a state of flux. There are examples of children younger than six years old being imprisoned for their involvement in serious cases, particularly homicides. Some rulers can be seen struggling with the difficulty of dealing with young offenders. The English king Athelstan (924–939) began one of his law codes by ordering that no thief who stole more than twelve pence and who was over twelve years old should be spared. Indeed, he declared, "we are to kill him and take all that he owns." At the end of the same document, however, he explained that he had taken more advice and that it now "seemed too cruel to him that a man should be killed so young, or for so small an offence, as he had learnt was being done everywhere." Consequently, he went on, "no man younger than fifteen should be killed unless he tried to defend himself or fled, and would not surrender."[39]

By the start of the fourteenth century, it was more widely accepted that young children were not to be condemned in this way. One English judge declared in 1302 that a child who committed a crime before the age of seven should not face trial, and, by the sixteenth century, this was more or less settled in English law. The associated and rebuttable presumption had also developed that a child who committed a crime between the ages of seven and twelve or fourteen could not be guilty of a serious crime. By the seventeenth century, the age of criminal responsibility had been fixed at fourteen.

CONCLUSION

What is perhaps most striking about the period 800–1400 as far as the history of the European family is concerned is the absence of direct state involvement in its development and organization. Families remained self-governing units by and large: there were no laws about how many children a family should contain, for example, and few dealing with how children should be reared, educated, or cared for in the absence of parental guidance. The church was much more directly involved in the administration and management of such family concerns. Church courts had the power to decide whether a marriage was valid and to decide questions of legitimacy, adultery, bigamy, and incest. In the absence of any form of state welfare provision, monasteries and hospitals cared for the poor and the orphaned. Lay rulers and their courts, meanwhile, kept their distance from these and other spiritual matters. That is not to say, of course, that secular authorities took no interest in families; quite the contrary. Secular courts regularly had to decide whether a child was entitled to inherit, for example, or whether a widow was entitled to her dower. The laws on such matters were complex, they differed across Europe, and they were constantly developing; but they clearly had a significant impact on the shape and future security of individual families and on the structure of the European family in general. At the heart of such secular concerns was not the welfare or happiness of the family but anxiety over property and how land could be kept and transferred between generations. In broad terms, secular involvement in family affairs served to support and institutionalize that shift away from clan-based property relationships toward the lineal transmission of land from generation to generation within (usually high-status) nuclear families.

This change could not have happened without the active cooperation of the church, and it occurred at different rates and took different forms in different places. In parts of Spain, Germany, and the Celtic parts of the British Isles, for example, clans and tribes continued to dominate well into the thirteenth century. In general, however, by 1100, the principle of patrilineal hereditary succession was largely established and acknowledged as the norm across Western Europe. For the rest of this period, the efforts of lay rulers and their agents were devoted to making this change irreversible. To this extent, state involvement in the development of the family during the high Middle Ages had momentous consequences.

CHAPTER EIGHT

Faith and Religion

VALERIE L. GARVER

Although most medieval parents cherished their offspring, religious institutions and leaders had a more ambivalent attitude toward children. At times, they valued children and placed great worth on preparing them to be pious Christians; at other times, they took a more suspect view. In the eyes of most clerics from late antiquity through the Middle Ages, Christians ought to have preferred celibacy to having children, but those same churchmen understood that universal celibacy was unrealistic. Ecclesiastical leaders therefore recognized the importance of family life and offered advice to the medieval laity to help them to lead virtuous lives. The desire to give children appropriate religious preparation—and, more importantly, to save their souls—united families and ecclesiastical authorities in the Middle Ages, producing a culture of faith surrounding children. Instructions and prescriptions concerning the piety of the young show that medieval Christians, both lay and religious, saw children as a distinct category. Accommodations to children within the family or religious house show the ways in which adults included them in religious practice. Specific views of children changed over the course of the Middle Ages and could vary even on a local level, but the idea that children needed special considerations to practice their faiths remained consistent.

Scholars have learned more about the religious life of children and their families than many would have believed possible twenty years ago, but certain problems limit possible areas of research. European Christians are the focus of this chapter, though, when possible, it will comment upon children and family among the Jewish minority in northwestern Europe. The Western focus results, in part, from the relative lack of scholarship on the faith of children and their families in the Byzantine Empire and Eastern Europe. By children, I mean those under the age of about twelve to fourteen. Because ecclesiastical authorities generally viewed early adolescence as the time when Christians became full members of the church, it is a logical stopping point when examining the faith and religion of medieval children. Like Christians, Jews saw children as distinct from adults, in need of special care and treatment; often their views of their offspring differed little from those of their Christian counterparts. Unlike Christians, they believed that each child matured at his or her own pace so that individual children would be ready for certain responsibilities and tasks at different ages. Much of this chapter also concerns elite children and their families because the most information survives for them and, particularly for the early Middle Ages, they are among the only individuals scholars can study. Although peasant families were listed in polyptychs, inventories of ninth-century Carolingian monastic estates, those documents provide little specific information about them and probably fail to list many children, especially girls. By the high and late Middle Ages, it becomes possible to discover more about peasant and urban families and children, yet the sorts of documents that survive for the non-elite do not often provide evidence for their faith.

INSTITUTIONS AS SPIRITUAL FAMILIES

Many children did not live with their natal families but rather became members of spiritual families at monasteries, convents, minsters, and orphanages. The first three institutions were generally open only to relatively wealthy children, and the last met the needs of perhaps the weakest members of medieval society. The children who served minsters as choristers and almoners received an education in return for their labors, as did those in the monastic life, whose main contribution to their houses and society was prayer. The experiences of boys and girls in these institutions varied, however, across the Middle Ages: an example is the move away from oblation after the early Middle Ages.

Oblates were children given to monasteries or convents by their parents so that they might someday take religious vows and then serve God and pray for their families. Many wealthy parents ensured that their young children entered the religious life by sending them to monasteries and convents, and by founding those institutions with the intention that their offspring might become the abbesses and abbots. Oblation had its roots in late antiquity and was relatively common in both East and West for much of the early Middle

Ages. Oblation was neither a form of child abandonment, nor was it a wholly positive experience for those children presented at the altar. Mayke de Jong has argued convincingly for the complexity of this form of religious donation, noting that some oblates eventually thrived as monks, but others suffered. Some of these monks, most famously Gottschalk of Orbais (d. 866/870), attempted to leave the religious life but often found that church authorities considered oblation to be irrevocable, despite an insistence that oblates take vows once they achieved the age of reason.[1]

By the twelfth century, male oblation was declining, due largely to monastic reform efforts. The Cistercians, for example, insisted that their order accept only adults, because a child could not make a conscious choice to enter the monastic life.[2] From late antiquity on, the various versions of the ages of man theory generally agreed that a child did not attain either reason or the ability to speak for himself or herself until at least the age of seven, resulting in the criticism that oblates could neither know what they were getting into nor object to it. In the Byzantine East, one could enter the monastic life at ten, according to the tradition established at the Council of Trullo (680–681), though the laws of Emperor Leo VI (886–912) stipulated that such children not be allowed to dispose of their goods until age sixteen or seventeen. Eastern hagiography of the fifth to eleventh centuries nevertheless presented children entering the religious life at various ages from three on.[3] By the twelfth century, theologians began to question not only oblation but also what aspects of Christianity a child who

FIGURE 8.1: *A boy being received into a monastery.* An early-fourteenth-century text of Gratian's *Decretum.* © The British Library Board (BL Royal MS. 10 D. VIII, f. 82v).

had not yet reached early adolescence could understand. Could a child sin if she or he did not understand sin? Some argued that baptism negated sin until adolescence since children were too young to control their impulses, much less understand the concept of sin. Though children in the early Middle Ages had taken communion and gone to confession, church leaders increasingly saw these sacraments as unnecessary for the very young. The Fourth Lateran Council of 1215 stated that children should begin to take communion and confess as young teenagers.[4] Thus, children participated less often in these church rites from the twelfth century on, and many fewer entered the religious life.

Although medieval sources on children in the monastic life generally focus on boys, we know little girls entered convents. Female oblation, however, needs more research. The sources for early medieval female oblation are relatively scant, but Carolingian legislation, for example, indicates that girls and their families may have wished, like Gottschalk, to view their time in the religious life as temporary. A capitulary (legal document) of 805–806 insisted that any family who sent a female relative to a convent could not take the girl back later.[5] Although it is possible to argue that female oblation increased from the twelfth to fourteenth centuries as male oblation declined, the fact that young girls had fewer opportunities for religious vocations in the same period means that, in real numbers, relatively few girls became oblates.[6] Providing a daughter with a dowry was expensive but so, too, was supplying the oblation gift necessary for entrance to a convent. Sending daughters to the religious life was not a cure for the costliness of having daughters. The expense of oblation also prevented the poor from sending their children into the religious life.

Boys served important liturgical functions in medieval religious houses. Among the earliest evidence for such roles are monastic customaries from the tenth to twelfth centuries, which outline the readings and chants oblates were to perform both on feast days and for regular services and therefore demonstrate the boys' need for instruction and practice in reading and singing. Serving as a chorister or an almoner was another means for boys from the thirteenth century on to participate in the liturgical life of the medieval church. Choristers did not take up their prominent, highly skilled singing role until the fifteenth century, when the widespread use of polyphony increased the complexity of musical liturgy. Choristers lived in special houses associated with minsters, churches staffed by canons. For much of the Middle Ages, churchmen believed that boys' voices were especially innocent and pure and therefore a worthy addition to musical liturgy. Choristers served the minsters by singing plain chant, which required some training, and by performing various menial tasks similarly to almoners, boys who were tonsured clerks at certain religious houses. Almoners often lived outside the cloister in a building called an almonery, where travelers and the poor could also receive hospitality and alms. Most often young teenagers, these boys had familial or local ties to their houses, and, like choristers, they received schooling from the houses they served.[7]

Orphans with some means usually had relatives, godparents, or other guardians to take them in, but poor orphans sometimes ended up in hospitals or orphanages, where they received care through Christian charity. Often the wealthy citizens of cities or aristocrats funded these institutions and sometimes worked in them. Duke William IX of Aquitaine, for example, founded the Hospital of Saint James in Bordeaux in order to assist pilgrims, but, in 1200, Pope Innocent III expanded its mission to serving abandoned children and poor women expecting babies—part of his promotion of such charity, which included founding in Rome the Hospital of Santo Spirito. Elizabeth of Hungary was recognized as a saint in part for her work on behalf of children, particularly at the hospital she founded in Marburg in 1228, where she ministered to the sick, fed the hungry, and, in one episode, rescued an infant from abandonment. These deeds made her a popular saint among those praying for children, especially mothers. Two stained glass windows erected in Marburg in 1235–1240 depict her engaged in these activities. In the Byzantine Empire, secular rulers and the church made efforts to find care for orphans with families, in monasteries, or in orphanages. Medieval people appear generally to have had great sympathy for orphans, but their weak social position meant that many orphans, even relatively well-off ones, were abused. Peter Damian, for example, was beaten and suffered neglect when sent to one of his brothers after the death of his parents; he moved on to another brother, who treated him well.[8]

RELIGIOUS EDUCATION

The distinction between children in the secular and religious worlds is often unclear, because they shared many common experiences, including education. Adults expected that both lay and religious children needed special treatment, and natal and spiritual families ensured that children received religious instruction designed to inculcate virtuous behavior and piety. Lay children sometimes went to monastic or church schools for a time. In the Byzantine East, as in the West, the age of seven marked when children could begin formal instruction.[9] Since late antiquity, ecclesiastical leaders had recognized *infantia* and *pueritia* as formative periods during which children required special care. Stipulations in *The Rule of Saint Benedict,* for example, required that abbots and monks treat children differently than adult members of religious communities.[10] Oblates received special treatment at monasteries, some indulgence for their misbehavior, and instruction to prepare them for the religious life. Their purity and lack of secular experience led many early medieval people to believe that oblates could become the most effective priests, nuns, and monks.

The early rearing of children, especially those younger than seven, took place mainly in the family home. Mothers were primarily responsible for the early instruction of their children, both boys and girls, in religious practices and beliefs. During the Carolingian civil war of 841–843, an aristocratic woman Dhuoda wrote a handbook for her teenage son, then hostage at the court of Charles the Bald. In it, she imparted practical advice as well as religious lessons, including detailed instructions on how to pray. From the very beginning of the handbook, she makes it clear that she would have taught William his religious precepts in person had it been possible. At her trial, Joan of Arc explained that her mother had taught her the Hail Mary, the Our Father, and the creed, along with Christian beliefs, which suggests that peasants like Joan might have received some religious instruction at home.[11] From an early age, by following their mother's example, daughters may have also learned how to perform virtuous (though often vital) domestic work, such as fabricating textiles and tending to the sick and dying. Byzantine widowers usually entrusted their young children, especially daughters, to female relatives for instruction.[12]

Church leaders throughout the Middle Ages often assumed and sometimes encouraged that the basic religious instruction for children ought to come from parents and godparents. Teaching children to pray would have ranked among the most important lessons. Some children would have had psalters or other religious books to teach them about Christian precepts, the saints, and salvation, including ones with illustrations, which could make a profound impression on the young. Wealthy parents by the later Middle Ages may have used primers, books that had prayers, short religious pieces, and sometimes an alphabet at the beginning to aid in teaching. Texts and sermons, which parents may have read or heard, may have helped them to understand that their children's souls were at stake. Books were also critical to the instruction of Jewish children; they were brought into close proximity to the sacred texts their fathers read even when they were infants. By the twelfth and thirteenth centuries, a rite to mark the beginning of a Jewish boy's education had developed.[13]

Relatively wealthy boys and girls, both legitimate and illegitimate, often attended monastic schools with the intention that one day they would enter the religious life, but even young male serfs could study at church schools to become clerks so that they might one day be ordained as priests. When children went to school away from home, parents may have provided necessary items. A ninth-century grammar book, possibly used at Ferrières, contains an inscription indicating that a mother obtained the text for her son.[14] Other important books at schools were psalters and primers: Latin lay at the center of a religious education until the thirteenth century, when schools began to introduce the study of the vernacular. That lay children educated at home learned from some of those same books highlights the centrality of the Psalms to the instruction of all medieval Christians. Education also aided in conversion to Christianity, strengthening its hold in areas new to the faith, such as Armenia and Georgia.[15]

MODELS AND PRESCRIPTIONS FOR
CHILDREN AND THEIR FAMILIES

In teaching children, medieval families and clerics drew on a rich tradition of instructive texts, especially in France. Books of advice for children usually demonstrated a concern for their souls in addition to their future secular success. Carolingian lay mirrors, including Dhuoda's handbook, may have been addressed to adolescent boys, while hagiography offered up images of heroic children as examples for their more ordinary counterparts. The theologian Peter Abelard wrote a didactic poem for his son Astralabe, *Carmen ad Astralabium*, in which he offered advice suitable for his age, including the lesson that he should use his reason in making religious choices. Louis IX, king of France (1226–1270), wrote *Enseignemenz* for his son and daughter. The French writer Christine de Pisan wrote a didactic poem for her son Jean du Caste, in which she urged him to use virtues to combat vices in addition to providing practical advice. She wrote, for example: "Another's wealth do not envy/The envious in this life may see/The flames of Hell and feel its pains."[16] In the late fourteenth century, a French nobleman wrote *The Book of the Knight of the Tower*, which offered his daughters examples of good and bad women.

Saints' lives and sermons also imparted religious lessons to families and children. The cult of saints remained popular throughout the Middle Ages, and children and families could play important roles in hagiography. The cult of the Virgin became increasingly popular from the high Middle Ages on. Although artistic depictions of medieval families with young children are relatively rare until the fourteenth century, the many artworks and literary descriptions of Mary with the infant Jesus and of her grief at the Crucifixion suggest an expectation of an ongoing emotional relationship between parent and child.[17] Sermons were also a means of instructing children and their families. The Dominican friar Humbert of Romans (1194–1277) wrote a guide for preachers that included suggestions about how to make a sermon appeal to children: focusing on the young Jesus or holding up child saints as models.[18]

Uniting many medieval people was the understanding that children needed guidance to grow into good Christians. Clerics frequently wrote that parents should take responsibility for the behavior of their children. In the Carolingian world, an emphasis on the correction of children prevailed in both the monastic and lay worlds that acknowledged that children could behave wickedly but that it was sometimes the result of natural exuberance and impulsiveness. Clerics therefore urged parents to punish errant children corporeally for their own good, though sometimes implying that parents were reluctant to do so. Such views lasted into the late Middle Ages, when the goal of schooling for children continued to be a moral one: to make them upright adults in control of their behavior.[19] The Dominican William of Tournai wrote in his work *De Instructione Puerorum* (ca. 1249–1264) that spiritual and biological parents were most responsible for the education of children. If they failed to set them on the right path, they were accountable for their child's future sins.[20]

Early medieval clerics believed the sins of parents might be visited upon their children. In the ninth-century *Vita Liutbirgae,* the recluse Liutberga discovered in a vision that a mother, whose children all died prior to baptism, was at fault for their deaths because she had been having sex on forbidden days.[21] The tenth-century reproductive miracles associated with the cult of Verena connect parental morality with bearing and raising children; parents often realized that their sins were preventing healthy offspring.[22] Western church authorities sometimes blamed parents for deformities or illnesses of their offspring. Early medieval parents therefore faced a situation in which others and they themselves might question whether their sins had caused their children's deaths. Certain medieval Jewish texts mention sin as cause for a child's death, and some sources note that parental grief could be a means to atone for sin.[23] During the high Middles Ages, Western church reformers emphasized how a parent's sin might taint the child, particularly in the cases of the illegitimate children of clerics. Although this idea went against the belief that baptism made the failings of parents moot, reformers worried that such children, themselves proof of sin, might likely repeat the wrongdoing of the parents. The sons of churchmen as well as other illegitimate sons could not, therefore, take church office, although a system of dispensations

FIGURE 8.2: *The Nativity*. The Virgin Mary breast-feeds the baby Jesus. A biblical illustration (ca. 1270–1280) inserted into a fourteenth-century Psalter, England. With permission of the master and fellows of St. John's College, Cambridge (St. John's College, Cambridge, MS. K. 26, f. 12).

developed, and, eventually by the thirteenth and fourteenth centuries, ordination of illegitimate men became relatively common.[24]

Medieval people did not share a consistent view of the relative innocence
of children. This inconsistency resulted in part from the difficultly of recon-
ciling the repercussions of original sin with the Christian emphasis on justice
and mercy for the weak. Some medieval writers emphasized a positive view of
children derived from ancient thought and influenced by Islamic ideas, while
others focused on the negative idea of the sin that children bore. Hildegard
of Bingen, for example, believed babies were free of sin, while Innocent III
noted that infants had a sinful genesis. Some churchmen wrote that a baby's
crying was a sign of sin or even of the devil; this belief was related to the idea
that the devil might sometimes replace an infant with a demonic being or
changeling.[25]

During the twelfth and thirteenth centuries, scholars, including Peter
Lombard, Albertus Magnus, and Thomas Aquinas, argued, in contrast to the
tradition inherited from Augustine of Hippo, that the incapacity of infants
to speak, reason, move themselves, and even to have teeth at birth resulted
mainly from nature, not just from original sin. Although they nevertheless
believed that original sin tainted each baby, they thought, for example, that
infants were naturally nescient and not ignorant as a penalty.[26] Thomas
Aquinas believed that any baptized child could achieve a spiritual maturity
on a par with an adult, but he also thought infants were "spiritually and
morally unformed."[27] In thirteenth-century encyclopedic works, scholars,
though recognizing the stain of original sin, wrote that babies could be
indulged, although once a child reached *pueritia* (age seven to fourteen),
parents and other caretakers must begin strict discipline to curb the child's
natural propensity to misbehave. Many saints from the twelfth century on
were depicted as exceptionally well-behaved babies, who sometimes vir-
tuously refused to suckle. Such stories probably resulted from new ideas
concerning infancy in the later Middle Ages. Because the young Jesus was
thought to be free of sin, he was rarely portrayed acting naughty. In later
medieval apocryphal literature, however, Jesus at times was willful and disobedient to his parents. Such depictions sometimes appear in contemporary
art, such as a fourteenth-century Simone Martini painting showing Mary
chastising a seemingly "annoyed" Jesus. These portrayals both answered
questions concerning the everyday life of Jesus and provided models to medieval parents about how they should ideally treat their children.[28]

Heretical families were a source of concern to ecclesiastical leaders. The
difficulties of interpreting inquisitorial records concerning heresy, however,

make any generalizations problematic, but it is safe to say that heretics viewed their children similarly to orthodox parents. The Cathar heretics of early-fourteenth-century Montaillou, for example, had quite a few children despite an alleged belief that having children was best avoided, and they mourned their dead children, worried through pregnancies, and showed great concern for the state of their offspring's souls, even if they had a rather different conception of the soul than Catholic families.[29]

Persecution not only of heretics but also of Jews at times resulted from the explanations parents and clerics sometimes offered for injuries to children. The profound horror aroused in medieval society when someone harmed a child demonstrates both affection for children and the emotion that attended them in much medieval discourse. Christians sometimes sought scapegoats among religious minorities to explain violent acts against the very young. Church leaders attributed to some heretics a desire to torture or kill orthodox Christian children; lay people believed the same to be true of Jews. Some eleventh- and twelfth-century French clerics wrote that heretics engaged in orgies that involved killing a child or consuming the ashes of dead children, though the resemblance of this accusation to ones leveled against early Christians means it cannot be accepted at face value.

Charges of child murder became a means to persecute Jews and to deal with major social, economic, and political changes across high medieval Europe. The best known was Saint William of Norwich, a tanner's apprentice who probably, like many children, died accidentally or by a random act of violence. Nineteen Jews were hanged for his murder, and around ninety more narrowly escaped the same fate. Although the papacy condemned the unfounded allegations that Jews wanted to murder Christian children for ritual purposes, such charges remained widespread among the laity. This belief may have resulted from the knowledge that some Jews had killed their own children during the Rhineland massacres of the First Crusade, causing a suspicion that Jews would happily murder Christian children since they had killed their own, but the practice was equally wrapped up in the cult of Corpus Christi. Jews were accused of abusing the Eucharist—that is, the body of Jesus, sometimes conceived of specifically as the Christ child. Anti-Semitism also found popular expression in a tale found in medieval sources from the sixth century on about a "converted" Jewish boy, whom the Virgin saved when his angry father tried to kill him by baking him in an oven.[30] Children also participated in the persecution of Jews. In some fourteenth-century towns in the Crown of Aragon, children insulted and threw stones at Jews during Holy Week. David Nirenberg has suggested that children learned how they should perceive Jews from this ritualized violence and that they could reveal how Christians thought of their Jewish neighbors since they were too young to yet be a part of the tangle of social relations.[31]

FAITH IN FAMILY LIFE

The combination of family and religious vocation was usually impossible, as evidenced by Elizabeth of Hungary, who sent her small daughter to a convent so that Elizabeth could lead a virtuous life without the hindrance of children. But one exception to this problem may be thirteenth-century communities associated with the Humilitati, which found ways to bring parents and children together into their communities.[32] Most medieval families found other means to express their religiosity, some at the behest of the church.

Baptism was the most crucial sacrament for medieval children and their families. As an ecclesiastical prescription concerning children, it stood above all others: Western and Eastern clerics, especially from the ninth century on, insisted that parents have their children baptized. It freed the infant from original sin, provided the child with a name, and made the child a member of the church and part of a social network through his or her godparents. During the eighth to tenth centuries, a liturgy for infant baptism and godparents developed in the West.[33] By the later Middle Ages, various customs had developed surrounding baptism, such as the priest placing salt in the baby's mouth to symbolize the reception of wisdom and the godparents wrapping a newly baptized infant in a little white robe.[34] Parents chose a child's godparents for various reasons, but the social connections they could provide were important considerations.

From the time of Augustine of Hippo until the twelfth century, Western Christians believed that unbaptized children went to hell. This danger caused Anglo-Saxon and Carolingian secular and lay leaders to promote infant and child baptism, urging parents not to delay bringing their children to receive this sacrament. Two ninth-century penitentials—handbooks for priests explaining the penance to be imposed for particular sins—identified killing an infant prior to baptism as a particularly heinous crime. As prescriptive texts, penitentials tell much more about medieval conceptions than reality; their mentions of children indicate the value placed upon baptism, inculcating good behavior, and protecting children from harm.[35] By the twelfth century, theologians believed such infants went to limbo, which, though perhaps a better fate than hell, still prevented them from reaching heaven. The logic for this new belief rested on the idea that unbaptized infants were not capable of sinning; they, therefore, did not deserve damnation, but original sin prevented their entrance to heaven.[36] Dante wrote of the unbaptized in the *Inferno*: "They did not sin; and yet, though they have merits, that's not enough, because they lacked baptism, the portal of [Christianity]."[37] Byzantine theologians, on the other hand, lacked the certainty of Western clerics concerning the ultimate fate of unbaptized babies and did not explain precisely what happened to them.[38]

Church leaders could show compassion for parents and children in their provision of baptism. Some clerics may have had warm feelings for the children they baptized. In the *Vita* of Bishop Hugh (prior to 1200), after a baptism, the infant took the bishop's hand and licked it for awhile. Though the onlookers were surprised by the scene, it shows the empathy some priests may have had for children. In the later Middle Ages, the church accepted that midwives, parents, or others attending a birth could baptize a baby in an emergency.[39] In this regard, ecclesiastical leaders were both responsive to the concerns of parents and determined to take measures to save as many souls as possible.

Medieval parents sometimes feared for their children's health, and they often sought healing through prayer. Clerics encouraged early medieval parents to bring children to shrines for healing. Both earlier and later medieval accounts of Nino, a woman missionary to the Georgians, emphasize her miraculous healing of children. These texts demonstrate not only affection for children in the Caucuses but also the idea that children were the means to pass on traditions, including those of faith. That role, however, often meant that parents and political authorities resisted, sometimes violently, the conversion of children to the new faith.[40] Western European miracle accounts from the twelfth to fifteenth centuries depict both the mothers and fathers of sick or injured children praying, going on pilgrimage, and obtaining a doctor's care. When coming upon a child who had suffered an accident, adults frequently made a vow so that God might heal the child. Mothers unsurprisingly made the most vows, but neighbors did so second most frequently, indicating community concern for children. The high level of detail in miracle accounts concerning children suggests the horror of a child's death and the desire to confer veracity. Thirteenth- and fourteenth-century hagiography as far afield as Scandinavia and northern Italy offers numerous accounts of miracles related to childbirth and childhood illnesses and accidents as well as peasant and urban parents who prayed to saints or went on pilgrimage in an effort to cure their children from disease or injury.[41]

A child's death was devastating to most medieval parents; ecclesiastical leaders appear to have tried to channel their mourning to appropriate times and forms. In sermons, priests, both to console and to discourage excessive grief, urged parents to remember that God had shown mercy in taking their children from this world. During most of the Middle Ages, dying children could receive the sacrament of unction, but, by the fourteenth century, church authorities came to believe it was unnecessary given children's lack of sin.[42] The Feast of the Innocents (December 28) had long been an appropriate occasion for parental displays of grief. Hucbald of Saint Amand, in his early-tenth-century *Vita* of Rictrud, noted that, while the saint deeply mourned the loss of her young daughter, Adalsindis, she waited until the Feast of the Innocents to grieve and withdrew from her sisters so as not to make an unseemly display of her sorrow.[43] Hucbald probably intended this passage concerning her heroic lack of mourning to encourage other mothers to follow her example. By the eleventh century, chapels were built in honor of the Innocents, housing relics that had been recently discovered, and medieval manuscript, stained glass, and sculptural depictions of this event from the fifth to fourteenth centuries elaborated on the original passage in the Gospel of Matthew, particularly in showing the mothers' grief.[44] Some wealthy parents had epitaphs composed for their children. Charlemagne and Hildegard, for example, had them written for a daughter and a son.[45] Although such poems may seem formulaic, they comprised a well-accepted form of mourning. *Pearl,* the late-fourteenth-century allegorical English poem, is perhaps the most complex medieval expression of grief for a lost child. The distraught poet falls asleep and dreams of his daughter in paradise, where she imparts various religious lessons to her father meant to help him find comfort in his faith. Western European Jewish parents from at least the eleventh century on worried for the health of their children, seeking the best possible medical care for them, and sometimes mourned so terribly when they died that Jewish texts urged parents not to grieve excessively.[46]

Christian leaders attempted to protect children from certain forbidden practices. The church in the West and civil authorities in the Byzantine Empire worked to limit the use of contraception, abortion, infanticide, abandonment, and exposure. Because most evidence concerning these acts is prescriptive, especially prior to the twelfth century, it is hard to measure how widespread they were. By the late Middle Ages, court records indicate that such cases were uncommon.[47] In the East, Byzantine civil authorities could punish acts of abortion and infanticide with penalties such as the confiscation of property and exile. In the West, the church took a dim view of these practices for the same reasons as the Byzantines: they contravened the Christian ideal that sex was for procreation among married couples.[48] Yet Christian authorities from late antiquity through the Middle Ages also genuinely wished to look after the welfare of children. Because the young were among the weakest in society, Christians had a duty to protect them from abuse and in particular to look after orphans. Among the Jewish minority, however, stories of infanticide to prevent the forcible baptism of Jewish children to Christianity became part of the written tradition of medieval martyrdom following the severe persecutions during and after the First Crusade (1096); it is impossible to estimate, however, how many Jewish parents actually took the lives of their children.[49]

Children became members of the church upon their baptism, and, throughout their early lives, most would have gone to their parish churches, often accompanying their mothers, to pray, attend services, or light a candle. Byzantine ecclesiastical leaders appear to have viewed twelve as the age of moral responsibility, with one twelfth-century patriarch insisting that, at that age, children begin to confess prior to communion. Confirmation made children adult members of the church, able to marry, take religious vows, and receive last rites. In the West, by the high Middle Ages, authorities encouraged parents to have children confirmed at around the ages of twelve to fourteen, though it appears to have been a relatively rare rite since bishops had to administer it. These leaders were often busy and sometimes away from their dioceses for extended periods. By the thirteenth century, calls for reforms resulted in mandates that bishops regularly provide opportunities for confirmation and appeals to parents not to neglect opportunities to have their children confirmed at puberty.[50]

Circumcision served similar purposes in the Jewish community as baptism did among Christians, except that Jews were understood to be Jews from birth. When newborn boys were eight days old, their circumcision was the moment when the Jewish community welcomed them and their fathers formally recognized them. As they aged and could take up certain religious responsibilities such as gesturing properly with their prayer shawls, Jewish children increasingly participated in worship and Jewish education. Some services and practices were meant to help children take part and pay attention, such as the congregation participation in the reading of the *Megillah* (Scroll of Esther) on Purim. Children also bore the responsibility of reciting the Kaddish or mourner's prayer for their deceased parents, even if they were not yet thirteen and thus not yet able to lead prayers. In these respects, Jewish children participated in worship and prayer at a similar level to Christian oblates, who themselves drew on Jewish traditions. At the same time that oblation fell out of favor, Jewish authorities began to insist that children reach their religious majority, around the age of thirteen, before they could participate in rites, and, in the fifteenth century, the rite of the bar mitzvah would be developed.[51]

As was the case with entry to the religious life, medieval religious leaders wished to ensure that children reach an age at which they understood and could logically choose marriage. Families across Europe sought church sanction for marriage, and, as described in the previous chapter, ecclesiastical law had a considerable effect upon medieval marriage. Both the Western and Eastern churches believed the mutual consent of the spouses and consummation were essential to marriage. From the twelfth century on, Western ecclesiastical leaders did not believe children capable of giving informed consent to marriage, much less making any oath. Following ancient tradition and civil law, Byzantine church authorities set the age for marriage at fourteen or fifteen for boys and twelve or thirteen for girls. Patrarich Alexis Studite (1025–1043), for example, invalidated the consent of a five-and-a-half-year-old girl and punished priests who blessed the marriage of anyone who was too young.[52] In practice, various individuals did not follow these laws. Child marriage was uncommon but could occur among the elite. In 1076, for example, seven-year-old Helen, the daughter of Robert Guiscard, arrived at the court of Constantinople, affianced to Constantine Doukas. (The marriage was never consummated.)[53]

CONCLUSION

Throughout the Middle Ages, families and religious leaders worked to inculcate piety in, and prepare children for participation in, their faith, despite variations over time and place. These efforts underline the ways in which medieval people understood children to be a distinct category. Religion was therefore important not only to oblates and choristers but to lay children, who were expected to participate in the culture of their faiths. Historians have learned a great deal about Jewish children and their families, but some areas demand further study. With the rich bounty of untapped sources, scholars hopefully will produce more works on children and religion, particularly for Eastern Europe and Byzantium. Assumptions about Christian children and families, particularly in the early Middle Ages, need questioning, since, too often, scholars have assumed a teleological view of children in the medieval West. Rather than assume that their lives have been constantly improving, scholars would do well to examine the evidence for the faith of children and their families more carefully, noting both the good and bad of living in the Middle Ages.

CHAPTER NINE

Health and Science

WILLIAM F. MACLEHOSE

Many possible narratives of childhood existed in the cultural repertoire of the Middle Ages: tales of innocence or corruption; tales of the exceptional or the ordinary child; tales of the spiritual or the physiological. It is with the last category that this chapter will be primarily concerned. Despite arguments put forward by early modern historians, children—and, in particular, their physical well-being—received considerable attention in the literature of the medieval West, especially in the scientific literature after the introduction of Arabic learning in the eleventh century.

The high Middle Ages witnessed a striking increase in awareness of, and interest in, the body, growth, and health of children. From the innumerable hagiographic tales of miraculous cures to chronicle accounts of pediatric disease and inquest reports as well as more learned medical traditions, materials on the lives and deaths of medieval children appeared in ever-increasing numbers from the twelfth century onward. Some of this, to be sure, is a product of the general profusion of sources over the course of the high and later Middle Ages, in contrast to the relative dearth of earlier materials. But, along with a quantitative increase in sources, one can identify a number of qualitative changes in the nature and tone of the materials about the family throughout Western Europe during this time. The child's uniquely weak and unstable nature was identified and continuously explored in the medical literature and provided the impetus for further scholastic debate.[1]

The birth and care of children was typically handled by women, caregivers outside the university-trained world of learned physicians, and, as such, remained largely undocumented and unknowable. However, within the written, learned medical tradition are references to contemporary folk practices, many of which receive praise for their efficacy. Because details of popular or domestic medical practice are so elusive, the primary means by which we can assess children's health care in the Middle Ages lie in the writings of the learned medical tradition. These sources are increasingly plentiful after 1100 but are difficult to contextualize; they are prescriptive in nature, providing an ideal method of healing rather than a reflection of actual medical practice.

Ancient Greek writers took an interest in children's health early in the history of the Western medical tradition, as seen in the scattered references to pediatric care in the Hippocratic corpus of the fifth and fourth centuries B.C.E. Large sections of the renowned Aphorisms are devoted to embryological and pediatric observations, and a small number of Hippocratic treatises are devoted exclusively to the same subjects.[2] By the second century C.E., more detailed discussions of birth and neonatal care appeared but were often subsumed under women's health, an acknowledgement that mothers, midwives, and wet nurses were the primary caregivers. Despite the relatively wide diffusion of one such text, the *Gynaecology* of Soranus, inclusion in such gynecological and obstetrical texts resulted in the relegation of children's health to a field considered to be secondary and largely artisanal in contrast to the theoretical and learned materials addressing general (that is, men's) health.

Despite some references to pediatric care in the large textbooks or compendia of medicine from the late antique and early Byzantine worlds, it is only with the rise of Islamic medicine that a coherent and extensive understanding of children's health and illness begins to be formulated. Medical authorities such as al-Razi (known as Rhazes in the West), al-Majusi (known as Hali Abbas), and Ibn Sina (Avicenna), writing in Baghdad and the intellectual centers of Persia during the tenth and eleventh centuries, produced enormous syntheses of the Greek, largely Galenic tradition and newer, Arabic materials.[3] The Arabic writings present a highly structured, comprehensive view of childhood as seen through a theoretical framework that distinguished the humoral and physiological characteristics of each of the primary ages of man. Although there is no consistent partitioning of the ages, childhood was usually divided into several phases, usually infancy (from birth to age seven) and childhood proper (from age seven to fourteen).[4] As in most fields of medical inquiry, the Arabic authorities brought a new cohesion to the Hippocratic and Galenic tradition, combining a heavily Aristotelian theory with the classical medical practice of pediatric care.

In the late eleventh century, some of the medicine of the Islamic world entered the West via southern Italy through the translations of Constantine the African at Monte Cassino, possibly in connection to the medical school at Salerno. But it is primarily after a second phase of translation took place in mid-twelfth-century Toledo, on the border of Christian and Muslim lands, that we find a greater understanding of the Galenic-Arabic views of the fetus and child. In the incipient scholastic environment of the urban universities, the speculative and theoretical elements of the new medical ideas mingled with Aristotelian natural philosophical traditions, which reappeared in the West via the same Arabic channels.[5]

Out of the early universities that arose in the thirteenth century, there appeared a variety of freshly composed treatises that, like the Islamic syntheses before them, sought to adapt the foreign materials to a new context (here, a Latin Christian academic setting). Latin encyclopedias, particularly those of Bartholomew the Englishman and Vincent of Beauvais in northern Europe from the 1230s through midcentury, sought to gather many traditions—moral, pedagogical, and theological as well as medical and natural philosophical—in order to present a unified vision of universal knowledge, incorporating childhood into the larger schemes of creation, nature, and world history.[6] Alongside the encyclopedias, another genre, the Regimen of Health (*regimen sanitatis*), arose and incorporated pediatric material. Devoted largely to preventative medicine, the genre seeks to prescribe how each person should eat, drink, exercise, and generally live a healthy life, regardless of his or her circumstances.[7] Accordingly, there always appear sections devoted to regimens for individuals of different complexions, sexes, and ages—the last category including often lengthy discussions of the care of infants and children.

By the late Middle Ages, we witness the beginnings of a specialist literature devoted to child care based on new observations as well as a critical appraisal of the Greek and Arabic authorities. While earlier child care materials were incorporated into larger treatises on general health or gynecology, there arose during the thirteenth century a new genre of independent treatises on pediatric disease. The earliest of these brief nosological texts is attributed to Rhazes (possibly correctly, although no manuscripts of the original Arabic text are known to have survived),[8] but later treatises borrow less from the Islamic tradition. We can trace the development of an interest in pediatric care, with an explosion of new materials on child care at the beginnings of Arabic influence from the late eleventh century onward, and a refinement of those materials by the years around 1300.

MAKING THE MEDIEVAL FAMILY:
PROCREATION AND PREGNANCY

In the 1280s, the northern Italian physician William of Saliceto wrote an account of the human life cycle that documented the health of man from the day of conception until the moment of death.[9] He explored the physiological development, regimen of health, and specific recipes of each stage of life, beginning with the embryo. What is unusual is the breadth of William's vision; such claims of complete coverage of health go far beyond the earlier schematic distinctions of the ages of man and are only possible after the thorough integration of the Arabic encyclopedic material in the thirteenth-century Latin West. Well before William, the processes of sexual intercourse, conception, and fetal development had inspired wide-ranging speculation scattered throughout natural philosophical and medical texts. Constantine the African had begun the renewed discussion with his treatise on sexual intercourse, *De Coitu*, in the late eleventh century and inspired further attempts to understand the human reproductive capacity.[10]

In the material on the generation of man, both male and female sexuality receive generally positive treatment, as the texts map out the physiology of pleasure and the mechanics of conception. In contrast to medieval moral traditions that problematized sexuality, medical materials argued for the importance of sexual intercourse in human generation and maintaining the health of the adult. Some medical writings viewed the male and female genitalia as complementary, the womb having an internal structure that was the exact inverse of the penis's shape. Similarly, the differences between male nature (hot and dry, external, active) and female nature (cold and humid, internal, passive) were seen as compatible rather than oppositional, and necessary to the process of conception and generation.[11]

Discussions of conception led to considerable controversy, built around a conflict between two radically distinct views of men's and women's roles in the process. The Hippocratic view had argued for a two-seed theory: both mother and father provided seed, which mixed together to form the fetus. In contrast to this understanding, which attributed to women an active role in conception, the Aristotelian view argued for a far more passive role for women. In the Aristotelian one-seed model, the man alone provided the seed, which used its formative, creative power to transform the woman's contribution, simply passive matter, into an embryo. The Aristotelian view, which became widespread in the early thirteenth century and triumphed by the end of the century, acknowledged that both were essential to creating a human fetus but saw the sperm as a sort of sculptor or artisan, transforming the raw material of the woman's contribution into a work of art.[12]

Once the child was conceived, the viability of the fetus and the possibility of miscarriage, intentional or otherwise, occupied the minds of medical and natural philosophical thinkers. In particular, the issue of abortion elicited extensive discussion. At stake was the issue of animation of the fetus: At what point was the soul infused into the body of the fetus? When, accordingly, did human life begin? If the soul entered the body at forty or sixty or ninety days, then prior to this period, there would be no serious ethical problem with choosing to end the pregnancy. Only after the entry of the soul into the body did such moral problems arise. By the end of the thirteenth century, the argument that this occurred at conception was becoming the most prominent view, thereby making contraception ethically and theologically untenable.[13] In less learned circles, the quickening of the child, the moment at which the mother first felt movement in her belly, was sometimes seen as the moment at which the soul (*anima*, hence animation) entered the body. Nonetheless, despite theoretical concerns, there continued to appear in the practical medical literature a wealth of recipes to induce miscarriage. At times, more surreptitiously, abortifacients could appear in the pharmacological literature as emmenagogues, medicines that produced the flow of menses.[14]

Menstruation itself played a crucial and increasingly contradictory role in the medical understandings of pregnancy. To Aristotelians advocating the one-seed theory, the matter that the mother contributed to generation was menstrual blood, which the male seed then thickened and transformed into the substance of the fetus. The fact that gravid women did not menstruate led to the argument that the menses served a further essential role in fetal development: it was the primary source of nourishment for the embryo. However, alarm over the possible deleterious effects of the menses on the fetus increased throughout the high Middle Ages, as the substance was perceived to be potentially harmful, toxic, and even deadly. While the Arabic authors viewed the menses as relatively unproblematic nourishment for the fetus, Western medical writers expressed concern over women's bodily functions, particularly the menses, which were considered too powerful for direct contact with the fetus.[15]

There is a lack of consensus over many issues relating to fetal development: When, and in what order, were the organs formed? Which was the most essential? Once again, Hippocratic-Galenic and Aristotelian views stood in opposition to one another. For Aristotelians, the heart was the central organ and necessitated priority in creation, while the Galenic tripartite division of the main organs into liver, heart, and brain brought a wider range of possibilities.[16]

The mother's role in the generation of children was problematized further in discussions of the influence of the pregnant woman's imagination: strong emotions, desires for specific foods, and even the sight of certain objects could affect the health and appearance of the fetus.[17] A constant theme throughout the literature on fetal growth is the agrarian metaphor of the fruit on a tree: just as the fruit can at first easily fall from the tree but becomes more firm as it ripens, so the fetus may be easily miscarried early in the pregnancy but becomes more durable as it grows inside the womb.[18] Concerns over proper development and suspicion over women's physiology was to be reduced by closer attention to the pregnant woman's regimen. Proper and moderate diet, exercise, emotions, and habits were the primary route by which the health of the fetus and a successful birth could be ensured.

MOTHERS, NURSES, AND NEWBORNS

The celebration of birth throughout medieval culture can be found in the innumerable joyous depictions and discussions of the birth of Christ and many saints as well as in the vernacular courtly romances of the high and later Middle Ages. But such joy presupposed a healthy, successful birth, and medical literature provided an extensive amount of information in an attempt to guarantee the safety of child and mother. The need for medical knowledge is clearest in the early stages of life: the risks inherent to the perinatal period, combined with a natural philosophical interest in physiological development, led to extensive discussions of pregnancy, birth, and the rituals associated with the newborn's postpartum existence. It was assumed that the primary actors in the events surrounding birth would be exclusively women: mother, midwife, and female attendants. For this reason, emphasis in medical literature lay on ensuring the proper training of the midwife (*obstetrix*). Evidence of the difficulty of birth can be found in the obstetrical advice dealing with the dangers of certain fetal positions and other complications of the birthing process. A literary and visual tradition associated with the *Gynaecology* of Soranus (written in Greek in the second century A.D. and translated multiple times into Latin in late antiquity) identified the various fetal positions, including those that could hinder a safe birth, and explained exactly how to overcome such problems.[19] The male physician is conspicuously absent from the birthing chamber, yet male medical authorities wrote extensively and highly practically on the process. We cannot know the full extent to which male authors borrowed information from women's practical knowledge, but it was most likely extensive throughout medieval medical writings, almost the entirety of which was written by men.

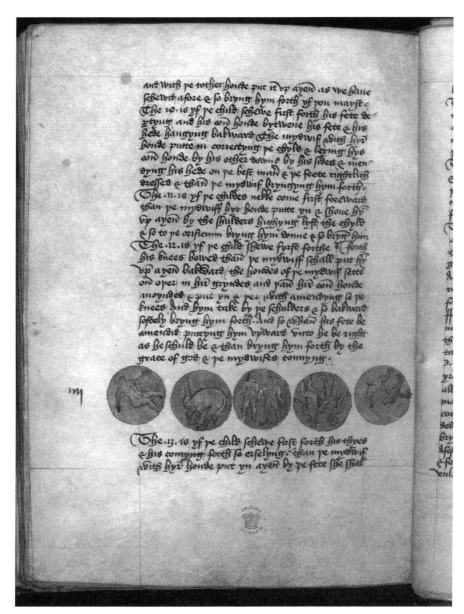

FIGURE 9.1: *Roundels showing five fetal positions, including two cases of twins.* A translation of a gynecological treatise extracted from the *Rogerina*, a thirteenth-century work on medicine, England, fifteenth century. © The British Library Board (BL Sloane MS. 2463, f. 218v).

Although a necessary stage in the creation of a normative adult, childhood (including infancy) is differentiated almost entirely from what comes after; the line between puerile and adult bodies is drawn extremely carefully and definitively. The medical sources stress the exceptional nature of the child and seek to explain the difficulties encountered in the early years of life. Most importantly, medical authors questioned how it was that a defenseless, essentially paralyzed creature could become an active, rational adult.[20] It is in this context that they developed a narrative of increasing solidity and stability, from a tender, flexible, fluid, vulnerable creature to a physically, mentally, and morally functioning adult.

The vulnerability of the newborn stands out as his most striking characteristic: the sources make very clear the fragility of the infant during the first moments outside the womb and draw parallels with the delicate first period after conception. Every action and ritual associated with the newborn reinforces the awareness of his weakness, from the minute attention to his physical well-being to the rites of infant baptism. The careful instructions on cutting the umbilical cord; removing the impurities of the birthing process; identifying healthy milk for sustenance; and creating a quiet, warm, and dark environment all reflect the complete passivity and brittle nature of the newborn.[21]

But the actions demanded of the midwife and nurse immediately after birth do more than underline the child's weakness; they also reassert a learned humoral interpretation of human physiology. According to the humoral tradition inherited from Galen and the Hippocratic writings, infancy and childhood were exceedingly hot and humid, far more so than any of the other ages of man. The quality of humidity takes on the greatest prominence here, as almost every action advocated by the medical sources was designed to reduce the extreme humidity of the newborn. As soon as the child was born, medical authors advocated opening the various orifices: removing any obstructions from the ears, mouth, and anus as well as pressing the bladder to begin the evacuation of fluids. The newborn's body had been surrounded by liquids in the womb, and these external humidities were to be removed by bathing the infant, an action that also sought to lower his temperature by immersion in tepid, but not cold, water.[22] What is for modern audiences perhaps the most striking aspect of the medieval rituals of birth is the advice that the newborn's body be rubbed with salt. The logic of salting follows directly from humoral theory, in that its explicitly stated purpose was to harness the desiccating properties of salt to dry the overly humid body.[23]

As for the infant's nourishment, there was general agreement that the mother's milk was best, but equally strong acknowledgement that her body was

FIGURE 9.2: *A noblewoman tests the breast of a wet nurse.* Aldobrandino of Siena, *Li Livres dou Santé*, France, late thirteenth century. © The British Library Board (BL Sloane MS. 2435, f. 28v).

too weak for the task immediately after giving birth. Instead, another woman, the wet nurse (*nutrix,* she who nourishes), would fill this essential role. Medical texts, following Arabic traditions, provide detailed information about the selection of the wet nurse: even more so than the expectant mother, the wet nurse should expect that her behavior, diet, emotions, and exercise would be monitored carefully. Her temperament, past history, and appearance were also to be considered, since it was recognized that the infant received much more than simple nourishment from his nurse; her habits and mores were imprinted on him, so much so that the medical and moral become inextricably linked in such discussions.[24] Such intermingling is made clear in the requirements that she should have recently given birth to a healthy boy, should not be of an irascible temperament, should be of good and consistent moral habits, and should avoid sharp food such as onions or garlic. Moderation in all things, a hallmark of the Galenic tradition, resurfaces here, as medical attention turns to the physical, psychological, and moral impact of the wet nurse on the infant. Her milk was essential to the suckling, but, because physiological theory identified human milk as transformed menstrual blood, the volatility of milk—as nourishment but also as potential pathogen—led to great concern and calls for closer inspection of the wet nurse in the later Middle Ages.[25]

FAMILY, CHILDHOOD, AND NURTURE

Although medical authorities could be vague about its chronology, the movement from infancy to childhood was sometimes identified with several important changes: the rejection of breast milk and the beginning of solid food; the acquisition of speech; and the first attempts at walking. All three of these transformations came to be understood as indicators not only of an essential transition but also of a distancing from the care of the nurse. Cognitive and physiological transformations accompanied the shift away from complete dependence on adults (women) to comparative independence (of movement, of nourishment, and of speech). There is considerable elasticity in medieval understandings of when, exactly, the transition from one stage to the other occurred. For example, weaning (*ablactatio*) could begin at two years of age, as Avicenna had advocated, or more often at three years of age, as argued by Galen and agreed upon by most Western medical writers.[26]

Dentition was a pivotal moment in the development of the child, because it led to several very different consequences. The growth of teeth served as proof that the body was successfully solidifying into something closer to the adult body. For Avicenna, the age of the planting of teeth was in itself a distinct phase of human growth. It was evidence, according to Bernard de Gordon, that the body had begun to crave solid food and move away from the breast.[27] Scattered throughout the medical literature are detailed instructions about how to make the shift from milk to hard food easier for the child. But dentition also served another purpose: it made speech possible. Prior to teething, the infant's attempts at speech were at best poor, but the acquisition of baby teeth allowed for crucial improvements in speaking, making the child's language intelligible to adults for the first time.[28] The mental process of language development had important physiological connections.

The growth of teeth was merely one manifestation of an increased solidity and strength in the child's body, which was also evident in the child's newfound ability to walk on his own. Medical texts provide extensive caveats about the new dangers that could befall the child learning to walk. Premature attempts at upright movement could lead to serious damage to the child, as could sharp objects left by a careless guardian.[29] Nonetheless, the child's eventual success at walking was an essential milestone in the narrative of solidification around which medieval medical discussions of pediatrics revolved.

Despite medical disagreements on the subject, Isidore of Seville and other theorists of the ages of man had considered the crucial transition from infancy to childhood to occur at age seven, a date chosen largely because the theorists understood the entire life cycle as part of a highly schematic and symbolic numerological system based on cycles of seven or fourteen years. The child had become more humorally stable than the infant, and consequently more capable of other forms of independence. Accordingly, age seven marked the moment at which, at least for boys, a clear differentiation from the realm of women occurred: seven-year-old boys began their formal education or training under the guidance of a (male) master. Although the pedagogical world of the young child may seem far removed from the world of pediatric health care, medico-scientific writers expressed considerable interest in the phenomenon. Medical advice indicated that the child was still relatively weak and that, accordingly, a slow transition to the realm of the teacher would be best for the child. Mentally and physically, the child would at first need considerable leniency from the *magister*.[30]

In the midst of the medical narratives of the child's growth is a discursive shift away from the predominantly physiological and toward a moralized interpretation of the child's character. In part, this may reflect the belief that the dangers to the child were considerably fewer than those that the newborn and infant had faced. The physical threats and crises of birth and the perinatal experience had passed and were replaced increasingly by an interest in the intellectual and moral development of the child from the age of seven onward.

Although medical discussions of the newborn and infant focused almost exclusively on physical care, advice on the health of the child consistently revolved around the need to attend to both his spiritual and his bodily care. The symbiosis of medicine and spirituality—in particular, morality—is made explicit often in texts from around 1300. Just as swaddling was thought to help to produce the ideal physical shape, so adults' proper behavior and their careful attention to the child's habits would help to produce the ideal morally upright character. Horticultural imagery enters the medical discourse in a parallel to the idea that the nurse and swaddling clothes shaped the newborn's body: as a twisted root will produce a twisted plant and an upright root an upright plant, so too can good or bad training produce a child of commensurate mores.[31]

Some medical figures claimed that the child's behavior was the realm of moral philosophers rather than of physicians or natural philosophers. But others refused to cede ground and instead argued that children's *actiones* and *passiones,* what they do and what they endure, can be subsumed under the rubric of medicine. Central to the argument was a quote from Avicenna, repeated often in thirteenth- and fourteenth-century medical works, that a bad complexion can influence or even cause bad mores, and vice versa.[32]

The belief that the humors and the complexions influenced moral behavior became a source of concern in several areas. Physical activity was a battleground in which the child's habits could be formed and natural inclinations curbed. Children of a colder complexion were thought to be lethargic, unwilling to exercise, and so should be compelled to do so, while intemperately hot children should avoid too much movement.[33] Because exercise was an essential part of the regimen of the child (and of all humans), the demands for control of the child's movements and awareness of his humoral makeup brought this aspect of child rearing into the medical realm. Other areas of medico-moral concern included the child's appetite and the use of wine. One topos of pedagogical and medical literature was that children often overate, a source of interest to moralists and physicians, who argued that their expertise could be enlisted to distinguish a physiological cause of this dilemma from mere childish gluttony.

Instead of invoking the image of the innocent child, medical and ethical writers agreed that there was a darker side to childhood, one that involved greed, obstinacy, disobedience, and a desire for forbidden or dangerous things.[34] The encyclopedists of the mid-thirteenth century began to fuse the moral and physiological traditions, a pattern that medical authors continued in the later Middle Ages. Debates over the appropriateness of children drinking wine, often consumed at meals and with medications, circled around both physiological and moral concerns; alcohol could further warm the already constitutionally hot child and could lead to dangerous or immoral behavior.[35] Just as the blood and breast milk that fed the fetus and newborn came under close scrutiny, so also the food and drink consumed by the child were to be scrupulously controlled by the child's minders. The consequences of improper sustenance for the child were no longer as life-threatening as they were for the embryo and infant, but the spiritual dimension now played a more prominent role.

Because the health of body and soul were at stake, the choice of the master who would instruct the boy took on an importance comparable to that of the wet nurse. The man's intellectual and ethical status were of great concern even to medical writers, who viewed the child as both mentally and physically weak, and thus advocated close attention to the boy's diet, psychology, and exercise regimen. By the ages of eleven or twelve, the rudimentary education given to all boys was—according to Bernard de Gordon—to be superseded by one of three options based on the child's future occupation: the military, the mechanical arts (meaning mercantile training), and philosophical study. This updating of the notion of the three orders, with bourgeois replacing peasants and scholastic students representing the clergy, necessitated medical intervention, because each of the three types required a distinct regimen that would produce the ideal body and mind appropriate to that path. The physical strength required of a warrior found its contrast in the soft body of the philosopher, for whom a weak body was the most conducive to rational thought. For each group, Bernard articulated a different regimen of food and exercise, particularly training the body through rubbing or massage to produce the proper physiognomy.[36]

The end of childhood was marked by both physical and intellectual changes, both of them with new moral implications. Adolescence or youth (generally interchangeable terms, with *adolescentia* being the more medical term in comparison with the less technical *juventus*) was thought to begin with sexual maturity and an increased ability to use rational thought. Girls were thought to reach menarche at twelve, while boys became capable of producing sperm two years later, at fourteen.[37] The same age marked the moment at which the young person developed intellectually and gained full use of his rational capacity. As a consequence of entering the age of reason, the youth was now fully responsible for his actions, with potentially dangerous consequences given the desires that arose at puberty.

That much closer to adulthood and humoral balance, the entry into adulthood entailed a transformation of the individual's humoral constitution. Although still prone to some humoral excesses, the youth was nonetheless more humorally balanced than the child. A theoretical debate over the constitutional differences between child and youth revolved around the nature of the heat that characterized both ages. Both were exceedingly hot, but the child's heat was hotter in quantity while the youth's was hotter in quality.[38] That is, the youth produced less but more refined heat than the child. As a consequence, the youth's humoral excess was easier to control or balance, further evidence that he was approaching the ideal of the fully formed, humorally balanced adult. For this reason, the conclusion that William of Saliceto reached was that, unlike the child, the youth had no distinct regimen but would be ruled in common with adults,[39] further evidence of the large gap between the child and the youth. In contrast, other medical authorities advocated a unique regimen for the youth, different from that of the child and closer to that of the adult.[40] For Bernard de Gordon, the age of youth was more temperate in terms of movement and intellect, but the child was more temperate in his ability to digest food, evidence of which was to be found in the remarkable physical growth of the child.[41] In this sense, his natural humidity and heat produced the positive result of stimulating growth and the proper development of the body, which was almost complete by the age of fourteen. Medieval medical writers contrasted the youth with the child in many ways: in physical structure, sexual potency, intellectual and rational capacity, and moral responsibility.

MEDICINE AND HEALTH CARE IN THE FAMILY

Scholars have generally assumed a very high infant and child mortality for the entirety of the premodern period—and, for that matter, through the nineteenth century in Western Europe. The possibility of death during the early years of life pervades much of the medieval material addressing the child. Awareness of the extent of infant mortality can be found in contemporary references to death rates as high as fifty percent. Despite the dramatic rhetoric in which such claims are couched, demographic historians generally agree with this assessment. An earlier generation of historians, following the thesis of Philippe Ariès, argued that medieval society exhibited a distanced, even callous attitude toward the death of children, but recent work has unearthed a considerable amount of material indicating deep concern and sadness over the loss of a child.

In the language and logic of learned medicine, the child's proclivity toward ill health stemmed from an imbalance of the humors. Just as we have seen with the care of the infant at birth, when almost every action sought to reduce the newborn's humoral excesses, so also many preventative and curative treatments of the infant and child were centered on reducing the heat and humidity, which were thought to cause and prolong illness in children.

Much of the practical material on child care may seem to be commonsensical, based on homespun or obvious advice. In fact, by 1300, medical writers indicate a clear awareness that some of their advice is unnecessary because the caregivers would know what to do and may have greater expertise. When discussing soiled swaddling clothes, Mayno or Magninus of Milan, writing around 1330 in Paris, notes that, since "mothers are more proficient in [this subject], I do not intend to discuss the matter further" and explains the source of women's expertise by wearily noting that the swaddling clothes are soiled almost as soon as they are changed.[42] Such observations beg the question of the extent of intervention by trained physicians as well as the nature of the boundaries between domestic and professional health care. Mayno refers extensively to practices by local women, all of which receive praise and are taken up by the author.[43] What may well have distinguished the (male) medical views of child care from (female) domestic care is the former's emphasis on a humoral prism through which to view the child's health. In dealing with the care of the infant, a thin veneer of Hippocratic-Galenic theory masks materials that, with rare exception, required only a slight familiarity with the learned medical tradition, particularly in pharmacology.

But humoral theory did not explain all pediatric illness, particularly perinatal problems. Given the possibility of death that loomed over the young child, it is not surprising that the medical literature often addresses the issue of the delicacy of the newborn's struggle to survive. The question of death at or immediately after birth appears in a number of ways. In embryological theory, this possibility arises in the argument that a child born at eight months' gestation would not survive while the child born at seven or nine months would live. The child at seven months sought to be born and struggled to exit the womb so laboriously that, if unsuccessful in the attempt, he would need to rest for the entire eighth month to recover his strength, so parturition in that month would entail certain death for the weakened fetus.[44] Given the difficulty of identifying the moment at which conception occurred, such arguments provided a conveniently elastic explanation for the inviability of certain fetuses.

Further evidence of an awareness of how precarious the newborn's life was can be found in the demands, ever increasing from the early thirteenth century onward, that the midwife be able to baptize the newborn. The mere possibility of the infant's death before baptism brought the possibility of eternal damnation, following an Augustinian tradition that led to the mid-thirteenth-century theological articulation of the category of the limbo of children, on the fringe of hell.[45] Church councils required some basic ability to pronounce the words of the baptismal rite, and medical materials occasionally echoed these requirements.[46]

After a successful birth, the fear of medical complications leading to death continued to hover over the infant and child. The wet nurse's milk was thought potentially to cause illness and death, and various diseases are identified as particularly likely to bring death to the young. The earliest pediatric texts of the twelfth through fourteenth centuries are generally organized as rudimentary nosological reference guides; they list the diseases of children, usually alphabetically, with a brief description of symptoms and more detailed instructions on treatment.[47] Many of the diseases are common to adults as well, although some—such as epilepsy—are associated most often with children. What differentiates children's diseases from those of adults is the extent of the danger faced by the young and the method of treatment. The pediatric treatises make it clear that children are more susceptible to these conditions and are more likely to die from them. But they also imply that methods of healing that are appropriate for adults, particularly oral delivery of medication, are not apposite for the child. Instead, ointments are generally rubbed externally around the afflicted part, and, if medicines must be taken by mouth to cure a suckling child, they should be taken by the nurse, whose milk will then bring the medication to the infant. Such a custom also provides some indication of aetiology; the nurse receives the medication in part because her milk may have been the corrupting factor that led to the illness.[48]

Although most diseases were understood through such epistemologies of illness, invoking humoral theory and suspicion of women's bodily fluids, other medical conditions proved harder to explain or treat. Infectious diseases, particularly the Black Death, affected children very differently from adults. Some diseases, such as leprosy, were generally not thought to affect children often (despite the famous case of King Baldwin IV of Jerusalem, who exhibited signs of the disease in his childhood), but the Black Death appeared to be distinctly virulent among children. Although the earliest and deadliest epidemic of 1347 to 1350 afflicted the entire population, regardless of age, it was with the later recurrences from the late 1350s onward that the rate of child mortality seemed to rise in relation to the death rates for other age groups. Many chroniclers and even the physician Guy de Chauliac noted the large number of children killed with each reemergence of the epidemic, some sources going so far as to indicate that the first signs of the plague's return appeared in the very young and very old.[49]

Even without such extraordinary circumstances as the Black Death, infants and children were recognized to be prone to more prosaic, though no less tragic, accidents and illnesses that could, and often did, prove fatal. Evidence of such occurrences is found in coroners' rolls and miracle tales associated with the shrines of saints across Europe.[50] The cult of Saint Guinefort, a greyhound venerated as a saint by peasants near Lyons, seems to have been entirely devoted to healing sick children, based on the folkloric belief that the sick child was a changeling.[51] Here and elsewhere, stories of severe diseases, life-threatening conditions, and accidental drownings or burnings served to remind medieval (and modern) audiences of the frailty of the infant's and child's condition. Whether because they were perceived to be prone to suffering illnesses or to exposing themselves to dangerous situations, children and their health were a source of considerable concern in medieval society.

CONCLUSION

The health of the family, and particularly the young, receives considerable attention in medieval sources from the late eleventh century onward. Evidence of a strong awareness of the unique physical nature of the child—a nature defined by weakness and helplessness—is amply available in many different types of materials addressing the medieval family. But it is the specialized medico-scientific literature of the high and later Middle Ages that delves most deeply into the details of the child's earthly condition and the dilemmas he faced.

Childhood stands as an example, along with old age, of the necessity of medical attention and theory. Unlike the more stable adult, both the young and the elderly are by definition so physiologically unbalanced and weak that they necessitate intervention. Old age was characterized by excessive cold and dryness, brought about by the loss of the heat and humidity that the child had in such abundance. Childhood required more medical care, because the physician's goal was not palliative but creative, based on the desire to produce a stable adult out of the imbalance and vulnerability of the infant and child. Pediatric theory demanded careful oversight of the humoral extremes that marked the nature of the child.

As imagined by medical writers, the child is best understood as an example of human frailty writ large. The weakness of the child, especially the newborn, forms one end of the spectrum of normative health, envisioned as a continuum between extreme fragility—of child or elderly person—and the lively vigor of the adult man. Childhood becomes a potential to be animated, a weakness that must be strengthened, a lack that must be filled. Childhood is accordingly an infirmity (in the sense of infirmity as lacking firmness, strength, or solidity), an incompleteness, not yet a fully formed adult. Intrinsic to the infant and child are the notions of superfluity and imbalance, which authorize medical intervention as essential and define its course of action. Whether in family practice or in learned theory, the health of the medieval child was an object of concern and study.

CHAPTER TEN

World Contexts

CAROL BARGERON

Other chapters within this volume have discussed the *problèmatique* of the study of the child and the family in the period before the European early modern era. It suffices to say here that the pioneering work of Philippe Ariès, nuanced and modified by Emmanuel Le Roy Ladurie and others, and the exemplary research of Nicholas Orme in the English context have painted a clear and detailed picture of the child in the premodern West.[1] By contrast, the medieval child in the world beyond Europe remains in chiaroscuro, heavily shadowed and enticingly impressionistic. This chapter approaches the study of children and childhood in the medieval non-Western world by relying on broad assumptions that positively linked diverse ethnic and racial groups who, while residing in disparate geographic regions, were bound together by a unitary cultural ethos. The difficult task here involves presenting an ethics of children and childhood in the context of the family relationship, as vast numbers of people lived that story according to the precepts of the world culture of Islam. The Arab conquests of the early Middle Ages, after all, significantly rewrote the map of the Mediterranean and the Middle East and brought the tenets of the Muslim faith, together with its understanding of childhood and family, to the borders of the Western world.

THE ADVENT OF CHILDHOOD

This volume's title, *A Cultural History of Childhood and Family in the Middle Ages,* underscores the idea that cultures create their own constructs of reality.

One of the most fundamental societal conceptualizations is that of childhood. The ideas of the child as a singular person and of childhood as a distinct stage in the life of an individual evolved very gradually over time, beginning in the Middle Ages.[2] This slow, incremental growth of ideas about children and childhood, however, accelerated not in the West but in the *dār al-islām* during its classical era, approximately 132–652 A.H./750–1258 C.E.[3] Childhood as a separate, different, and special stage of life; the place of the child within the family unit; parental responsibilities toward children; and children's duties within the family all constituted important issues toward which Muslim intellectuals devoted thought and time. They expressed their ideas in scholarly prose and poetry—in familiar idiom and sublime metaphor. The medieval Islamic world valued and invested in children. Thinkers within that tradition of civilization paid attention to children and importantly emphasized varying aspects of the child's life and development. Their work expressed emphatically their society's cultural ideals of the child and of childhood, underscoring Muslim emotion toward children and emphasizing the depth of feeling and sociocultural capital that Islamic society invested in children and families, and with which Muslim parents surrounded their children. Islam also gave voice to the rights and privileges with which the child was innately and divinely endowed. The traditional adage that held that wealth and children are the riches of this world resonated throughout every sector of the Muslim world.

Medieval Islamic treatises in law, theology or *kalām*, mysticism or Sufism, and medicine all considered children in their own milieu, as beings who were specifically different from adults, with their own interests and concerns. These source materials show definitively that medieval Muslim parents perceived children in ways that diverged importantly from their European counterparts. Although the work of historical discovery and integration is much less advanced in the case of the Muslim child and its family, an eminent European Islamicist in the early post–World War II era studied one aspect of child development. More recently, the depth of Muslim parental emotional attachment to their children has been illustrated through an examination of bereavement and consolation manuals.[4] These advice treatises were composed to provide solace and prayerful guidance for Muslim parents who loved and lamented the death of a child or children.

Modern scholarship typically has focused on the formal education of children, both religious and practical.[5] In broad compass, we know what educational practices were approved and implemented within the Islamic context. Often, however, scholars are unable to capture a real emotional *feel* for Muslim children, for the cultural and social values with which their parents and other

adults struggled to imbue them, and for the human sensibilities that so enliv-
ened and warmed Islamic civilization in the past and that remain vital and
vibrant today. This author has not found any historical studies of the child
or of childhood per se in the premodern era. This scholarly lacuna is striking.
Significant materials exist to illuminate how medieval Muslims thought about
children and families. Certain types of textual materials are available. These
offer insight, often scanty and incomplete, into the physical needs of children
and the arrangements made to fulfill those requirements; the appropriate socialization, education, and acculturation of the young; and the wellsprings of
feeling that a child's birth and loss occasioned within his or her family. These
texts, nevertheless, are mute when the task is to discover the Muslim conception of childhood. Treatises on marriage, however, comprise a potentially
rich source of materials relating to childhood, as do expositions designed to
mold character. The polymath Muslim intellectual abū Hāmid Muhammad al-
Ghazālī (d. 505/1111) developed a full understanding of the child and of childhood as medieval Muslim parents experienced, as well as shaped, its contours
for their children, families, and societies.

GEOGRAPHICAL EXTENT OF THE MUSLIM PARADIGM

A prolific author, al-Ghazali wrote his masterwork *Ihyā' ʿulūm al-dīn* (Revival
of the sciences of religion) during his first period of retreat for contemplation
and spiritual regeneration, which lasted eleven years, beginning when he left
Baghdad in Dhū'l-Qaʿda 488/November 1095 and ending with his return to
teaching at Nishapur in 499/1105–1106. Most likely a product of the early
years of his retirement from public life, the *Ihyā'* contains several treatises
that provide data for the construction of an Islamic conceptual paradigm of
childhood. The most significant texts are the *Kitāb ādāb al-nikāh* (On etiquette
[good practices] in marriage, II: 2, 19–55) and the *Kitāb riyādat al-nafs wa
tahdīb al-akhlāq wa muʿālajat amrād al-qalb* (Book on spiritual discipline, the
shaping of the character, and the treatment of the ailments of the heart, III: 2,
42–68). The sources start with the touchstone of all speculation and law in
Islām, the Qur'an, and its prescriptions regarding children. In addition, the
biography of the Prophet Muhammad, particularly with its details concerning
his infancy and childhood, as well as the traditions or reports (hadith) concerning what the Prophet Muhammad said and did during his governance of the
first Muslim community at Medina offer further material. These initial sources
must be investigated, because they formed the elemental references for the construction of the unitary cultural ethos that was universally Islamic.

FIGURE 10.1: *The frontispiece of Sultan Baybar's Qur'an, Cairo, 1304–1306.* © The British Library Board (BL Add. MS. 22406, ff. 1v-2r).

The cultural and societal goals of Islam percolated widely throughout the vast expanse of territory, stretching over parts of several continents—Asia, Africa, and Europe—that early Muslim rulers brought under their control. Islam ultimately spread to the Indian subcontinent, Malaysia, and Indonesia before the end of the classical period. Geographic expansion of Islam entailed the extension of a distinctly "Islamicate" cultural ethos, although each of the diverse racial and ethnic groups, who in full or large measure embraced Islam, created their singular Muslim societies.[6] One element of Islam that contributed to its extraordinarily swift pace of acceptance was its willingness and ability to incorporate cultural beliefs, traits, and traditions of non-ethnically Arab peoples under the broadly inclusive umbrella of Islam. The sole bar to inclusion was the incompatibility of specific beliefs, traditions, practices, and traits with the fundamental principles of Islam. As a consequence, not only Arabs, but Persians, Africans, Turks, Indians, Chinese, and Malays—as well as many numerically smaller groups—played their part in the construction of a unitary high Islamic civilization to which all belonged, in which all participated, and to which all uniquely contributed.

Intercontinental trade brought the European and Middle Eastern intellectual and cultural domains into closer connection with one another. The religious, intellectual, and medical institutions of *al-Andalus* opened other pathways through which people, ideas, practices, and techniques traveled for over seven hundred years until January 1492, when Muhammad XII of Granada surrendered complete control of the Muslim ruled kingdom of Granada to the Catholic sovereigns, Ferdinand and Isabella. The First Crusade preached in 1096 and its aftermath, the consolidation of the Latin Kingdom of Jerusalem, which Salah-ad-Din recaptured in 1171, contributed as well to this cross-continental exchange. The literary genre of the romance in addition to specific poetic forms and the books of manners or courtesy moved in the same direction, from the Middle East and Islamic Africa across the eastern Mediterranean to southern Europe and then, northward. Despite later political and sectarian fragmentation, essential Islamic unity of viewpoint and perspective continued in arenas of primordial meaning. This was especially true in the cultural ethos surrounding the family and its most treasured members, the young.

Two issues especially concerned medieval thinkers: the inherent nature of the child and the subsequent malleability of that character. Prescriptive literature in the West concentrated upon the child as intrinsically evil and thus in need of coercive discipline, although some saw the child as basically good but still requiring strong guidance. The view that al-Ghazālī notably expressed went unarticulated in the West until the end of the late medieval era. The concept of the child as a blank slate, neither inherently good nor intrinsically evil, and thus requiring instruction and guidance toward the good, began to find voice, however, in the early fifteenth century with Giovanni Dominici's *Regola del Governo di Cura Familiare,* written between 1400 and 1405. Until the early eighteenth century, the Christian West then vacillated between two approaches, one that was sternly Augustinian and the other that emphasized the faith and innocence of the child that nurturing affection and education only helped to refine and modulate.

THE ELEMENTS OF THE PARADIGM OF CHILDHOOD

Although the incomparable and essential basis of all speculation within Islam is the Qur'an, the hadith (traditions or reports) of the Prophet Muhammad's customary or habitual practices (sunna) further explicated and amplified the ethical, moral, and cultural values that suffused God's injunctions and prohibitions, particularly as earlier generations of Muslims heard and understood them. Together, these constitute the first two sources or principles that have guided the formulation of law in Islam, and their outlook must be placed in evidence.

In the Muslim context, children typically are described as "the delight of our eyes." Muslim scholars (ʿulamāʾ) debated the religious virtue of marriage (nikāh).[7] Some maintained that the state of celibacy was preferable for the worship of God, while others stressed that marriage was superior to seclusion. The weight of scripture, the Prophetic exemplar, and the sunna-hadith preponderated on the side of marriage. God commanded:

> And marry off the single among you and those of your male and female slaves who are righteous [fit for marriage]. If they are poor, God will provide for them from His bounty: God's bounty is infinite and He is all-knowing. Those who are unable to marry should keep chaste until God gives him enough out of His bounty. (Qur'an 24: 32–33)

Elsewhere, God enjoined the believers to understand the merit of marriage by reminding them that "We sent messengers before you and gave them wives and children" (Qur'an 13: 38). Accordingly, the Creator of the heavens and earth "made mates for you from among yourselves—and the animals too—so that you may multiply" (Qur'an 42: 11). Islam importantly recognized marriage as one of the two essential bases of human society. Both divinely instituted, the blood relationship and the marriage relationship possessed coeval significance, as the Qur'an emphasized: "It is He who creates human beings from fluid, then makes them kin by blood and marriage" (Qur'an 25: 54).

Marriage was understood to provide a fortress (hisn) of chastity, a spur to virtuous behavior, and a sanctified means through which satisfaction of sexual urges could be attained. "And the Prophet said: 'Whoever has the means, let him get married, for it will avert the eyes and assure more relief and virtuousness,' and who does not, 'let him fast for fasting to him is [a form of] castration (wijāʾ)'" (Bukhārī, Sahīh 7: 3; also 30: 11). Marriage entailed active defense of Islamic religious faith, for the Prophet said "whoever marries safeguards half of his faith, let him fear God for the second half." Adherence to the Prophet's example was urged upon believers; accordingly, marriage was viewed as part of the Prophetic sunna: "Marriage is of my sunna, whoever refrains from my sunna refrains from me" (Bukhārī, Sahīh 67: 1).[8]

Both sources stressed the importance of procreation within the legal and spiritual foundations that marriage provided for the attainment of religious virtue, moral uplift, individual status, as well as conjugal warmth, affection, and support. Fulfillment of dīn—the full practice of religion in every aspect of life—is accomplished through marriage. The Prophet is reported to have urged the Muslims to "marry and multiply for I will boast about you above other nations on the day of resurrection, even about the least of you." Scripture reminded believers that God acted purposefully in establishing the institution of marriage, as well as by making it the legitimate channel of sexual desire, in this way: "People, be mindful of your Lord, who created you from a single soul, and from it created its mate, and from the pair of them spread countless men and women far and wide" (Qur'an 4: 1). The emphasis on procreation in marriage underscored the medieval Muslim perception of the child as the critical generational link within the family unit. The child tied the present to the past as well as to the future, for the child embodied the key to the family's continuation as well as to its material and spiritual advancement. The Prophet's biography offered a descriptive guide to the early care and feeding of the newborn child.

INFANT CARE AND CHILD REARING

Following pre-Islamic peninsular Arab practice and the Muslim model of the Prophet's early infancy, strict attention was devoted to the selection of the nurse. Āmina, the Prophet's mother, nursed him initially, and after several days, Thaubīyah did so. Because it was customary for those with resources to send their infants into the Bedouin Arab villages, Halīmah Saʿdīyah then received the baby Muhammad. But there is a twist here. Before his birth, Muhammad's father had died while on a business trip. Āmina then was not economically comfortable; thus, a woman who had recently given birth, but was herself destitute and starving, received the care of Muhammad. The famine-induced shortage of Halīmah's milk proved a source of divine mercy for her. Despite knowing that she could expect very little payment for nursing the baby, she accepted him. Halīmah told her husband that "it did not look proper for her to leave the city and return to the village empty-handed," so I decided that "I better take this orphan child."

Halīmah took the baby, and, immediately upon starting to feed him, the blessings began to manifest themselves—not just for Halīmah and her family including Muhammad, but also for their female camel and sheep. The family received these divine favors for the full two-year term of Muhammad's nursing. Muhammad had benefited from being nursed by a good Bedouin woman: he had grown robust and had attained good health in the village and he had learned the pure Arabic language. Halīmah now set out for Mecca to deliver Muhammad to his mother. Plague, however, engulfed the city, forcing a return to the countryside. After an incident in which Halīmah was frightened that she could not sufficiently protect the child Muhammad, she brought him to Āmina.

Muslims understood how influential were the earliest intimate contacts of the newly born with adults. Parents at all levels of the socioeconomic ladder took great pains to ensure their child's emotional and psychological well-being over the long term, beginning with the child's delivery by an experienced older woman, the midwife, who, then, at frequent intervals, checked the infant and adjusted the baby's environmental conditions (temperature and ventilation of the room), washed, dressed, and made certain with the mother that the newborn was adequately fed. The warmth and affection of the midwife, mother, and nurse—if utilized—were closely monitored, because the child's initial experiences played a basic role in his or her adaptation to life outside the womb. The father petted, held, and thanked God for his child.

The care and feeding of the newborn was the father's financial obligation, even in the case of divorce. God prescribed:

> Mothers shall suckle their children for two whole years, for him [the infant] who desires to complete the time of suckling. And their maintenance and their clothing must be borne by the father according to usage. No soul shall be burdened beyond its capacity. Neither shall a mother be made to suffer harm on account of her child, nor [shall] a father on account of his child; and a similar duty [devolves] on the [father's] heir. But if both desire weaning by mutual consent and counsel, there is no blame on them. And if you wish to engage a wet-nurse for your children, there is no blame on you so long as you pay what you promised according to usage. (Qur'an 2: 233)

Daughters as well as sons were valued as divine gifts, and female infanticide was condemned (Qur'an 42: 49; 16: 59; 43: 17; 81: 8–9).[9]

Parents of a newborn benefited from instructional treatises on practical topics such as infant feeding, swaddling, methods of comforting a crying baby, and techniques of playing with the baby and making the baby coo. These advice books demonstrated the Muslim awareness of infants as unique creatures, gifts from God, who deserved special understanding and treatment. Newborns then required special protection and care. Because the infant was a blank slate (*sazājah*) whose innate nature was completely impressionable—either for good or for ill—medieval Muslims were especially mindful of the character, physical habits, and mental traits of those who would come into the most intimate contact with the infant.

A child's birth, whether boy or girl, occasioned happiness and hope for the parents. The Prophet cautioned the Muslims not to lament the birth of a daughter, and, although boys were preferred, especially for a first child, the birth of a daughter did not cause unmitigated sorrow. A child was a gift from God, not simply to its parents but to its entire extended family, who anticipated the birth with delight, pleasure, and hopeful expectation. Babies were extravagantly indulged and petted by all, not just the mother and the baby's female relatives. The period of maternal indulgence ended with the birth of the next child; however, others, especially older sisters, continued to lavish affection upon younger siblings.

Patrilineally organized, all members of the Muslim extended family participated in the process of rearing the child to be *mu'addab(a)*, or well-mannered—that is, properly socialized to Muslim cultural norms. The child's socialization took place primarily within the home, and the parents bore ultimate responsibility for their children. However, grandparents, aunts, uncles, and cousins participated in a child's rearing, acting alternatively either to provide discipline or to offer additional affection for the child. Class mattered, as did urban or rural residence, where neighbors were actively engaged with the local children; in every context, Qur'anic teachers, and private tutors in the case of wealthy girls, played a role in children's maturation.

The high value placed upon children found cogent expression in the development of a normative model that articulated the cultural ideal of the value and place of the child within the family, nuclear as well as extended; succinctly explored the needs of the child; and wisely advised parents of their duties toward children and children's obligations toward their parents. Stories about the Prophet's birth, his childhood, and his relationships with young members of his own family as well as with the community's children often provided the popular medium for the transmission of the behavioral standard. The Prophetic exemplar served as a singular source, not simply of appropriate names for the newly born, but also of how they should be presented to God and to their communities, reared, and acculturated to various age-related activities, tasks, and responsibilities. Medieval Muslim parents thus possessed an awareness of the different nature and special character of the child. That consciousness originated in observation, culture-based sensitivity, pre-Islamic customary tradition, scriptural injunction, and Prophetic example; all of these strands resonate in two texts within al-Ghazālī's body of work.

Al-Ghazālī's texts provide an early and full theoretical conception of the child and childhood. They offer important data from which to reconstruct a theory of childhood as a distinct stage in the ages of life, a period that imposed special

FIGURE 10.2: *The birth of the Prophet Muhammad.* The *Jami' al-Tawarikh* of Rashid al-Din, circa 1307, Islamic School. With permission of the University of Edinburgh/The Bridgeman Art Library (Edinburgh University Library, Scotland, MS. Or 20, f. 42).

duties upon parents. The Ghazālian texts comprise a thorough account of genuinely Muslim belief, spirit, sentiment, and practice with regard to children. The Muslim world inherited, assimilated, elaborated, and transmitted the corpus of Hellenic theoretical and empirical knowledge. Yet al-Ghazālī's work does not merely repeat classical and postclassical Greek theories about the practical education of children. Biographies of child saints within the Sufi tradition also provide data on the special attributes that Muslims ordinarily ascribed to children. In the case of blessed children, these qualities were heightened or otherwise highlighted in marvelous ways. Nor does his text simply copy earlier Muslim models.[10] The traditions of learning—non-Muslim and Muslim—that were contained in philosophical speculation, empirical observation, actual medical practice, as well as legal precedent and religious norms all resound within the Ghazālian corpus.

The first lines of the section entitled *Bayān al-tarīq fī riyādat al-sibyān fī awwal nushrū'ihim wa wajh ta'dibihim wa tahsīn akhlāqihim* (Clarification on the training of infant children, their education, and the improvement of their character) enunciate in tender language a developmental understanding of the infant and young child that, as is immediately evident, seems remarkably Piagetian in its observations, proscriptions, and prescriptions. Toward the beginning of the sixth Islamic/twelfth Christian century, al-Ghazālī expressed in full the modern notion of childhood as a dependent state, a condition in which the child:

is an empty depository confided to the care of his parents, his pure soul is a precious substance, innocent, stripped bare of any inscription or image.

The child's soul receives all that is written upon it; thus, his soul leans toward that to which one [parent, teacher, governess, nurse] inclines it. Habituate the child to the good, teach the child the good, and all his early infancy will be thus marked.[11]

The Ghazālian materials lay out a system of values, a body of moral rules, and a code of conduct that demarcate the lines between ethical and unethical practices in child rearing in the Muslim system. They permit us to reconstruct a medieval Islamic model of the child, childhood, and parental obligations. This model indicates that, well before the late Middle Ages and the humanisms of the Renaissance era, medieval Muslims recognized the sanctity of the child, the special character of childhood—especially the earlier phases, which were designated as a carefree period in which playtime was required and certain types of play were recommended—and the specific stages and the education that was appropriate to each period within infancy, childhood, and adolescence. Muslims also emphasized the unique opportunities that proper child-rearing practices offered to parents in their quest to attain eternal salvation. As his work clarifies, medieval Muslim parents valued their children, but not simply for the pleasure and entertainment that they could derive from the antics of their offspring or for the future aid that good children might render to parents. Medieval Muslim *abā* and *ummāt* were distinctly attentive and devoted, because they saw that children were fragile creatures of God who needed to be both safeguarded and perfected. Al-Ghazālī's work also offers the first extensive treatment of the psychology of the child; he recognized that, before parents could attempt to guide their children's behavior, they first had to understand it. The wisdom of his fundamental insight is strikingly modern.

According to Ghazālian teaching, the child is neither an adult in miniature nor someone simply to be petted and cuddled, without regard to his needs or intrinsic nature as human. Although the child is inherently noble, by his God-given nature, the newly born and young infant is neither naturally good nor naturally bad. The child is simply innocent. Thus, at birth, his mind is a clean slate on which parents and those others who play a role in his rearing may write whatever they please. The child is unique, and parental recognition of the special qualities of the child influenced the care and affection given to the child. Muslim parents exhibited love, affection, and emotional attachment to children, although seemingly to a somewhat lesser degree to their daughters than to their sons. Scripture and Prophetic example strictly admonished Muslims against female infanticide and urged similar treatment of both boys and girls in terms of cuddling and other displays of physical affection toward infants and young children.[12]

Gender differentiation in terms of treatment began at the age when small responsibilities were allotted to children. The tasks of acculturation and socialization by gender were seen by Muslim parents as part of their roles as good parents; most met the expectations of their families, neighborhoods, and wider social networks. Little girls participated in tasks around the home, including those related to babies; by contrast, boys ran errands, tended to animals, or did chores in the father's shop or on the family farm. Both young boys and young girls were expected to know how to take basic care of infants, and both were expected to be responsible for the well-being of younger members of the family and the larger kin group. By approximately seven years of age, gender sorting in terms of responsibilities and freedoms became a more seriously pursued task among parents and other adult relatives. The Prophet Muhammad traditionally urged Muslims to "be gentle to your children the first seven years and in the following seven be firm." By that time, boys went regularly to the mosque and girls covered their hair.

As a child grew, personhood evolved through several stages, each of which was characterized by the emergence of a specific faculty. As al-Ghazālī described the child's development, sensation emerged first, and after birth, the child possessed the ability to receive information via the five physical senses. These sensory abilities did not emerge all at once, but instead in closely joined phases. The sense of touch appeared first in the child, followed by sight, hearing, taste, and, finally, speech. Second, the child's faculty of imagination (al-wahm) came forth. Imagination is "the recorder of the information conveyed by the senses" and "it is not found in the infant at the beginning of its evolution." Clearly an experienced parent, al-Ghazālī further explained that

> this is why an infant wants to get hold of an object when he sees it, yet forgets about this object when it is out of his sight. No conflict of desire arises in his soul for something out of sight until he gets a little older, when he begins to cry for it, because its image is still with him, preserved in his imagination.[13]

Sometime between the ages of five and seven, the child received the third faculty of reason or discernment. Reason or intellect (al-ʿaql) allowed the child to "apprehend ideas beyond the spheres of sense and imagination. Intellect is the specifically human faculty, [and] it is not found in the lower animals nor yet in infants and toddlers," for its emergence constitutes a fresh stage in the child's development. Reason permits the child to distinguish the good from the bad, the obviously true from the obviously false, and so forth.[14]

The fourth faculty of discursive reason began to appear gradually during mid-adolescence. According to al-Ghazālī, the young person now comes to possess the ability to "take the data of pure reason and combine them, arrange them as premises, and deduce from them informing knowledge. [The pre-teen] thus may take, for example, two conclusions thus learned, combine them again, and learn a fresh conclusion." The individual then may go on multiplying knowledge (acquired) in this way ad infinitum. This fourth faculty of discursive reasoning in the *Munqidh min addalāl* (The deliverer from error) is labeled *al-ᶜaql,* while the faculty enumerated as the third is simply called *al-tamyīz,* or the power of distinguishing or differentiating.[15]

Parents must adapt their attempts to influence or incline their child's behavior to the specific stage of human development that the child's actions suggest. Small children wish to imitate the behaviors they see around them. Muslim parents built upon this knowledge of children's desire to model adult behavior; occasionally, little girls were allowed to wear a head scarf and little boys were permitted to accompany the men to the mosque, field, grove, or shop. Honed through observation, adult knowledge of developmental child psychology also served as the foundation of effective teaching once instruction passed into the hands of the professional teacher, as al-Ghazālī emphasized. In addition to entering upon a new stage of intellectual life with the dawning of the ability to reason, the child between five and seven years of age also develops the capacity to feel shame (*haya'*). Emotional maturation becomes a process when the child's capacity to be ashamed of an action that he or she has performed or of a thought that has occurred to him or her first emerges. According to al-Ghazālī, shame is that emotion which the child displays when blushing and hanging one's head low over uncommendable actions.

Al-Ghazālī allotted an important place to shame in his exploration of the psychology of children, because, for him, shame determined especially when the formal moral education of a young person should begin. Informal education in moral virtue or ethics, however, must commence earlier in a child's life, when the simple inculcation of good habits through unreflected imitation should be encouraged. Before the child is able to reason, habituation toward the good can be stimulated by having him or her simply imitate kindness toward other people and animals or by having the small girl or boy copy charity toward the unfortunate and the poor by allowing the child to extend a coin to a beggar.[16] At this point, the child cannot reflect upon or think about why the performance of good deeds is important, both for the individual as well as for society; all the child can do is model the appropriate behavior. The advent of shame and guilt, by contrast, signals the emergence within the child of a newfound capacity to understand the moral qualities of actions and to adjust his or her conduct to virtuous patterns of behavior.

Shame *(haya')* works in the effort to rear the "good citizen" of the ideal Islamic community. One of the oldest and most enduring of Muslim ethical and religious precepts stipulates that each Muslim is personally obligated before God to "command the right and to forbid the wrong." In the hierarchy of obligations, jurists classified duties as belonging to either of two categories: (1) a *fard kifāyah* duty was one that obligated the community as a whole to fulfill. The mosque, for example, must be kept clean; if delegated to a custodian who does his job well, then the community's obligation is met; (2) with a *fardᶜayn* duty, the responsibility is incumbent upon each individual to fulfill. Each Muslim must perform the ritual prayers *(salat)* five times daily; this duty cannot be delegated to someone else to perform. Similarly, each Muslim is personally responsible before God to command that which is right and to prevent evildoing among other Muslims and to do the same within the larger society. Institutionalized as public ostracism, shame functioned then in at least two ways: the virtuous reminded backsliders of their duty to behave according to the Islamic code of ethics, while the recalcitrant were at least minimally persuaded to restrain their tendencies toward evildoing in the hope of avoiding socioreligious guilt for bad deeds.

Far from undermining an individual's sense of self-esteem, feeling ashamed, according to Ghazālian doctrine, vindicated the child's inherent nobleness of character and sense of self-respect. These two together acted strongly both to prevent as well as to correct the temptation to do evil. Further, shame expressed the child's feeling of utter disgrace and humiliation about doing what he or she should not have done. Shame, moreover, reflected the child's quiet but firm resolve not to repeat the unworthy or bad act in the future. Finally, this emotion's appearance demonstrated the child's amenability to discipline and instruction. In al-Ghazālī's eyes, it is only in so far as the child is capable of feeling shame that there exists any hope that education may improve or perfect the child. A child who is impudent has lost his or her self-respect. As a result, this child may be far beyond the powers of human assistance, whether given by parents or outside professionals, to help the young person regain the straight path.

The defining characteristics of *haya'* consequently show that shame and self-respect are equivalents. Should a child be so unfortunate as to lose entirely the ability to be ashamed, al-Ghazālī insists that the very first help the child requires consists of aid in restoring his or her self-respect. Al-Ghazālī encouraged developing the emotion of shame into an "unerring conscience," which required protection against all such vicious influences that may damage it.[17] For this reason, al-Ghazālī strongly condemned all authoritarian and coercive methods of making children learn through physical abuse, corporal punishment, force and threat, pain and fear. With equal vigor, al-Ghazālī also proscribed pedantic exhortations on the part of parents and teachers. What he was condemning, of course, is the universal anthem of "do as I say, and not as I do."

Ghazālian theorizing about children reminds us that the basic fact about children is that they learn by persuasion and not by rational demonstration. According to him, children imitate what appeals to their imagination rather than to their reason. Children are fond of fairy tales and fanciful stories; thus, by making thoughtful and judicious comments on these tales and stories, parents and teachers may communicate the basic knowledge of good and evil to their children and to their students. Parents are advised even to use poetry and song to soften children's hearts and refine their imaginations. In practical terms, parents are advised that they must always praise children for whatever little bit of good that they do. Praise will serve as recognition for children and will save them from suffering humiliation at being ignored. Praise, moreover, helps children to build a strong moral conscience on the basis of the natural emotion of shame.

Al-Ghazālī's teaching advised that children must be praised generally, but reproved or reprimanded only sparingly. When children conceal little misdeeds, they should not be exposed to the disgrace of being detected or found out. Even when censure seems unavoidable, reproof must be always indirect and benevolent. Correction, al-Ghazālī said, may be carried out first by attributing the lapse on their part to oversight or ignorance and then second by warning the child not to repeat the act. Open and violent censure, as far as possible, must be avoided, "for it only helps to destroy children's candor, inducing them to duplicity and hypocrisy, and turning them into impudent rebels."[18]

When physical punishment becomes inevitable, al-Ghazālī urged that such correction be administered in privacy. Under the condition of privacy, children may take corporal punishment to be a natural and logical consequence of the behavioral lapses on their part. Privacy, however, never provided concealment for adult excess in dispensing bodily punishment. Parents and teachers must never administer more than three whacks of the cane and then never to the face or to the head. The humiliation of publicly given corporal punishment results in disgrace, and public humiliation leads only, he tells us, to the extinction of the innate sense of shame.

In the education of young children, al-Ghazālī seemingly placed an inordinate stress on shame. His advocacy of stimulating the emotion of shame was not equivalent to urging the development of neurotic, guilt-ridden children. For him, shame possessed the primary characteristics of rational discrimination, self-respect, humiliation, self-reproach, and amenability to discipline. Equivalent to self-respect, the flowering of this innate emotion into a strong moral conscience comprised the central task of education and the primary obligation of the parents, the guardians of the innocent child.[19]

Childhood, so pleasant a stage in life, had a natural terminal point. Between the ages of nine and eleven at the very latest, fitting of a child for his or her adult roles and responsibilities began. The Islamic ethic demanded that parents prepare their offspring for the essentially gender-assigned roles that society expected boys and girls to fulfill. Boys primarily were groomed to earn a living to support themselves, their families, and their parents in old age and infirmity. Girls were prepared to be married and, in that context, to be good wives, mothers, and competent stewards of the family's resources. The Prophetic tradition emphasized that both sexes had similar but differently fulfilled responsibilities: "All of you are guardians and are responsible for your words [and deeds]. The ruler is a guardian and the man is a guardian of his family; the lady is a guardian and is responsible for her husband's house and his offspring. And thus all of you are guardians and are responsible for your words [and deeds]."[20]

Al-Ghazālī provided advice regarding the formal instruction of children. Boys as well as girls were expected to learn the Qur'an, and this normally was achieved through rote memorization. Ideally, girls were taught the fundamentals of reading and counting; this minimum constituted enough learning to allow them to serve as good custodians of their future husbands' resources and sage guardians of their children's upbringing. Socioeconomic class influenced girls' educational achievement heavily and positively, as did urban residence. Al-Ghazali was known as *abū'l-banāt* because he was the father of daughters for whom he made the appropriate financial provisions when he left his professorial position at the Baghdad *nizāmīya* initially in 488/1095.[21] A girl ordinarily was not expected to earn a living; she was fitted, however, to "earn" and to keep a husband's attention and his devotion, and that naturally flowed from her talents and skills at managing a household, keeping his parents— especially his mother and older women relatives—favorably disposed toward her, and raising his children well, so that he, as father and husband, would have compliments and not complaints bestowed upon him. These skills and talents were among those with which an accomplished wife secured her so-called independent status.

Islamic education typically fulfilled two functions. Education prepared the child to take his or her place not just in earthly society but in the hereafter as well.

Muslims quickly learned that the religious ideal of producing the God-fearing believer required a complement. By the second/eighth century, they recognized that, in addition to proper conduct in this life and preparation for the next, Muslim boys and girls had "to learn in order to earn." The gradual development of this "secular" aim eventually came to be expressed quite nicely. The early modern Turkish scholar, Hajjī Khalīfa taught that "there is something to be derived from every branch of knowledge, something to benefit [the believer] for the next world, for earning his living [in this world], and for perfecting the human being."[22]

CONCLUSION

Several centuries before their counterparts in the West, medieval Muslims emphatically voiced the ideas of the child as a separate and special individual and of childhood as a distinct stage of life. The singular quality and character of the child demanded of both parents that they devote serious and careful attention to child rearing within the family, including the obligation to give a child an appropriate name and not one that would expose him or her to ridicule and scorn. A cultural and religious ethic sanctioned procreation within the context of marriage and provided guidelines for the spouses and potential parents. Medieval Muslims prepared for the conception, growth of the fetus, and arrival of the new person; pregnancy, birth, the "welcoming" of the child, and the naming, all followed the formal and customary rules of the diverse Islamicate. The rearing and preparation of the child through the preadult stages of life to become a good citizen of the Muslim community demonstrated norms of behavior, socialization, and relational patterns that were not identical but similar throughout the geographically, racially, ethnically, and linguistically disparate communities that constituted the living world civilization of Islam in the Middle Ages. From one corner of the Islamicate at its peak to the other, Muslims understood the intrinsic significance of children and manifested that consciousness of children as different and separate from adults in every aspect of being. Cardinal ideas about the nature of the child, the unique character of childhood, and the special requirements of proper child rearing and instruction bloomed first in the Muslim world of the Middle Ages. Many of these concepts and practices made their way across the eastern Mediterranean basin to Christian Europe through a variety of channels. Nonetheless, the distinctly modern insights into the intrinsic character of the child and the special quality of childhood that Muslim thinkers, specifically al-Ghazali, articulated moved into the Western consciousness at glacial speed.

Medieval Muslim mothers and fathers revered the child and recognized the unique responsibilities and opportunities that parenthood bestowed upon them. Loving parents attempted to model that particular devotion to children that scriptural injunction and Prophetic example enjoined. In the medieval Islamic world, whether born to high status or into a more lowly one, children were wanted, welcomed, and valued as a divine gift and a sacred trust. Qur'anic injunction stipulated fair and equitable treatment for children, including wards; urged charity and kindness toward orphans; and mandated a minimal level of education as a duty incumbent upon parents to fulfill to the extent of their capacities. Al-Ghazali articulated that "special devotion" in *Ihyā' ̣ulūm al-dīn*:

> Parents are responsible for looking after their children properly. To their hands the innocent child is confided with a pure conscience and stainless soul. His heart, resembling a mirror, is ready to reflect anything put before it, and he imitates carefully whatever he watches. He may be an ideal citizen if he is educated well; and he may be a harmful person if he is ill-trained or neglected. His parents, relatives, as well as teachers will share with him his happiness or suffer from his being evil. So, it is the duty of parents or guardian to pay full attention to the child. Teach him good behavior, edify him and keep him away from bad company.
>
> The child must be accustomed to a spare and hard life, and not luxury. Self-respect, modesty and sincerity must be among his outstanding qualities. The child should not be encouraged to be fond of money or material things, as this is the first step toward useless quarrels.
>
> When the child is grown up, he is due to be handed over to an excellent and good instructor to teach him useful and necessary learning, and to lead him by the right way to the right end.[23]

His words and the ethic of the child that they represented remain as soundly emblematic of good parenting in the twenty-first century as they did toward the beginning of the sixth Islamic century, the twelfth century C.E.

NOTES

Introduction

1. Ariès 1962: 125.
2. Ariès 1962: 16–47.
3. Ariès 1962: 48, 69, 91–92.
4. Ariès 1962: 37, 125.
5. Ariès 1962: 353–357.
6. See, for example, Alexandre-Bidon and Lett 1999; Classen 2005; Crawford 1999a; Finucane 1997; Hanawalt 1986; Heywood 2001; Orme 1984; Orme 2001; Alexandre-Bidon and Riché 1994; Schultz 1995; Shahar 1990. A splendid online exhibition on medieval childhood, hosted by the Bibliothèque nationale de France, is available at http://classes.bnf.fr/ema. For childhood in medieval Byzantium, see Mitchell 2007: ch. 3; Hennessy 2008.
7. Shahar 1990: 1.
8. Hanawalt 1986: 171.
9. Hanawalt 1986: 171, 180.
10. Oosterwijk 2008: 230–235.
11. Orme 2001: 9.
12. Duby 1988: 56.
13. These figures are cited by Crawford 1999b: 343.
14. Classen 2005: 16–19; Shahar 1990: 126–128, 139–140; Hanawalt 1986: 177, 184–185.
15. Finucane 1997: 3–6, 9–10, 40–41, 50, 155–158.
16. Barthélemy 1988: 85.
17. Herlihy 1985: 2–3, 44–51; Blanks 2001: 222.
18. Herlihy 1985: 49; McCarthy 2004: 14; Mitchell 2007: 68–70.
19. Herlihy 1985: 57–62.
20. Mitchell 2007: 84–85.
21. Ephesians 5: 22–23.

22. 1 Corinthians 7: 8–9; Richards 1990: 23; Karras 2005: 28.
23. Bullough et al. 1988: 53; Salisbury 1996: 84; Salisbury 1992: 21.
24. Brundage 1996: 36; Herlihy 1985: 103–111.
25. Ward 2006: 21–22.
26. Murray 1995: 9–15.
27. Gold 1985: ch. 2.
28. Leyser 1995: 223.
29. All figures are cited in Jordan 2001: 5–8.
30. Jordan 2001: 27–29; Dyer 2003: 101.
31. Dyer 2003: 36–37; Jordan 2001: 10–11.
32. Bouchard 1998: 7–27, 28.
33. Bouchard 1998: 68–69.
34. Herlihy 1985: 82–83, 86–98. See also Crouch 2005: ch. 4 for the scholarly debates on these developments.
35. Duby 1983: 19.
36. McCarthy 2004: 5. See also Brooke 1989: ch. 6; Herlihy 1985: 86.
37. Dyer 2003: 272–281.
38. Boccaccio [d. 1375] 2002: 10–12.

Chapter 1

1. This observation is based on a survey of a number of periodicals, including *Early Medieval Europe* (founded 1992); *Journal of Family History* (founded 1976); *The History of the Family* (founded 1996).
2. Herlihy 1985: 70–72.
3. Stafford 1998: 103–125.
4. Devroey 2000: 19.
5. Herlihy 1985: 76–77.
6. Rheubottom 2000: 80–101.
7. Razi 1980: 50–64, 135–138.
8. Goldberg 2005: 77–79.
9. Hollingsworth 1958: 4–26.
10. Biller 1982: 3–26.
11. Riddle 1991: 3–32.
12. Ariès 1962.
13. Hanawalt 1977: 1–22; see Goldberg 2008: 249–262.
14. Swanson 1990: 309–331.
15. Schultz 1991: 519–539.
16. Halsall 1995.
17. Bray 2003 discusses the meaning of such joint burials at length.

Chapter 2

1. Rubin 1991: 133–136; Watt 1997: 7–16.
2. Farmer 1997: 274–275.

3. Green 1988–1989: 449–450.

4. *Calendar of Inquisitions Post Mortem,* 7. 1909: 341–343.

5. Amt 1993: 142–149.

6. Kellum 1974: 367–388; Helmholz 1974–1975: 379–390; Poos 1994–1995: 585–607; Chew and Weinbaum 1970: 53; Hunnisett 1961: 4.

7. Baumgarten 2004: 52–54.

8. Amt 1993: 123–129; Jewell 2007: 139–141; Dhuoda [841–843] 1991: 1–106; Goldberg 1995: 97–103; Riddy 1996: 70–83; *The book of the knight of the tower* [1371–1372] 1971: 13–19; Bonney 1973: 138–140.

9. Kristensson 1974: 76; Swanson 1990: 309–331; Baumgarten 2004: 1; Goldin 2004: 42–43.

10. Shahar 1990: 22–30.

11. Orme 1995: 51–64; Orme 2001: 167–183; Klapisch-Zuber 1985: 311–321; Egan 1998: 281–283.

12. Douglas and Greenaway 1953: 960–961; *Calendar of Inquisitions Miscellaneous,* 1. 1916: 562–563, 592.

13. Hanawalt 1986: 113–117, 158–162, 201–202.

14. Prestwich 2004: 921.

15. Bartlett 2000: 250, 632–633; Ward 2006: 115; McFarlane 1973: 243–244.

16. Harris 1907–1913: 561–562.

17. Vincent of Beauvais [d. 1264] 1938: 172–197; Morgan 1993: 44; Scase 1993: 83.

18. Barron 1996: 139–143; Ward 2002: 18–19.

19. Herlihy and Klapisch-Zuber 1985: 202–211; Watkins 1969: 208–228.

20. Goldberg 1986a: 208–228.

21. Klapisch-Zuber 1986: 72–73; Klapisch-Zuber 1985: 106–107, 173–174; Stouff 1986: 1, 127; Romano 1996: 152–153; Goldberg 1992: 159–164; Reyerson 1992: 355–366; Nicholas 1995: 1107–1114; Barron 1996: 144–146; Dixon 1895: 209–228; Wensky 1982: 631–650; Kowaleski and Bennett 1988–1989: 481–483.

22. Flandrin 1991: 54–57; Goldberg 1986b: 141–169; Goldberg 1995: 103–129; Bennett 2003: 131–162.

23. Orme 1994: 571–577; Adam 1964: 252–254; Nelson 1994: 91; Bossy 1983: 35–43.

24. Orme 1994: 582–583; French 1998: 399–425; Orme 2001: 221–223.

25. Orme 1994: 578–582; Orme 1995: 69–71; Nelson 1994: 96; Zika 1988: 38–43.

26. Klapisch-Zuber 1985: 117–131; Amt 1993: 208–210; Hanawalt 1993: 89–93; Nicholas 1985: 109–118.

27. Altschul 1965: 160; Amt 1993: 55; Menuge 2000: 77–103.

28. Du Boulay 1966: 144–145; Lock 1998: 51–52.

29. Rawcliffe 1984: 2; Geremek 1987: 170–171; Klapisch-Zuber 1985: 104–106; Pullan 1988: 188; Nicholas 1985: 115.

30. Nicholas 1987: 41–42; Henderson 1994: 260–277.

31. Kermode 1998: 82–84, 89.

32. Keen 1984: 83–94, 200–207; Orme 1984: 182–191; Barber and Barker 1989: 206–207; Barron 2002: 219–226.

33. Nichols 1780: 177–186; Ward 1997: 189–198.

Chapter 3

1. Saint-Germain-des-Prés: see, for instance, Goetz 1999: 863, n. 6; Macedonia: Laiou-Thomadakis 1977: 78–81; Tuscany: Klapisch-Zuber 2000: 149; Italy, more generally: Menant 2005a: 150; Scandinavia: see, for instance, the figures in Jordan 1996: 129–130.

2. Thorner et al. 1986; for comment on Chayanov, see, for instance, Menant 2005b: 206–210. Postan 1973a: 114–115, quote at 114.

3. On the peasant family and economy, see, for instance, Smith 1984: 22–38; Catalonia: To Figueras 1997: 96–102.

4. Dyer 1989: 134; Kitsikopoulos 2000: 238; see also Briggs 2003: 231–233.

5. Carr 1982: 195; Dyer 1989; Smith 1991: 48–55.

6. Shahar 1990: 77–120; on weaning and nursing, Shahar 1983: 183–186; Shahar 1990: 55–76; on the debate relating to infanticide, see Kellum 1974; Helmholz 1974–1975; Shahar 1983: 184–185; Shahar 1990: 121 ff.; on the Great Famine and ejection of servants, see Lucas 1962: 57. On charity, Tierney 1959: 57.

7. Halesowen: Razi 1980: 83–85; royal households: Woolgar 1999: 9–10.

8. Tilly and Scott 1989: 60.

9. See, for instance, Goldberg 1995: 169–170.

10. Hanawalt 1986: 145–147.

11. See, for instance, Bennett 2006: 86–107.

12. See, for instance, Herlihy 1990: 185–191 and, on the differing experience of women in the later Middle Ages, a period Herlihy identifies as essentially one of economic restriction for women, 154–184.

13. Kussmaul 1981; Tilly and Scott 1989.

14. de Lacy: Wilkinson 2003: 302–306; Guidiccioni: Blomquist 2005b: 23–25.

15. But note the interesting reflections on aspects of the same for later periods in Pfister 1995.

16. On wage labor: Dyer 1989: 212–217; Poos 1991: 141–148, for discussion of neo-locality in a medieval context—that is, the association of household formation and marriage with property acquisition; Halesowen: Razi 1980: 77–78.

17. Porto: Melo 2003; labor legislation: Cohn 2007.

18. Rebel 1998: 206–207.

19. Poll taxes: Goldberg 1992: 158–202; catasto: Klapisch-Zuber 1985: 167–170; on the migration of the non-inheriting, Razi 1993; narrative accounts of food shortage: Lucas 1962: 63.

20. On lords and the search for possible heirs, Raftis 1996: 33–46; on early modern and modern families and the support of those living away from the hearth, see, for instance, Engerman 1995: 247. See also Herlihy and Klapisch-Zuber 1985: 137.

21. Lucca: Blomquist 2005a: 151; Blomquist 2005b: 19–22; "circular tour of rural wealth": Postan 1973b: 54–59; for an assessment that reduces the significance of landed status for merchants, Kermode 1998: 276–290.

22. Poos 1991: 142.

23. Goetz 2005; Scandinavia: Gaunt 1998: 327; dowry: Bourgard et al. 2002.

24. Howell 2003.

25. Woolgar 1999; Harvey 1993; Bridport: Wood-Legh 1956.
26. Luxury goods: see, for instance, Hinton 2005; foodstuffs: see, for instance, the essays in Woolgar, Serjeantson, and Waldron 2006; Italian town houses: Wickham 2005: 650–651; on investment in housing in southern Europe, see also Bazzana and Hubert 2000.
27. Florence: Kuehn 1991: 112–113; Redon: Davies 1999: 888; Languedoc: Amado 1999: 903.

Chapter 4

1. Epstein 2004: 109.
2. Richards 2004: 84–90.
3. Fleming 2001: 65–70; Schofield 2003: 82–83.
4. Owen-Hughes 2004: 126, 129.
5. Madureira Franco 2003: 271, 290.
6. Alexandre-Bidon and Lett 1999: 100; Alcock 2003: 455.
7. Santangeli Valenzani 2007: 133; Vésteinsson 2007: 156; Alcock 2003: 466; Pearson 2007: 55.
8. Roesdahl and Scholkmann 2007: 174–175; Kirby 1998: 29; Schofield and Vince 2003: 117.
9. Gilchrist 1999: 109–145.
10. Fresco 2003: 189–190.
11. Gilchrist 1996: 50; Blackmore 2003, 259–260.
12. Gilchrist 1999: 138–143.
13. Lafuente 2007a: 157.
14. Fleming 2001: 64; Bennett 1987: 20–22; Altenberg 2003: 257–258, 262.
15. Bennett 1987: 27.
16. Martin McLaughlin 2004: 38; Shahar 1990: 53–54.
17. Lewis 2002: 56.
18. Lewis 2002: 9.
19. Martin McLaughlin 2004: 47; Lewis 2002: 56.
20. Karg 2007: 196; Hammond 1993: 37; Lafuente 2007b: 182.
21. Dembińska 1999: 103; Karg 2007: 194.
22. Barrett 2007: 201–202.
23. Karg 2007: 200.
24. Moisà 1997: 20–21; Dyer 1994: 77–87.
25. Dyer 1994: 91.
26. Albarella 2007: 144–145.
27. Ariès 1962: 48.
28. Owen-Crocker 2004: 266. Pictorial examples include the abduction of Helen, possibly by Zanobi Srozzi (in the National Portrait Gallery, London); a child running across the scene wears an open-sided tunic over a shirt like the adult men except with bare legs rather than hose. A few surviving examples of children's garments can be found in the Museum of London Collections.

29. Owen-Crocker 2004: 266.
30. Museum of London Collections.
31. Leahy 2003: 61. The illustration for June from *Les Très Riches Heures* by the Lumbourg Brothers (in the Musée Condé), circa 1415, shows male and female harvest workers with bare legs and feet.
32. Leahy 2003: 62.
33. Bridgeford 2004: 156–157; Mosher Stuard 2006: 116.
34. Riikonen 2007: 250.
35. Riikonen 2007: 251.
36. Owen-Crocker 2004: 219–223.
37. Mosher Stuard 2006: 73–74, 79.
38. Reeves 2000: 17.
39. Alexandre-Bidon and Lett 1999: 83.

Chapter 5

1. Verger 1999: 256; Jordan 2001: ch. 8.
2. Clanchy 1993: 1–3.
3. Verger 1999: 264.
4. Cited by McKitterick 2005: 153.
5. McKitterick 2005: 156–157; Orme 2006: 35–37; McKitterick 2003: 16; Jaeger 1994: 47–48; Murray 1978: 216.
6. Alexandre-Bidon and Lett 1999: 121.
7. Luscombe 2004: 467–468, 470–477; McKitterick 2005: 159; Orme 2006: 262; Verger 1999: 257–260.
8. Shahar 1990: 225.
9. Youngs 2006: 83; Shahar 1990: 188.
10. All figures: Shahar 1990: 225 and Youngs 2006: 83–85. See also Shahar 1990: 187; Orme 2006: 68–70, 131.
11. Alexandre-Bidon and Lett 1999: 121; Orme 2006: 141–142.
12. Orme 2006: 139, 143–144; Alexandre-Bidon and Lett 1999: 128–129.
13. Barthemely L'Anglais [thirteenth century] 1999: 143.
14. Vincent 1996: 154–156; Matthæi Parisiensis [d. 1259] 1872–1883: v, 235.
15. Christine de Pisan [d. ca. 1431] 1985: 67.
16. Cited by Cherewatuk 1988–1991: 52; McKitterick 1989: 223–224.
17. Allen 2006: 667; *The book of the knight of la Tour-Landry* [1371–1372] 1868: 1–3.
18. Murray 2001: 74.
19. Cited by Riché 1993: 309.
20. Cited by Alexandre-Bidon and Lett 1999: 44.
21. The Goodman of Paris [ca. 1393] 2006.
22. Labarge 1965: 42; *The book of the knight of la Tour-Landry* [1371–1372] 1868: 65–67; Sponsler 1997: 15–16.
23. Labarge 1965: 43; Murray 2001: 74.
24. Cited by Kanarfogel 2008: 16.

25. Murray 2001: 74; Orme 2006: 35; Jaeger 1994: 49.
26. McKitterick 1989: 222.
27. Shahar 1990: 209–210, 215; Ward 2006: 56.
28. Bell 1988: 162–163.
29. Christine de Pisan [d. ca. 1431] 1985: 68.
30. Bell 1988: 163–165; Donovan 1991: ch. 1.
31. Lloyd-Morgan 1998: 160.
32. Bell 1988: 151, table 1.
33. Meale 1996: 128–158; Bell 1988: 152.
34. Lloyd-Morgan 1998: 160; Beach 2004. See also Dronke 1984: 55–83, 144–201; Wilson 1998: 2–18; Hildegard of Bingen [d. 1179] 1990: 9; Flanagan 1989; Orme 1984: 158, 160; Bell 1988: 165.
35. Shahar 1990: 226–227, 232.
36. Bardsley 2007: 72, 75.
37. Hanawalt 1986: 13, 158–161.
38. Cressy 1980: 176.

Chapter 6

1. Bloch 1961: 73.
2. Youngs 2006: 11; Le Goff 1988: 168.
3. Christine de Pisan [d. ca. 1431] 1985: 67.
4. Higounet-Nadal 1978: 289; Klapisch-Zuber 2000: 140.
5. Dubois 1995: 349; Lorcin 1981; Youngs 2006: 131–139.
6. Razi 1980: 83–88, 140–146.
7. Thrupp 1948: 199–200.
8. Razi 1980; Dubois 1995: 349; Lorcin 1981: 14.
9. Klapisch-Zuber 2000: 135.
10. Röhrkasten 2001: 209; Razi 1980: 45; Nightingale 2005.
11. Alexandre-Bidon and Lett 1999: 33; Benedictow 1993: 30, 40.
12. Mays 1998: 67–70.
13. Cohn 2002.
14. Lewis 2002: 40, 52–53.
15. Gilchrist and Sloane 2005: 208; Benedictow 1993: 37; Loschky and Childers 1993: 91–95.
16. Dyson and Schofield 1981: 78.
17. Rosenthal 1973: 290.
18. Leyser 1979: 52–58; Benedictow 1993: 56–75; Fleming 2006: 36–38; Crawford 1999a: 63.
19. Fossier 2004: 15; Youngs 2006.
20. Mays 1998: 50, 71; Gilchrist and Sloane 2005.
21. Davies 1998.
22. Fleming 2006: 42.
23. Razi 1980: 150.
24. Dubois 1995: 362–363.

25. Burrow 1986; Sears 1986.
26. Biller 2000: 257–259; Sears 1986: 27–28.
27. Burrow 1986.
28. Thompson 2004: 10.
29. Seymour et al. 1975: 300.
30. Dobozy 1999: 112.
31. Burns and Parsons 2000: 881, 957.
32. Orme 2001: 322.
33. Thorpe 1969: 59.
34. Tobin 1989: 63; Schultz 1995: 240.
35. Schultz 1995: 200–228.
36. France 1989; Nagy and Schaer 2001: 22.
37. Harris 1990; Raymond of Capua [d. 1399] 2003.
38. Eadmer [d. 1124?] 1962: 3; Benton 1995.
39. Froissart [d. 1410?] 2001: line 246.
40. Schultz 1995: 248, 251.
41. Harris 1990: 72; Raymond of Capua [d. 1399] 2003: 26.
42. Christine de Pisan [d. ca. 1431] 1985: 68.
43. Voaden and Volf 2000; McEvoy 1981: 387, 402.
44. Suger [d. 1151] 1992: 25.
45. Holden 2002: 1, 553, 560.
46. Douie and Farmer 1961–1962: i, 1, 128–130.
47. Benton 1995.
48. Van Gennep 1960.
49. Taglia 1998: 260; Orme 2001: 23–24, 31–33.
50. Harris 1990: 36.
51. Kauper and Kennedy 1996: 166–171.
52. Shenton 2003: 110.
53. Youngs 2006: 199.
54. Taglia 1998: 259; Mays 1998: 25; Gilchrist and Sloane 2005: 209.
55. Orme 2001: 119; Arnold 1980: 38–39.
56. Binski 1996: 106; Oosterwijk 2003: 191; Orme 2001: 120–121.

Chapter 7

1. Smith 2005: 125–135.
2. Matthew 1:25.
3. 1 Corinthians 7:1–2.
4. McCarthy (ed. and trans.) 2004: 32.
5. McCarthy (ed. and trans.) 2004: 44–53.
6. Whitelock 1968: 358, 426.
7. Hall 1993: 87.
8. For one recent restatement of this view, see Aurell 2006: 47–54.
9. Whitelock 1968: 431.
10. Brooke 1989: 136–143.
11. Whitelock et al. 1981: I ii, 991; Douie and Farmer 1961–1962: ii, 20–27.

12. Hall 1993: 85; Rothwell 1975: 318; Woodbine 1968: ii, 257.
13. Brooke 1989: 51–52.
14. Waugh 1988: 159.
15. Ephesians 5:22–24, 33.
16. On this subject generally, see Brundage 2000: 183–195.
17. Brundage 2000: 187–195.
18. Brundage 2000: 187 and n. 28.
19. Pollock and Maitland 1911: ii, 436.
20. Hanawalt 2000: 206–207.
21. 1 Corinthians 7:9; Mark 10:8–9; McCarthy (ed. and trans.) 2004: 103.
22. McCarthy (ed. and trans.) 2004: 52.
23. Bede [d. 735] 1969: 84–85; McCarthy (ed. and trans.) 2004: 103 (I Cnut 7); Rothwell 1975: 318 (Magna Carta [1215], cap. 6).
24. Duby 1983: esp. ch. 1.
25. Bartlett 2000: 557; Brooke 1989: 125.
26. Orderic Vitalis [d. ca. 1142] 1969–1980: vi, 552–555.
27. See, for example, Rothwell 1975: 317 (Magna Carta [1215], cap. 4).
28. Hall 1993: 88.
29. Rothwell 1975: 353–354 (Statute of Merton, 1236, cap. 9).
30. Hanawalt 1993: ch. 6.
31. Shahar 1990: 127.
32. Hanawalt 1993: 43.
33. For the view that the relationship between parents and their children in premodern periods was a more detached one, see Ariès 1962. For the story about Princess Katherine, see Matthæi Parisiensis [d. 1259] 1872–1883: v, 632.
34. Proverbs 13:24: "He that spareth his rod hateth his son: but he that loveth him chasteneth him betimes."
35. Sharpe 1913: 83.
36. Hall 1993: 82.
37. Woodbine 1968: ii, 351–353.
38. Orderic Vitalis [d. ca. 1142] 1969–1980: v, 221.
39. Whitelock 1968: 387, 391 (VI Athelstan, 1.1, 12.1).

Chapter 8

1. Boswell 1988: 228–255; Quinn 1989: 10; de Jong 1996: 73–99.
2. Orme 2001: 225.
3. Antoniadis-Bibicou 1973: 78; Patlagean 1973: 90.
4. Orme 2001: 214–215.
5. *Capitula Ecclesiastica ad Salz data* 1881: 6, 119.
6. Boswell 1988: 319–320.
7. Boynton 1998: 195–204; Wright 1989: 165–195; Robertson 1991: 311–313; Orme 2001: 226–228.
8. Stingre 1991: 21; Bolton 1994: 153–167; Shahar 1990: 155–161, 184–185; Goodich 2004: 19–22; Miller 2003.

9. Riché 1989: 293–294; Crawford 1999a: 148; Shahar 1990: 183; Antoniadis-Bibicou 1973: 78.

10. *Regula Benedicti* [sixth-century] 1972: chs. 30, 37, 39; 554, 572, 576–578.

11. Hobbins 2005: 50.

12. Herrin 1999: 91–102; Kalogeras 2005: 139–141.

13. Kanarfogel 1992: 37–40; Goldin 2004: 34; Marcus 1996: 35–46.

14. McKitterick 1976: 225–231.

15. Horn 2007: 292–296.

16. Christine de Pisan [d. ca. 1431] 1994: 60.

17. Classen 2005: 33–38.

18. Goodich 2004: 14.

19. Garver 2005: 78–83; Hanawalt 1993: 85–86.

20. Goodich 1983: 1.

21. *Vita Liutbirgae Virginis* [ninth century] 1937: 37–40.

22. *Ex miraculis Sanctae Verenae* [tenth century] 1841: 459–460.

23. Baumgarten 2004: 165–166.

24. Wertheimer 2006: 382–407.

25. Goodich 2004: 8; Alexandre-Bidon and Lett 1999: 12.

26. Reynolds 2006: 89–132.

27. Traina 2001: 104–105.

28. Goodich, 1983: 6–7; Bejczy 1994: 143–151; Dzon 2005: 135–157.

29. Ladurie 1978: 205–213.

30. Moore 1987: 36–38; Auslander 2005: 114; Marcus 1996: 100–101; Rubin 1999: 7–28, 35, 77–78.

31. Nirenberg 1996: 223–227.

32. Andrews 2004: 73–84.

33. Lynch 1986: 285–304; Nelson 1994: 97–98.

34. Shahar 1990: 45–49; Hanawalt 1993: 45–46.

35. Stortz 2001: 78–99; Crawford 1999a: 85–87; Lutterbach 2003: 17; Meens 1994: 53–64.

36. Traina 2001: 114.

37. Canto 4, lines 34–36.

38. Baun 1994: 115–125.

39. Hanawalt 1993: 44; Finucane 1997: 43–44.

40. Horn 2007: 270–285.

41. Finucane 1997: 56–95, 102–140, 148–149; Katajala-Peltomaa 2005: 145–155; Lett 1997b: 32–39, 362–364; Hanawalt 2002: 447; Krötzl 1989: 28–36; Webb 1994: 183–195.

42. Orme 2001: 215.

43. Hucbald of Saint Amand [early tenth century] 1680: 85–86.

44. Alexandre-Bidon and Lett 1999: 22; Nolan 1996: 95–119.

45. *Monumenta Germaniae Historica Poetae* 1 1881: 59, 71–73.

46. Baumgarten 2004: 165–168; Goldin 2004: 32–33.

47. Kellum, 1974: 371; Hanawalt 1993: 44–45.

48. Antoniadis-Bibicou 1973: 79; Brundage 1987: 138–139, 182, 240, 260.

49. Baumgarten 2004: 181–183; Goldin 2004: 26–27.
50. Patlagean 1973: 88; Orme 2001: 211–213, 217–221.
51. Goldin 2004: 36–40; Marcus 1996: 17, 117–126.
52. Patlagean 1973: 86–89.
53. Antoniadis-Bibicou 1973: 83.

Chapter 9

1. Goodich 1975, ch. 4; MacLehose 2006: ch. 1.
2. Stroppiana 1970: 77–95; Dasen 2004: articles by Vincent Barras, Danielle Goure-vitch, and Ann Ellis Hanson.
3. Demaitre 1977: 461–490.
4. Goodich 1989; Sears 1986.
5. Jacquart and Micheau 1990; Lemay 1978: 1–12.
6. Goodich 1975: 75–84.
7. Arnaldus de Villanova [d. 1311] 1996: introduction.
8. Sudhoff 1925. *Tafeln* 2–8, Passalacqua 1959. 26–53.
9. William of Saliceto [1280s] 1476.
10. Constantine the African [d. 1087] 1983.
11. Jacquart and Thomasset 1988.
12. See Thomas of Cantimpré [d. 1272] 1973: 1.72 (*De semine generationis*, p. 72); Cadden 1993.
13. William of Conches [1080–ca. 1150] 1997: 6.9 (*De conceptione et formatione foetus*, p. 212). See also Biller 1982: 3–26.
14. Riddle 1992: 118–134.
15. MacLehose 2006; Lemay 1992.
16. Nardi 1938; Vico 2002.
17. Huet 1993.
18. Vincent of Beauvais [d. 1264] 1964: liber 31, ch. 54.
19. Temkin 1956. For illustrations, see Jones 1998: 39–40; Alexandre-Bidon and Riché 1994: 42–43.
20. William of Conches [1080–ca. 1150]: 4.14; William of Conches [1080–ca. 1150] 1997: 6.10 (*De nativitate et infantia*, p. 216).
21. The use of the masculine pronoun to describe the child reflects a desire to remain faithful to the tenor of the primary sources, which consistently refer to the fetus, infant, and child as *he*. See MacLehose 2006: ch. 1, fn. 39.
22. Bartholomaeus Anglicus [thirteenth century; 1601 edition] 1964: 6.4, p. 237; Vin-cent of Beauvais [d. 1264] 1964: 31.57, vol. 1, col. 2335. For medical illustrations of the bath, see Aldobrandino of Siena [thirteenth century] 1911: 74.
23. Mayno of Milan [ca. 1330] 1502, 6r.
24. Vincent of Beauvais [d. 1264] 1964: 31.79, vol. 1, col. 2337.
25. MacLehose 2006, ch. 1.
26. See the overview of authorities in Vincent of Beauvais [d. 1264] 1964: 31.60, vol. 1, col. 2337.

27. Avicenna [d. 1037] 1527: 1.3.2.3; Vincent of Beauvais [d. 1264] 1964: 31.75, vol. 1, col. 2348–2349 *(De gradibus aetatum)*; Aldobrandino of Siena [thirteenth century] 1911: 79 *(Comment on doit le cors garder en cascun aage).*
28. MacLehose forthcoming.
29. For late medieval images of children taking their first steps in wheeled walkers, see Alexandre-Bidon and Riché 1994: 79.
30. Vincent of Beauvais [d. 1264] 1938.
31. Bernard de Gordon [d. ca. 1318] 1570: ch. 4, 29.
32. Avicenna [d. 1037] 1527: 1.3.2.4.
33. Bernard de Gordon [d. ca. 1318] 1570: ch. 5, 28–29 (quoting Avicenna).
34. Bartholomaeus Anglicus [thirteenth century; 1601 edition] 1964: 6.5 *(De puero,* p. 239).
35. Bernard de Gordon [d. ca. 1318] 1570: question 3, pp. 156–158.
36. Bernard de Gordon [d. ca. 1318] 1570: ch. 5, 29–31.
37. Amundsen and Diers 1973: 363–369; Goodich 1989: ch. 6.
38. Avicenna [d. 1037] 1527: 1.1.4.3.
39. William of Saliceto [1280s] 1476.
40. This is the majority opinion of medical authors. See Avicenna [d. 1037] 1527; Bartholomaeus Anglicus [thirteenth century; 1601 edition] 1964; Aldobrandino of Siena [thirteenth century] 1911.
41. Bernard de Gordon [d. ca. 1318] 1570: 206–208.
42. Mayno of Milan [ca. 1330] 1502: fo. 6v.
43. Mayno of Milan [ca. 1330] 1502: fos. 6r–v. See also Bernard de Gordon [d. ca. 1318] 1570: ch. 1, p. 12.
44. Hanson 1987: 589–602; MacLehose 2006: ch. 1 at note 86.
45. Lett 1997a: 77–92.
46. Taglia 2001: 77–90; Baumgarten 2004: 43–54.
47. Sudhoff 1925; MacLehose 2006: ch. 1 at note 139.
48. See the brief pediatric text of the thirteenth century, *Ut testatur Ypocras*: Sudhoff 1915: 443–458.
49. Cohn 2002: 214.
50. Lett 1997b; Finucane 1997. For the medical elements of these tales, see Gordon 1986: 502–522.
51. Schmitt 1983: 68–72.

Chapter 10

1. Ariès 1962: 128; Ladurie 1974, 1980; Orme 2001: 1–10.
2. Although the modern notions of the child and of childhood do emerge in the medieval period, there is significant information in the antique sources, especially in medical material, to suggest that the Greeks certainly perceived the child as its own person, subject to frailties and maladies that were not observed in adults.
3. I have given the *hijrī* years first followed by the Western dating. Subsequently, the dates are given in the same order but without the designations.
4. Rosenthal 1952: 1–22; Gil'adi 1990: 345–368; Gil'adi 1989: 121–152.

5. See, for example, Makdisi 1981, 1990.

6. This is Marshall Hodgson's term: Hodgson 1974–1975.

7. Scriptural citations directly follow the quoted Qur'anic passages.

8. The citations are given in short form immediately following the quotations in the text. Muhammad ibn Ismaʿil al-Bukhārī (194–256/810–870) compiled what Sunni Muslims regard as the most authentic collection of hadith, *al-Jamīʿ al-sahīh* (The sound collection), a work more popularly known as the *Sahīh Bukhārī*. The *Sahīh* consists of over seven thousand verified or "tested" traditions, which are arranged in chapters for easier use by lawyers in the process of juridical decision making. Bukhārī is perceived as second only to the Qur'an in authenticity and authoritative weight.

9. See Quran 4: 11; *Ihyā'* II: 2, 46, lines 30–35.

10. This text partially relies on Ibn Miskawayh's (d. 420/1030), *Tahdhīb al-akhlāq* [The cultivation of morals], which incorporated sections of the *Oikonomikos* treatise of Bryson of Heraclea: Ibn Miskawayh [d. 430/1030] 1966.

11. *Ihyā'* III: 2, 48, lines 13–15.

12. Qur'an 16: 59, 43: 17, and 81: 8–9 condemn female infanticide.

13. *Mishkāt*, 76, lines 11–20.

14. *Mishkāt*, 77, lines 6–8. *Munqidh*, 41, lines 6 ff. to which the *Mishkāt* passages should be compared.

15. *Mishkāt*, 77, lines 9–13; *Munqidh*, 41, lines 10–13.

16. *Ihyā'*, III: 2, 49, lines 15–19.

17. *Ihyā'*, III: 2, 54, lines 21–24.

18. *Ihyā'*, II: 2, 46, lines 1–5; *Ihyā'*, III: 2, 54, lines 26–29.

19. *Ihyā'*, III: 2, 54, lines 30–33, 55, lines 1–3.

20. Bukhārī, *Sahīh* VII, 62: 128.

21. Bargeron 2003: 32–78.

22. His given name was Mustafa ibn ʿAbdallah Kātib Chelebi (d. 1068/1658).

23. *Ihyā'* III: 2, 56, lines 5–15.

BIBLIOGRAPHY

Adam, Paul. 1964. *La vie paroissiale en France au quatorzième siècle*. Paris: Sirey.

Albarella, Umberto. 2007. "Meat production and consumption in town and country." In *Town and country in the Middle Ages: Contrasts, contacts and interconnections, 1100–1500*, eds. Kate Giles and Christopher Dyer. Leeds: Maney.

al-Bukhārī, Muhammad. [194–256/810–870] 2007–2009. *al-Jamī῾ al-sahīh* [Beirut]. Translated by M. Khan. USC-MSA Compendium of Muslim Texts. Available at: http://www.usc.edu/dept/MSA/fundamentals/hadithsunnah/bukhari/. Accessed November 12, 2008. Now at http://www.msawest.net/islam/.

Alcock, N. W. 2003. "The medieval peasant at home: England, 1250–1550." In *The medieval household in Christian Europe c. 850–c. 1550: Managing power, wealth and the body*, eds. Cordelia Beattie et al. Turnhout, Belgium: Brepols.

Aldobrandino of Siena. [thirteenth century] 1911. *Régime du corps*. Paris: Champion.

Alexandre-Bidon, Danièle, and Didier Lett. 1999. *Children in the Middle Ages, fifth to fifteenth centuries*. Translated by Jody Gladding. Notre Dame, IN: University of Notre Dame Press.

Alexandre-Bidon, Danièle, and Pierre Riché. 1994. *L'enfance au Moyen Age*. Paris: Seuil.

al-Ghazālī, abū Hāmid. 1933. *Ihyā' ῾ulūm al-dīn* [The revival of the sciences of religion]. Cairo: al-Matba῾at al-῾uthmānīyat al-misrīya.

al-Ghazālī, abū Hāmid. 1959. *al-Munqidh min addalāl* [The deliverer from error]. Beirut: al-Lajnah al-Duwalīyah li-Tarjamat al-Rawā'῾ [UNESCO Collection of Representative Works. Arabic Series].

al-Ghazālī, abū Hāmid. 1964. *Mishkāt al-anwār* [Niche for lights]. Cairo: al-Maktabat al-῾arabīya.

Allen, Prudence. 2006. *The concept of woman: The early humanist reformation, 1250–1500, Part 2*. Cambridge: Eerdmans.

Altenberg, Karin. 2003. *Experiencing landscapes: A study of space and identity in three marginal areas of medieval Britain and Scandinavia*. Stockholm: Almqvist & Wiskell International.

Altschul, Michael. 1965. *A baronial family in medieval England: The Clares, 1217–1314*. Baltimore: Johns Hopkins University Press.

Amado, C. 1999. "Circulation des diens à l'intérieur de la famille aristocratique de la Gothie au xve siècle." *Mélanges de l'Ecole française de Rome: Moyen Age* 111 (2): 895–910.

Amt, Emilie, ed. and trans. 1993. *Women's lives in medieval Europe: A sourcebook*. New York and London: Routledge.

Amundsen, D. W., and C. J. Diers. 1973. "The age of menarche in medieval Europe." *Human Biology* 45 (3): 363–368.

Andrews, Frances. 2004. "A safe-haven for children? The early Humiliati and provision for children." In *Youth in the Middle Ages*, eds. P. J. P. Goldberg and Felicity Riddy. Woodbridge: York Medieval Press.

Antoniadis-Bibicou, Hélène. 1973. "L'enfant de la moyenne epoque Byzantine." *Annales de démographie historique*, 77–84.

Ariès, Phillipe. 1962. *Centuries of childhood*. Translated by Robert Baldick. London: Jonathan Cape.

Arnaldus de Villanova. [d. 1311] 1996. "Regimen sanitatis ad regem Aragonum." In *Arnaldi de Villanova Opera medica omnia*, eds. Luis García-Ballester and Michael R. McVaugh. Barcelona: Universitat de Barcelona.

Arnold, Klaus. 1980. *Kind und Gesellschaft in Mittelalter und Renaissance*. Paderborn, Germany: Ferdinand Schöningh.

Aurell, Martin. 2006. "Society." In *The short Oxford history of Europe: The central Middle Ages. Europe 950–1320*, ed. Daniel Power. Oxford: Oxford University Press.

Auslander, Diane Peters. 2005. "Victims or martyrs: Children, anti-Judaism, and the stress of change in medieval England." In *Childhood in the Middle Ages and the Renaissance*, ed. Albrecht Classen. Berlin: DeGruyter.

Avicenna. [d. 1037] 1527. *Liber canonis*. Venice: Junta.

Barber, Richard, and Juliet Barker. 1989. *Tournaments: Jousts, chivalry and pageants in the Middle Ages*. Woodbridge: Boydell Press.

Bardsley, Sandy. 2007. *Women's roles in the Middle Ages*. Santa Barbara, CA: Greenwood Publishing Group.

Bargeron, Carol. 2003. "Sufism's role in al-Ghazālī's first crisis of knowledge." *Medieval Encounters* 9 (1): 32–78.

Barrett, James H. 2007. "Sea fishing and long-term socio-economic trends in northwestern Europe." In *The archaeology of medieval Europe*. Vol. 1, *Eighth to twelfth centuries AD*, eds. James Graham-Campbell with Magdalena Valor. Aarhus, Denmark: Aarhus University Press.

Barron, Caroline M. 1996. "The education and training of girls in fifteenth-century London." In *Courts, counties and the capital in the later Middle Ages*, ed. Diana E. S. Dunn. Stroud: Alan Sutton.

Barron, Caroline M. 2002. "Pageantry and merchant culture in medieval London." In *Heraldry, pageantry and social display in medieval England*, eds. Peter Coss and Maurice Keen. Woodbridge: Boydell Press.

Barthélemy, Dominique. 1988. "Kinship." In *A history of private life: Revelations of the medieval world*, ed. Georges Duby, trans. Arthur Goldhammer. Cambridge, MA: Belknap Press of Harvard University Press.

Barthemely L'Anglais [Bartholomew the Englishman]. [thirteenth century] 1999. *Le livre des propriétés des choses: Une encyclopédie au xive siècle [sic]*. Translated by Madeleine Jeay and Kathleen Garay. Paris: Stock. Available at: http://mw.mcmaster.ca/scriptorium/barthol.html. Accessed March 4, 2010.

Bartholomaeus Anglicus [Bartholomew the Englishman]. [thirteenth century; 1601 edition] 1964. *De proprietatibus rerum*. Frankfurt: Minerva.

Bartlett, Robert. 2000. *England under the Norman and Angevin kings, 1075–1225*. Oxford: Clarendon Press.

Baumgarten, Elisheva. 2004. *Mothers and children: Jewish family life in medieval Europe*. Princeton, NJ: Princeton University Press.

Baun, Jane. 1994. "The fate of babies dying before baptism in Byzantium." In *The church and childhood*, ed. Diana Wood. Studies in Church History 31. Oxford: Blackwell.

Bazzana, A., and E. Hubert, eds. 2000. *Maisons et espaces domestiques dans le monde méditerranéen au Moyen Age*. Rome: Ecole française de Rome; Madrid: Casa de Velázquez.

Beach, Alison I. 2004. *Women as scribes: Book production and monastic reform in twelfth-century Bavaria*. Cambridge: Cambridge University Press.

Bede [d. 735] 1969. *Bede's ecclesiastical history of the English people*. Edited by Bertram Colgrave and R.A.B. Mynors. Oxford: Clarendon Press.

Bejczy, István P. 1994. "The *sacra infantia* in medieval hagiography." In *The church and childhood*, ed. Diana Wood. Studies in Church History 31. Oxford: Blackwell.

Bell, Susan Groag. 1988. "Medieval women book owners: Arbiters of lay piety and ambassadors of culture." In *Women and power in the Middle Ages*, eds. Mary Erler and Maryanne Kowaleski. Athens: University of Georgia Press.

Benedictow, Ole Jørgen. 1993. *The medieval demographic system of the Nordic countries*. Oslo: Middelalderforlaget.

Bennett, Judith M. 2006. *History matters: Patriarchy and the challenge of feminism*. Philadelphia: University of Pennsylvania Press.

Bennett, Judith M. 1987. *Women in the medieval countryside: Gender and household in Brigstock before the plague*. Oxford: Oxford University Press.

Bennett, Judith M. 2003. "Writing fornication: Medieval leyrwite and its historians." *Transactions of the Royal Historical Society*, sixth series, 13: 131–162.

Benton, John F. 1995. *Self and society in medieval France: The memoirs of Abbot Guibert of Nogent*. Toronto: University of Toronto Press.

Bernard de Gordon. [d. ca. 1318] 1570. *De conservatione*. Leipzig: J. Rhamba.

Biller, P. P. A. 1982. "Birth control in the West in the thirteenth and early fourteenth centuries." *Past and Present* 94: 3–26.

Biller, P. P. A. 2000. *The measure of multitude: Population in medieval thought*. Oxford: Oxford University Press.

Binski, Paul. 1996. *Medieval death: Ritual and representation*. London: British Museum.

Blackmore, Lyn. 2003. "The iron objects." In *Middle Saxon London: Excavations at the Royal Opera House 1989–99*, eds. Gordon Malcolm and David Bowsher with Robert Cowie. London: Museum of London Archaeological Service.

Blanks, David R. 2001. "Family." In *Medieval Germany: An encyclopedia*, ed. John M. Jeep. New York: Routledge.

Bloch, Marc. 1961. *Feudal society.* Translated by L. A. Morgan. London: Routledge and Kegan Paul.

Blomquist, T. W. 2005a. "La famiglia et gli affair: Le Compagnie Internazionsli Lucchesi al Tempo di Castruccio Castracani." In *Merchant families, banking and money in medieval Lucca,* ed. T. W. Blomquist. Aldershot: Ashgate.

Blomquist, T. W. 2005b. "Lineage, land and business in the thirteenth century: The Guidiccioni family of Lucca." In *Merchant families, banking and money in medieval Lucca,* ed. T. W. Blomquist. Aldershot: Ashgate.

Boccaccio, Giovanni. [d. 1375] 2002. *The Decameron.* Translated by Mark Musa and Peter Bondanella. London: Signet Classics.

Bolton, Brenda. 1994. "'Received in his name': Rome's busy baby box." In *The church and childhood,* ed. Diana Wood. Studies in Church History 31. Oxford: Blackwell.

Bonney, F. 1973. "Jean Gerson: Un nouveau regard sur l'enfance." *Annales de démographie historique,* 138–140.

The book of the knight of la Tour-Landry. [1371–1372] 1868. Edited by Thomas Wright. London: Early English Text Society.

The book of the knight of the tower. [1371–1372] 1971. Translated by William Caxton. Edited by M. Y. Offord. Early English Text Society, supplementary scrics, 2. Oxford: Oxford University Press.

The book of the knight of the tower. [1371–1372] 2006. Translated by Rebecca Barnhouse. New York: Palgrave.

Bossy, John. 1983. "The mass as a social institution 1200–1700." *Past and Present* 100: 35–43.

Boswell, John. 1988. *The kindness of strangers: The abandonment of children in Western Europe from late antiquity to the Renaissance.* New York: Pantheon Books.

Bouchard, Constance Brittain. *Strong of body, brave and noble: Chivalry and society in medieval France.* Ithaca, NY: Cornell University Press.

Bourgard, F., et al., eds. 2002. *Dots et douaires dans le haut Moyen Age.* Rome: L'Ecole française de Rome.

Boynton, Susan. 1998. "The liturgical role of children in monastic customaries from the central Middle Ages." *Studia Liturgica* 28: 194–209.

Bray, Alan. 2003. *The friend.* Chicago: University of Chicago Press.

Bridgeford, Andrew. 2004. *1066: The hidden history of the Bayeux tapestry.* London: Fourth Estate.

Briggs, C. 2003. "Credit and the peasant household economy in England before the Black Death: Evidence from a Cambridge manor." In *The medieval household in Christian Europe, c. 850–c. 1550: Managing power, wealth and the body,* eds. Cordelia Beattie et al. Turnhout, Belgium: Brepols.

Brooke, Christopher N. L. 1989. *The medieval idea of marriage.* Oxford: Oxford University Press.

Brundage, James A. 2000. "Domestic violence in classical canon law." In *Violence in medieval society,* ed. Richard W. Kaeuper, Woodbridge: Boydell Press.

Brundage, James A. 1987. *Law, sex, and Christian society in medieval Europe.* Chicago: University of Chicago Press.

Brundage, James A. 1996. "Sex and canon law." In *Handbook of medieval sexuality,* eds. Vern L. Bullough and James A. Brundage. New York: Garland.

Bullough, Vern, et al. 1988. *The subordinated sex: A history of attitudes toward women.* Athens: University of Georgia Press.

Burns, Robert I., and Samuel Parsons Scott. 2000. *Las siete partidas.* Vol. 4, *Family, commerce and the sea.* Philadelphia: University of Pennsylvania Press.

Burrow, J. A. 1986. *The ages of man: A study in medieval learning and thought.* Oxford: Clarendon Press.

Cadden, Joan. 1993. *Meanings of sex difference in the Middle Ages.* Cambridge: Cambridge University Press.

Calendar of inquisitions miscellaneous, 1. 1916. London: His Majesty's Stationery Office.

Calendar of inquisitions post mortem, 7. 1909. London: His Majesty's Stationery Office.

Capitula ecclesiastica ad salz data. 1881. Edited by Alfred Boretius. In *Monumenta Germaniae Historica Capitularia* 1, no. 42. Hanover: Impensis Bibliopolii Hahniani.

Carr, A. D. 1982. *Medieval Anglesey.* Llangefni, Wales: Anglesey Antiquarian Society.

Cherewatuk, Karen. 1988–1991. "*Speculum matris.* Dhuoda's manual." *Florilegium* 10: 49–64.

Chew, Helena M., and Martin Weinbaum, eds. 1970. *The London eyre of 1244.* London Record Society, 6.

Christine de Pisan. [d. ca. 1431] 1985. *The treasure of the city of ladies, or the book of the three virtues.* Translated by Sarah Lawson. Harmondsworth: Penguin.

Christine de Pisan. [d. c. 1431] 1994. *The writings of Christine de Pizan.* Translated by Charity Cannon Willard. New York: Persea.

Clanchy, Michael. 1993. *From memory to written record: England 1066–1307.* Oxford: Blackwell.

Classen, Albrecht. 2005. "Philippe Ariès and the consequences. History of childhood, family relations, and personal emotions; where do we stand today?" In *Childhood in the Middle Ages and the Renaissance,* ed. Albrecht Classen. Berlin: DeGruyter.

Cohn, Samuel K. 2007. "After the Black Death: Labour legislation and attitudes towards labour in late-medieval Western Europe." *Economic History Review* 60 (3): 457–485.

Cohn, Samuel K. 2002. *The Black Death transformed: Disease and culture in early Renaissance Europe.* London: Arnold.

Constantine the African. [d. 1087] 1983. *Constantini Liber de coitu, El tratado de andrología de Constantino el Africano.* Edited by Enrique Montero Cartelle. Santiago de Compostela, Spain: Universidad de Santiago de Compostela.

Crawford, Sally. 1999a. *Childhood in Anglo-Saxon England.* Stroud: Sutton.

Crawford, Sally. 1999b. "Children, death and the afterlife in Anglo-Saxon England." In *The archaeology of Anglo-Saxon England,* ed. Catherine E. Karkov. London: Garland.

Cressy, David. 1980. *Literacy and the social order: Reading and writing in Tudor and Stuart England.* Cambridge: Cambridge University Press.

Crouch, David. 2005. *The birth of nobility: Constructing aristocracy in England and France, 900–1300.* Harlow: Longman.

Dante Alighieri. [1308–1321] 1980. *Inferno.* Translated by Allen Mandelbaum. Berkeley: University of California Press.

Dasen, Véronique, ed. 2004. *Naissance et petite enfance dans l'antiquité: Actes du colloque de Fribourg, 28 Novembre – 1er Décembre 2001*. Fribourg: Academic Press; Göttingen: Vandenhoeck and Ruprecht.

Davies, Virginia. 1998. "Medieval longevity: The experience of members of religious orders in late medieval England." *Medieval Prosopography* 19: 111–124.

Davies, W. 1999. "Intra-family transactions in south-eastern Brittany." *Mélanges de l'Ecole française de Rome: Moyen Age* 111 (2): 881–894.

de Jong, Mayke. 1996. *In Samuel's image: Child oblation in the early medieval West*. Leiden: Brill.

Demaitre, Luke. 1977. "The idea of childhood and child care in medical writings of the Middle Ages." *Journal of Psychohistory* 4 (4): 461–490.

Dembińska, Maria. 1999. *Food and drink in medieval Poland: Rediscovering a cuisine of the past*. Philadelphia: University of Pennsylvania Press.

Devroey, J.-P. 2000. "Men and women in early medieval serfdom: The ninth-century north Frankish evidence." *Past and Present* 166: 3–30.

Dhuoda. [841–843] 1991. *Handbook for William*. Translated by Carol Neel. Lincoln: University of Nebraska Press.

Dixon, E. 1895. "Craftswomen in the *Livre des Métiers*." *Economic Journal* 5: 209–228.

Dobozy, Maria, trans. 1999. *The Saxon mirror: A sachenspiegel of the fourteenth century*. Philadelphia: University of Pennsylvania Press.

Donovan, Claire. 1991. *The de Brailes hours*. London: British Library.

Douglas, David C., and George W. Greenaway, eds. 1953. *English historical documents II 1042–1189*. London: Eyre and Spottiswoode.

Douie, Decima L., and Dom Hugh Farmer, eds. 1961–1962. *Magna vita Sancti Hugonis: The life of St Hugh of Lincoln*. 2 vols. Edinburgh: Nelson.

Dronke, Peter. 1984. *Women writers of the Middle Ages: A critical study of texts from Perpetua (d. 203) to Marguerite Porete (d. 1310)*. Cambridge: Cambridge University Press.

Dubois, H. 1995. "La depression (xvie et xve siècles)." In *Histoire de la population française*. Vol. 1, ed. Jacques Dupâquier. Paris: Presses Universitaires de France.

Du Boulay, F. R. H. 1966. *The lordship of Canterbury*. London: Nelson.

Duby, Georges. 1988. "The aristocratic households of feudal France." In *A history of private life: Revelations of the medieval world*, ed. Georges Duby, trans. Arthur Goldhammer. Cambridge, MA: Belknap Press of Harvard University Press.

Duby, Georges. 1983. *The knight, the lady, and the priest: The making of modern marriage in medieval France*. Translated by Barbara Bray. New York: Pantheon Books.

Dyer, Christopher. 1994. *Everyday life in medieval England*. London: Hambledon Press.

Dyer, Christopher. 2003. *Making a living in the Middle Ages: The people of Britain 850–1520*. London: Penguin.

Dyer, Christopher. 1989. *Standards of living in the later Middle Ages: Social change in England, c. 1200–1520*. Cambridge: Cambridge University Press.

Dyson, A., and J. Schofield. 1981. "Excavations in the city of London, second interim report 1974–8." *Transactions of the London and Middlesex Archaeological Society* 32: 24–81.

Dzon, Mary. 2005. "Joseph and the amazing Christ child of late-medieval legend." In *Childhood in the Middle Ages and the Renaissance*, ed. Albrecht Classen. Berlin: DeGruyter.

Eadmer. [d. 1124?] 1962. *The life of St Anselm, archbishop of Canterbury.* Translated by R. W. Southern. Cambridge: Cambridge University Press.

Egan, G. 1998. *The medieval household: Daily living, c. 1150–c. 1450.* London: Museum of London.

Engerman, S. L. 1995. "Family and economy: Some comparative perspectives." In *The European peasant family and society: Historical studies*, ed. R. L. Rudolph. Liverpool: Liverpool University Press.

Epstein, Stephan R. 2004. *Town and country in Europe, 1300–1800.* Cambridge: Cambridge University Press.

Ex miraculis Sanctae Verenae. [tenth century] 1841. Edited by Georg Waitz. In *Monumenta Germaniae Historica Scriptores* 4, ed. Georg Heinrich Pertz. Hanover: Impensis Bibliopolii Hahniani.

Farmer, David H. 1997. *The Oxford dictionary of saints.* Oxford: Oxford University Press.

Fernea, Elizabeth W. 1995. "Children in the Muslim Middle East." In *Children in the Muslim Middle East*, ed. Elizabeth W. Fernea. Austin: University of Texas Press.

Finucane, Ronald C. 1997. *The rescue of the innocents: Endangered children in medieval miracles.* Basingstoke: Macmillan; New York: St. Martin's Press.

Flanagan, Sabina. 1989. *Hildegard of Bingen, 1098–1179: A visionary life.* London: Routledge.

Flandrin, Jean-Louis. 1991. *Sex in the Western world: The development of attitudes and behaviour.* Chur, Switzerland: Harwood Academic Publishers.

Fleming, Peter. 2001. *Family and household in medieval England.* Basingstoke: Palgrave.

Fleming, Robin. 2006. "Bones for historians: Putting the body back into biography." In *Writing medieval biography, 750–1250*, eds. David Bates et al. Woodbridge: Boydell & Brewer.

Fossier, Robert. 2004. "The rural economy and demographic growth." In *The new Cambridge medieval history.* Vol. 4, *c. 1024–c. 1198*, eds. David Luscombe and Jonathan Riley-Smith. Cambridge: Cambridge University Press.

France, John, ed. 1989. *Rodulfus Glaber.* Oxford: Clarendon Press.

French, Katherine L. 1998. "Maidens' lights and wives' stores: Women's parish guilds in late medieval England." *Sixteenth Century Journal* 29: 399–425.

Fresco, Karen L. 2003. "Gendered household spaces in Christine de Pizan's *Livre des trois vertus.*" In *The medieval household in Christian Europe c. 850–c. 1550: Managing power, wealth and the body*, eds. Cordelia Beattie et al. Turnhout, Belgium: Brepols.

Froissart, Jean. [d. 1410?] 2001. *Jean Froissart: An anthology of narrative and lyric poetry.* Translated by Kirstin M. Figg and R. Barton Palmer. New York and London: Routledge.

Garver, Valerie. 2005. "The influence of monastic ideals upon Carolingian conceptions of childhood." In *Childhood in the Middle Ages and the Renaissance*, ed. Albrecht Classen. Berlin: DeGruyter.

Gaunt, D. 1998. "The peasants of Scandinavia, 1300–1700." In *The peasantries of Europe from the fourteenth to the eighteenth centuries*, ed. T. Scott. Harlow: Longman.

Geremek, Bronislaw. 1987. *The margins of society in late medieval Paris.* Cambridge: Past and Present.

Gil'adi, Avner. 1989. "Concepts of childhood and attitudes towards children in medieval Islam: A preliminary study with special reference to reaction to infant and child mortality." *Journal of the Economic and Social History of the Orient* 32 (2): 121–152.

Gil'adi, Avner. 1990. "Infants, children, and death in medieval Muslim society: Some preliminary observations." *Social History of Medicine* 3 (3): 345–368.

Gilchrist, Roberta. 1996. "Ambivalent bodies: Gender and medieval archaeology." In *Invisible people and processes: Writing gender and childhood into European archaeology*, eds. Jenny Moore and Eleanor Scott. London: Leicester University Press.

Gilchrist, Roberta. 1999. *Gender and archaeology: Contesting the past.* London: Routledge.

Gilchrist, Roberta, and Barney Sloane. 2005. *Requiem: The medieval monastic cemetery in Britain.* London: Museum of London Archaeology Service.

Goetz, H-W. 1999. "La circulation des biens à l'intérieur de la famille: Rapport introductif." *Mélanges de l'Ecole française de Rome: Moyen Age* 111 (2): 861–879.

Goetz, H-W. 2005. "Coutume d'héritage et structures familiales au haut Moyen Age." In *Sauver son âme et se perpétuer: Transmission du patrimoine et mémoire au haut Moyen Age*, eds. F. Bougard, C. la Rocca, and R. le Jan. Rome: L'Ecole française de Rome.

Gold, Penny Schine. 1985. *The lady and the virgin: Image, attitude and experience in twelfth-century France.* Chicago: University of Chicago Press.

Goldberg, P. J. P. 2008. "Childhood and gender in later medieval England." *Viator* 39: 249–262.

Goldberg, P. J. P. 1986a. "Female labour, service and marriage in northern towns during the later Middle Ages." *Northern History* 22: 25.

Goldberg, P. J. P. 1986b. "Marriage, migration, servanthood and life-cycle in Yorkshire towns in the later Middle Ages: Some York cause paper evidence." *Continuity and Change* 1: 141–169.

Goldberg, P. J. P. 2005. *Medieval England: A social history 1250–1550.* London: Arnold.

Goldberg, P. J. P. 1992. *Women, work and life cycle in a medieval economy: Women in York and Yorkshire c. 1300–1520.* Oxford: Clarendon Press.

Goldberg, P. J. P., ed. and trans. 1995. *Women in England, 1275–1525.* Manchester: Manchester University Press.

Goldin, Simha. 2004. "Jewish society under pressure: The concept of childhood." In *Youth in the Middle Ages*, eds. P. J. P. Goldberg and Felicity Riddy. Woodbridge: York Medieval Press.

Goodich, Michael E. 1975. "Bartholomaeus Anglicus on child-rearing." *History of Childhood Quarterly* 3 (1): 75–84.

Goodich, Michael E. 1983. "Encyclopaedic literature: Child-rearing in the Middle Ages." *History of Education* 12: 1–8.

Goodich, Michael E. 1989. *From birth to old age: The human life cycle in medieval thought, 1250–1350.* Lanham, MD: University Press of America.

Goodich, Michael E. 2004. "A saintly child and a saint of children: The childhood of Elizabeth of Thuringia (1207–1231)." In *Lives and miracles of the saints: Studies in medieval Latin hagiography,* ed. Michael E. Goodich. Aldershot: Variorum.

The Goodman of Paris. [ca. 1393] 2006. *A treatise on moral and domestic economy by a citizen of Paris, c. 1393.* Translated by Eileen Power. Woodbridge: Boydell Press.

Gordon, E. V., ed. 1953. *Pearl.* Oxford: Clarendon Press.

Gordon, Eleanora. 1986. "Child health in the Middle Ages as seen in the miracles of five English saints, A.D. 1150–1220." *Bulletin of the History of Medicine* 60: 502–522.

Green, M. 1988–1989. "Women's medical practice and health care in medieval Europe." *Signs* 14 (2): 449–450.

Hall, G. D. G., ed. 1993. *The treatise on the laws and customs of England commonly called Glanvill.* Oxford: Clarendon Press.

Halsall, Guy. 1995. *Settlement and social organization: The Merovingian region of Metz.* Cambridge: Cambridge University Press.

Hammond, Peter W. 1993. *Food and feast in medieval England.* Gloucestershire: Alan Sutton.

Hanawalt, Barbara A. 1977. "Childrearing among the lower classes in late medieval England." *Journal of Interdisciplinary History* 8: 1–22.

Hanawalt, Barbara A. 1993. *Growing up in medieval London: The experience of childhood in history.* Oxford: Oxford University Press.

Hanawalt, Barbara A. 2002. "Medievalists and the study of childhood." *Speculum* 77 (2): 440–460.

Hanawalt, Barbara A. 1986. *The ties that bound: Peasant families in medieval England.* Oxford: Oxford University Press.

Hanawalt, Barbara A. 2000. "Violence in the domestic milieu of late medieval England." In *Violence in medieval society,* ed. Richard W. Kaeuper. Woodbridge: Boydell Press.

Hanson, Ann Ellis. 1987. "The eight months child and the etiquette of birth: Obsit omen!" *Bulletin of the History of Medicine* 61: 589–602.

Harris, M. T., ed. 1990. *Birgitta of Sweden: Life and selected revelations.* New York: Paulist Press.

Harris, Mary Dormer, ed. 1907–1913. *The Coventry leet book.* London: Early English Text Society, original series, 134–135, 138, 146.

Harvey, B. F. 1993. *Living and dying in England 1100–1540: The monastic experience.* Oxford: Oxford University Press.

Helmholz, R. H. 1974–1975. "Infanticide in the province of Canterbury during the fifteenth century." *History of Childhood Quarterly* 2 (3): 379–390.

Henderson, John. 1994. *Piety and charity in late medieval Florence.* Oxford: Clarendon Press.

Hennessy, Cecily. 2008. *Images of children in Byzantium*. Aldershot: Ashgate.

Herlihy, David. 1978. "Medieval children." In *Women, family and society in medieval Europe: Historical essays, 1978–1991*, ed. A. Molho (1995). Oxford: Berghahn.

Herlihy, David. 1985. *Medieval households*. Cambridge, MA: Harvard University Press.

Herlihy, David. 1990. *Opera muliebria: Women and work in medieval Europe*. New York: McGraw-Hill.

Herlihy, David, and Christiane Klapisch-Zuber. 1985. *Tuscans and their families: A study of the Florentine catasto of 1427*. New Haven, CT, and London: Yale University Press.

Herrin, Judith. 1999. "L'enseignement maternal à Byzance." In *Femmes et pouvoirs des femmes à Byzance et en Occident (vie–xiie siècles)*, eds. Stéphane Lebecq et al. Lille: Centre de recherche sur l'histoire de l'Europe du Nord-Ouest.

Heywood, Colin. 2001. *A history of childhood: Children and childhood in the West from medieval to modern times*. Cambridge: Polity.

Higounet-Nadal, Arlette. 1978. *Périgueux aux xive et xve siècles: Etude de démographie historique*. Bordeaux: Fédération Historique du Sud-Ouest.

Hildegard of Bingen. [d. 1179] 1990. *Scivias*. Edited and translated by Columba Hart et al. Mahwah, NJ: Paulist Press.

Hinton, D. 2005. *Gold and gilt, pots and pins: Possessions and people in medieval Britain*. Oxford: Oxford University Press.

Hodgson, Marshall G. 1974–1975. *The venture of Islam*. Chicago: University of Chicago Press.

Holden, A. J., ed. 2002. *History of William Marshal*. London: Anglo-Norman Text Society, No. 4.

Hollingsworth, T. H. 1958. "A demographic study of British ducal families." *Population Studies* 11: 4–26.

Horn, Cornelia B. 2007. "The lives and literary roles of children in advancing conversion to Christianity: Hagiography from the Caucasus in late antiquity and the Middle Ages." *Church History* 76 (2): 262–297.

Howell, Martha. 2003. "The properties of marriage in late medieval Europe: Commercial wealth and the creation of modern marriage." In *Love, marriage and family ties in the later Middle Ages*, eds. I. Davis et al. Turnhout, Belgium: Brepols.

Hucbald of Saint Amand. [early tenth century] 1680. *Vita Sanctae Rictrudis*. In *Acta Sanctorum mai III*. Brussels: Société des Bollandistes.

Huet, Marie-Hélène. 1993. *Monstrous imagination*. Cambridge, MA: Harvard University Press.

Hunnisett, R. F., ed. 1961. *Bedfordshire coroners' rolls*. Bedfordshire Historical Record Society, 41.

Ibn Miskawayh [d. 430/1030]. 1966. *Tahdhīb al-akhlāq* [The cultivation of morals]. Edited and translated by C. Zurayk. Beirut: American University of Beirut.

Jacquart, Danielle, and Françoise Micheau. 1990. *La médecine arabe et l'Occident médiéval*. Paris: Maisonneuve et Larose.

Jacquart, Danielle, and Claude Thomasset. 1988. *Sexuality and medicine in the Middle Ages*. Translated by M. Adamson. Cambridge: Polity.

Jaeger, C. Stephen. 1994. *The envy of angels: Cathedral schools and social ideals in medieval Europe, 950–1200*. Philadelphia: University of Pennsylvania Press.

Jewell, Helen M. 2007. *Women in Dark Age and early medieval Europe c. 500–1200*. Basingstoke: Palgrave Macmillan.

Jones, Peter Murray. 1998. *Medieval medicine in illuminated manuscripts*. London: British Library.

Jordan, William Chester. 2001. *Europe in the high Middle Ages*. London: Penguin.

Jordan, William Chester. 1996. *The Great Famine: Northern Europe in the early fourteenth century*. Princeton, NJ: Princeton University Press.

Kaeuper, Richard W., ed. 2000. *Violence in medieval society*. Woodbridge: Boydell Press.

Kalogeras, Nikos. 2005. "The role of parents and kin in the education of Byzantine children." In *Hoping for continuity: Childhood, education and death in antiquity and the Middle Ages*, eds. Katariina Mustakallio et al. Rome: Institutum Romanum Finlandiae.

Kanarfogel, Ephraim. 1992. Reprinted 2008. *Jewish education and society in the high Middle Ages*. Detroit: Wayne State University Press.

Karg, Sabine. 2007. "Food. Part 2: The rest of Europe." In *The archaeology of medieval Europe*. Vol. 1, *Eighth to twelfth centuries AD*, eds. James Graham-Campbell with Magdalena Valor. Aarhus, Denmark: Aarhus University Press.

Karras, Ruth Mazo. 2005. *Sexuality in medieval Europe: Doing unto others*. London: Routledge.

Katajala-Peltomaa, Sari. 2005. "Parental roles in the canonisation processes of Saint Nicola of Tolentino and Saint Thomas of Cantilupe." In *Hoping for continuity: Childhood, education and death in antiquity and the Middle Ages*, eds. Katariina Mustakallio et al. Rome: Institutum Romanum Finlandiae.

Kauper, Richard, and Elspeth Kennedy. 1996. *The book of chivalry of Geoffroi de Charny: Text, context and translation*. Philadelphia: University of Pennsylvania Press.

Keen, Maurice. 1984. *Chivalry*. New Haven, CT, and London: Yale University Press.

Kellum, Barbara A. 1974. "Infanticide in England in the later Middle Ages." *History of Childhood Quarterly* 1 (3): 367–388.

Kermode, Jenny. 1998. *Medieval merchants: York, Beverley and Hull in the later Middle Ages*. Cambridge: Cambridge University Press.

Kirby, Joan. 1998. "Gentry households and the concept of service in the later Middle Ages." *Medieval Life* 9: 25–29.

Kitsikopoulos, H. 2000. "Standards of living and capital formation in pre-plague England: A peasant budget model." *Economic History Review* 53 (2): 237–261.

Klapisch-Zuber, Christiane. 1985. "Female celibacy and service in Florence in the fifteenth century." In *Women, family and ritual in Renaissance Italy*, ed. Christiane Klapisch-Zuber. Chicago: University of Chicago Press.

Klapisch-Zuber, Christiane. 2000. "Plague and family life." In *The new Cambridge medieval history*. Vol. 6, *c .1300–c. 1415*, ed. M. Jones. Cambridge: Cambridge University Press.

Klapisch-Zuber, Christiane. 1986. "Women servants in Florence during the fourteenth and fifteenth centuries." In *Women and work in preindustrial Europe*, ed. Barbara A. Hanawalt. Bloomington: Indiana University Press.

Kowaleski, Maryanne, and Judith M. Bennett. 1988–1989. "Crafts, gilds and women in the Middle Ages: Fifty years after Marian K. Dale." *Signs* 14 (2): 481–483.

Kristensson, G. 1974. *John Mirk's instructions for parish priests*. Lund: C. W. K. Gleerup.

Krötzl, Christian. 1989. "Parent-child relations in medieval Scandinavia according to Scandinavian miracle collections." *Scandinavian Journal of History* 14 (1): 21–37.

Kuehn, T. 1991. *Law, family and women: Toward a legal anthropology of Renaissance Italy*. Chicago: University of Chicago Press.

Kussmaul, A. 1981. *Servants in husbandry in early modern husbandry*. Cambridge: Cambridge University Press.

Labarge, Margaret. 1965. *A baronial household of the thirteenth century*. London: Eyre and Spottiswoode.

Ladurie, Emmanuel Le Roy. 1980. *Montaillou: Cathars and Catholics in a French village, 1294–1324*. Translated by Barbara Bray. Harmondsworth: Penguin.

Ladurie, Emmanuel Le Roy. 1978. *Montaillou: The promised land of error*. Translated by Barbara Bray. New York: Random House.

Ladurie, Emmanuel Le Roy. 1974. *The peasants of Languedoc*. Translated by John Day. Urbana: University of Illinois Press.

Lafuente, Pilar. 2007a. "The Andalusian house." In *The archaeology of medieval Europe*. Vol. 1, *Eighth to twelfth centuries AD*, eds. James Graham-Campbell with Magdalena Valor. Aarhus, Denmark: Aarhus University Press.

Lafuente, Pilar. 2007b. "Food. Part 1: The south." In *The archaeology of medieval Europe*. Vol. 1, *Eighth to twelfth centuries AD*, eds. James Graham-Campbell with Magdalena Valor. Aarhus, Denmark: Aarhus University Press.

Laiou-Thomadakis, A. E. 1977. *Peasant society in the late Byzantine empire: A social and demographic study*. Princeton, NJ: Princeton University Press.

Le Goff, Jacques. 1988. *Medieval civilization 400–1500*. Translated by Julia Barrow. Oxford: Basil Blackwell.

Leahy, Kevin. 2003. *Anglo-Saxon crafts*. Stroud: Tempus.

Lemay, Helen. 1978. "Arabic influence on medieval attitudes toward infancy." *Clio Medica* 13 (1): 1–12.

Lemay, Helen. 1992. *Women's secrets: A translation of Pseudo-Albertus Magnus De secretis mulierum with commentaries*. Saratoga Springs: State University of New York Press.

Lett, Didier. 1997a. "De l'eerrance au Deuil: Les enfants morts sans baptème et la naissance du limbe puerorum aux xiie–xiiie siècles." In *La petite enfance dans l'Europe médiévale et moderne*, ed. Robert Fossier. Toulouse: Presses Universitaires du Mirail.

Lett, Didier. 1997b. *L'enfant des miracles: Enfance et société au Moyen Age (xiie–xiiie siècle)*. Paris: Aubier.

Lewis, Mary. 2002. *Urbanisation and child health in medieval and post-medieval England: An assessment of the morbidity and mortality of non-adult skeletons from the cemeteries of two urban and two rural sites in England (AD 850–1859)*. Oxford: Archaeopress.

Leyser, Henrietta. 1995. *Medieval women: A social history of women in England, 450–1500*. London: Weidenfeld and Nicolson.

Leyser, K. J. 1979. *Rule and conflict in an early medieval society*. London: Arnold.

Lloyd-Morgan, Ceridwen. 1998. "More written about than writing? Welsh women and the written word." In *Literacy in medieval Celtic societies*, ed. Huw Pryce. Cambridge: Cambridge University Press.

Lock, Ray, ed. 1998. *The court rolls of Walsham le Willows 1303–50*. Suffolk Records Society, 41.

Lorcin, Marie-Thérèse. 1981. *Vivre et mourir en Lyonnais à la fin du Moyen Age*. Paris: Editions du CNRS.

Loschky, David, and Ben D. Childers. 1993. "Early English mortality." *Journal of Interdisciplinary History* 24 (1): 85–97.

Lucas, H. S. 1962. "The great European famine of 1315, 1316 and 1317." In *Essays in economic history*, Vol. 2, ed. E. Carus-Wilson. London: Arnold.

Luscombe, David. 2004. "Thought and learning." In *The new Cambridge medieval history*. Vol. 4, *c. 1024–1198*, eds. David Luscombe and Jonathan Riley-Smith. Cambridge: Cambridge University Press.

Lutterbach, Hubertus. 2003. 'Der Zivilisationsgeschichtliche Beitrag der frühmittelalterlichen Bussbücher zum christlichen Kinderschutz." *Historisches Jahrbuch* 123: 3–25.

Lynch, Joseph H. 1986. *Godparents and kinship in early medieval Europe*. Princeton, NJ: Princeton University Press.

Lynn Martin, A. 2001. "Old people, alcohol and identity in Europe 1300–1700." In *Food, drink and identity: Cooking, eating and drinking in Europe since the Middle Ages*, ed. P. Scholliers. Oxford: Berg.

MacLehose, William F. forthcoming. "The holy tooth: Dentition, child development and the cult of the Christ child." In *The Christ child: Collected essays*, ed. Mary Dzon. Toronto: University of Toronto Press.

MacLehose, William F. 2006. *A tender age: Cultural anxieties over the child in the twelfth and thirteenth centuries*. New York: Columbia University Press.

Madureira Franco, Isabel M. 2003. "Les dynamiques familiales et sociales dans un village de Pêcheurs des environs de Porto (1449–1497)." In *The medieval household in Christian Europe c. 850–c. 1550: Managing power, wealth and the body*, eds. Cordelia Beattie et al. Turnhout, Belgium: Brepols.

Makdisi, George. 1981. *The rise of colleges: Institutions of learning in Islam and the West*. Edinburgh: Edinburgh University Press.

Makdisi, George. 1990. *The rise of humanism in classical Islam and the Christian West*. Edinburgh: Edinburgh University Press.

Marcus, Ivan G. 1996. *Rituals of childhood: Jewish acculturation in medieval Europe*. New Haven, CT: Yale University Press.

Martin McLaughlin, Mary. 2004. "Survivors and surrogates: Children and parents from the ninth to the thirteenth centuries." In *Medieval families: Perspectives on marriage, household and children*, ed. Carol Neel. Toronto: University of Toronto Press.

Matthæi Parisiensis, monachi Sancti Albani. [d. 1259] 1872–1883. *Chronica Majora*. Edited by H. R. Luard. London: Rolls Series. 7 vols.

Mayno of Milan. [ca. 1330] 1502. *Regimen sanitatis Magnini Mediolanensis.* Lyon: François Fradin.

Mays, Simon. 1998. *The archaeology of human bones.* London: Routledge.

McCarthy, Conor. 2004. *Marriage in medieval England: Law, literature and practice.* Woodbridge: Boydell Press.

McCarthy, Conor, ed. and trans. 2004. *Love, sex and marriage in the Middle Ages: A sourcebook.* London: Routledge.

McEvoy, James. 1981. "Notes of the prologue of St Aelred of Rievaulx's *De spirituali amicitia* with a translation." *Traditio* 37: 396–411.

McFarlane, K. B. 1973. *The nobility of later medieval England.* Oxford: Clarendon Press.

McKitterick, Rosamond. 2005. "The Carolingian renaissance." In *Charlemagne: Empire and society,* ed. J. Story. Manchester: Manchester University Press.

McKitterick, Rosamond. 1989. *The Carolingians and the written word.* Cambridge: Cambridge University Press.

McKitterick, Rosamond. 2003. "Continuity and innovation in tenth-century Ottonian culture." In *Intellectual life in the Middle Ages: Essays presented to Margaret Gibson,* eds. Lesley Smith and Benedicta Ward. London: Hambledon Continuum.

McKitterick, Rosamond. 1976. "A ninth-century schoolbook from the Loire Valley: Phillipps MS 16308." *Scriptorium* 30 (2): 225–231.

Meale, Carol M. 1996. "'... alle the bokes that I haue of latyn, englisch and frensch': Laywomen and their books in late medieval England." In *Women and literature in Britain, 1150–1500,* ed. Carol M. Meale. Cambridge: Cambridge University Press.

Meens, Rob. 1994. "Children and confession." In *The church and childhood,* ed. Diana Wood. Studies in Church History 31. Oxford: Blackwell.

Melo, A. Sousa. 2003. "Women and work in the household economy: The social and linguistic evidence from Porto, c. 1340–1450." In *The medieval household in Christian Europe, c. 850–c. 1550: Managing power, wealth and the body,* eds. Cordelia Beattie et al. Turnhout, Belgium: Brepols.

Menant, F. 2005a. *L'Italie des communes (1100–1350).* Paris: Belin.

Menant, F. 2005b. "Comment le marché de la terre est devenu un thème pour les historiens du Moyen Age." In *Le marché de la terre au Moyen Age,* eds. L. Feller and C. Wickham. Rome: L'Ecole française de Rome.

Menuge, Noël J. 2000. "A few home truths: The medieval mother as guardian in romance and law." In *Medieval women and the law,* ed. Noël J. Menuge. Woodbridge: Boydell Press.

Miller, Timothy S. 2003. *The orphans of Byzantium: Child welfare in the Christian empire.* Washington, DC: Catholic University of America Press.

Mitchell, Linda E. 2007. *Family life in the Middle Ages.* Westport, CT: Greenwood Press.

Moisà, Maria. 1997. "Waste and pilfering: Competing for the scraps in the black economy of the medieval poor." *Medieval Life* 7: 19–25.

Monumenta Germaniae Historica Poetae 1. 1881. Edited by Ernst Dümmler. Berlin: Weidmann.

Moore, R. I. 1987. *The formation of a persecuting society.* Oxford: Blackwell.

Morgan, Nigel. 1993. "Texts and images of Marian devotion in fourteenth-century England." In *England in the fourteenth century,* ed. Nicholas Rogers. Stamford: Harlaxton Medieval Studies, 3.

Mosher-Stuard, Susan. 2006. *Gilding the market: Luxury and fashion in fourteenth-century Italy.* Philadelphia: University of Pennsylvania Press.

Murray, Alexander. 1978. *Reason and society in the Middle Ages.* Oxford: Clarendon Press.

Murray, Jacqueline. 1995. "Thinking about gender: The diversity of medieval perspectives." In *Power of the weak: Studies on medieval women,* eds. Jennifer Carpenter and Sally-Beth MacLean. Urbana and Chicago: University of Illinois Press.

Murray, Jacqueline, ed. 2001. *Love, marriage and family in the Middle Ages.* Peterborough, ON: Broadview Press.

Nagy, Balázs, and Frank Schaer, eds. 2001. *Autobiography of Emperor Charles IV and his legend of St Wenceslas.* Budapest: Central European University Press.

Nardi, G. M. 1938. *Problemi d'embriologia umana antica e medioevale.* Florence: Sansoni.

Nelson, Janet L. 1994. "Parents, children, and the church in the earlier Middle Ages." In *The church and childhood,* ed. Diana Wood. Studies in Church History 31. Oxford: Blackwell.

Nicholas, David. 1995. "Child and adolescent labour in the late medieval city: A Flemish model in regional perspective." *English Historical Review* 110: 1107–1114.

Nicholas, David. 1985. *The domestic life of a medieval city: Women, children and the family in fourteenth-century Ghent.* Lincoln: University of Nebraska Press.

Nicholas, David. 1987. *The metamorphosis of a medieval city: Ghent in the age of the Arteveldes, 1302–90.* Lincoln: University of Nebraska Press.

Nichols, J. 1780. *A collection of all the wills of the kings and queens of England.* London.

Nightingale, Pamela. 2005. "Some new evidence of crises and trends of mortality in late medieval England." *Past and Present* 187: 33–68.

Nirenberg, David. 1996. *Communities of violence: Persecution of minorities in the Middle Ages.* Princeton, NJ: Princeton University Press.

Nolan, Kathleen. 1996. "*Ploratus et ululatus:* The mothers in the massacre of the innocents at Chartres Cathedral." *Studies in Iconography* 17: 95–141.

O'Connell, David. 1979. *The instructions of Saint Louis: A critical text.* Chapel Hill: University of North Carolina Press.

Oosterwijk, Sophie. 2008. "The medieval child: An unknown phenomenon?" In *Misconceptions about the Middle Ages,* eds. Stephen J. Harris and Bryon Lee Grigsby. New York: Routledge.

Oosterwijk, Sophie. 2003. "'A swithe feire Graue': The appearance of children on medieval tomb monuments." In *Family and dynasty in late medieval England,* eds. Richard Eales and Shaun Tyas. Donington: Shaun Tyas.

Orderic Vitalis. [d. ca. 1142] 1969–1980. *The ecclesiastical history of Orderic Vitalis.* Edited and translated by Marjorie Chibnall. 6 vols. Oxford: Clarendon Press.

Orme, Nicholas. 1994. "Children and the church in medieval England." *Journal of Ecclesiastical History* 45: 571–582.

Orme, Nicholas. 1995. "The culture of children in medieval England." *Past and Present* 148: 51–64.

Orme, Nicholas. 1984. *From childhood to chivalry: The education of the English kings and aristocracy 1066–1530*. London: Methuen.

Orme, Nicholas. 2001. *Medieval children*. New Haven, CT: Yale University Press.

Orme, Nicholas. 2006. *Medieval schools: From Roman Britain to Renaissance England*. New Haven, CT: Yale University Press.

Owen-Crocker, Gale R. 2004. *Dress in Anglo-Saxon England*. Woodbridge: Boydell Press.

Owen-Hughes, Diane. 2004. "Domestic ideals and social behaviour: Evidence from medieval Genoa." In *Medieval families: Perspectives on marriage, household and children*, ed. Carol Neel. Toronto: University of Toronto Press.

Passalacqua, V. T. 1959. "La 'Practica Puerorum' di Rhazes." *Pagine di storia della medicina* 3: 26–53.

Patlagean, Evelyne. 1973. "L'enfant et son avenir dans la famille byzantine." *Annales de démographie historique*, 85–93.

Pearson, Sarah. 2007. "Rural and urban houses 1100–1500: "'Urban adaptation' reconsidered." In *Town and country in the Middle Ages: Contacts, contrasts and interconnections, 1100–1500*, eds. Kate Giles and Christopher Dyer. Leeds: Maney.

Pfister, U. 1995. "The proto-industrial household economy: Toward a formal Analysis." In *The European peasant family and society: Historical studies*, ed. R. L. Rudolph. Liverpool: Liverpool University Press.

Pollock, Frederick, and Frederic William Maitland. 1911. *The history of English law before the time of Edward I*. 2 vols. Cambridge: Cambridge University Press.

Poos, L. R. 1991. *A rural society after the Black Death: Essex 1350–1525*. Cambridge: Cambridge University Press.

Poos, L. R. 1994–1995. "Sex, lies and the church courts of pre-Reformation England." *Journal of Interdisciplinary History* 25: 585–607.

Postan, M. M. 1973a. "The charters of the villeins." In *Essays on medieval agriculture and general problems of the medieval economy*, ed. M. M. Postan. Cambridge: Cambridge University Press.

Postan, M. M. 1973b. "Some social consequences of the Hundred Years War." In *Essays on medieval agriculture and general problems of the medieval economy*, ed. M. M. Postan. Cambridge: Cambridge University Press.

Prestwich, J. O. 2004. "Orderic Vitalis." *Oxford dictionary of national biography*, 41. Oxford: Oxford University Press.

Pullan, Brian. 1988. "Support and redeem: Charity and poor relief in Italian cities from the fourteenth to the seventeenth century." *Continuity and Change* 3: 177–208.

Quinn, Patricia A. 1989. *Better than the sons of kings: Boys and monks in the early Middle Ages*. New York: Peter Lang.

The Qur'an. 2005 edition. Translated by Muhammad Abdel Haleem. New York: Oxford University Press.

Raftis, J. A. 1996. *Peasant economic development within the English manorial system*. Montreal: McGill-Queen's University Press.

Rawcliffe, Carol. 1984. "The hospitals of later medieval London." *Medical History* 28 (1): 1–21.

Raymond of Capua. [d. 1399] 2003. *The life of St Catherine of Siena*. Translated by George Lamb. London: Harvill Press.

Razi, Zvi. 1980. *Life, marriage and death in a medieval parish: Economy, society and demography in Halesowen, 1270–1400*. Cambridge: Cambridge University Press.

Razi, Zvi. 1993. "The myth of the immutable English family." *Past and Present* 140: 3–44.

Rebel, H. 1998. "Peasantries under the Austrian Empire, 1300–1800." In *The peasantries of Europe from the fourteenth to the eighteenth centuries*, ed. T. Scott. Harlow: Longman.

Reeves, Compton. 2000. "The sumptuary statute of 1363: A look at the aims and effectiveness of English legislation on diet and clothing." *Medieval Life* 16: 16–19.

Regula Benedicti, La régle de Saint Benoît. [sixth century] 1972. Edited by Adalbert de Vogüé and Jean Neufville. Sources Chrétiennes 181–182. Paris: Editions du Cerf.

Reyerson, Kathryn L. 1992. "The adolescent apprentice/worker in medieval Montpellier." *Journal of Family History* 17 (4): 355–366.

Reynolds, Philip L. 2006. "The infants of Eden: Scholastic theologians on early childhood and cognitive development." *Mediaeval Studies* 68: 89–132.

Rheubottom, David. 2000. *Age, marriage, and politics in fifteenth-century Ragusa*. Oxford: Oxford University Press.

Richards, Jeffrey. 1990. *Sex, dissidence and damnation: Minority groups in the Middle Ages*. London: Routledge.

Richards, Julian D. 2004. *Viking Age England*. Stroud: Tempus.

Riché, Pierre. 1993. *The Carolingians: A family who forged Europe*. Translated by Michael Idomir Allen. Philadelphia: University of Pennsylvania Press.

Riché, Pierre. 1989. *Ecoles et enseignement dans le haut Moyen Age: De la fin du ve siècle—milieu du xie siècle*. Paris: Picard.

Riddle, John M. 1992. *Contraception and abortion from the ancient world to the Renaissance*. Cambridge, MA: Harvard University Press.

Riddle, John M. 1991. "Oral contraceptives and early-term abortifacients during classical antiquity and the Middle Ages." *Past and Present* 132: 3–32.

Riddy, Felicity. 1996. "Mother knows best: Reading social change in a courtesy text." *Speculum* 71: 70–83.

Riikonen, Jaana. 2007. "Women's costume in south-western Finland from grave goods." In *The archaeology of medieval Europe*. Vol. 1, *Eighth to twelfth centuries AD*, eds. James Graham-Campbell with Magdalena Valor. Aarhus, Denmark: Aarhus University Press.

Robertson, Anne Walters. 1991. *The service-books of the Royal Abbey of Saint-Denis*. Oxford: Clarendon Press.

Roesdahl, Else, and Barbara Scholkmann. 2007. "Housing culture." In *The archaeology of medieval Europe*. Vol. 1, *Eighth to twelfth centuries AD*, eds. James Graham-Campbell, with Magdalena Valor. Aarhus, Denmark: Aarhus University Press.

Röhrkasten, Jens. 2001. "Trends of mortality in late medieval London, 1348–1400." *Nottingham Mediaeval Studies* 45: 172–209.

Romano, Dennis. 1996. *Housecraft and statecraft: Domestic service in Renaissance Venice, 1400–1600*. Baltimore: Johns Hopkins University Press.

Rosenthal, Franz. 1952. "Child psychology in Islam." *Islamic Culture* 26: 1–22.

Rosenthal, Joel T. 1973. "Medieval longevity and the secular peerage, 1350–1500." *Population Studies* 27: 287–293.

Rothwell, Harry, ed. 1975. *English historical documents III, 1189–1327*. London: Eyre and Spottiswoode.

Rubin, Miri. 1999. *Gentile tales: The narrative assault on late medieval Jews*. New Haven, CT: Yale University Press.

Rubin, Miri. 1991. "Small groups: Identity and solidarity in the late Middle Ages." In *Enterprise and individuals in fifteenth-century England*, ed. J. Kermode. Stroud: Alan Sutton.

Salisbury, Joyce E. 1992. *Church fathers, independent virgins*. London: Verso.

Salisbury, Joyce E. 1996. "Gendered sexuality." In *Handbook of medieval sexuality*, eds. Vern L. Bullough and James A. Brundage. New York: Garland.

Santangeli Valenzani, Riccardo. 2007. "Rome." In *The archaeology of medieval Europe*. Vol. 1, *Eighth to twelfth centuries AD*, eds. James Graham-Campbell with Magdalena Valor. Aarhus, Denmark: Aarhus University Press.

Scase, Wendy. 1993. "St Anne and the education of the Virgin: Literary and artistic traditions and their implications." In *England in the fourteenth century*, ed. Nicholas Rogers. Stamford: Harlaxton Medieval Studies, 3.

Schmitt, Jean-Claude. 1983. *The holy greyhound*. Translated by Martin Thom. Cambridge: Cambridge University Press.

Schofield, John, and Alan Vince. 2003. *Medieval towns: The archaeology of British towns in their European setting*. London: Equinox.

Schofield, Phillipp R. 2003. *Peasant and community in medieval England 1200–1500*. Basingstoke: Palgrave Macmillan.

Schultz, James A. 1995. *The knowledge of childhood in the German Middle Ages, 1100–1350*. Philadelphia: University of Pennsylvania Press.

Schultz, James A. 1991. "Medieval adolescence: The claims of history and the silence of the German narrative." *Speculum* 66: 519–539.

Sears, Elizabeth. 1986. *The ages of man: Medieval interpretations of the life cycle*. Princeton, NJ: Princeton University Press.

Seymour, M. C., et al., eds. 1975. *On the properties of things: John Trevisa's translation of Bartholomaeus Anglicus De proprietatibus rerum: A critical text*. Oxford: Clarendon Press.

Shahar, S. 1990. *Childhood in the Middle Ages*. London: Routledge.

Shahar, S. 1983. *The fourth estate: A history of women in the Middle Ages*. London and New York: Methuen.

Sharpe, R. R., ed. 1913. *Calendar of coroners' rolls of the city of London, 1300–1378*. London: Richard Clay and Sons.

Shenton, Caroline. 2003. "Philippa of Hainault's churchings: The politics of motherhood at the court of Edward III." In *Family and dynasty in late medieval England*, eds. Richard Eales and Shaun Tyas. Donington: Shaun Tyas.

Smith, Julia M. H. 2005. *Europe after Rome: A new cultural history 500–1000*. Oxford: Oxford University Press.

Smith, R. M. 1991. "The manorial court and the elderly tenant in late medieval England." In *Life, death and the elderly: Historical perspectives,* eds. M. Pelling and R. M. Smith. London and New York: Routledge.

Smith, R. M. 1984. "Some issues concerning families and their property in rural England 1250–1800." In *Land, kinship and life-cycle,* ed. R. M. Smith. Cambridge: Cambridge University Press.

Sponsler, Claire. 1997. *Drama and resistance: Bodies, goods and theatricality in late medieval England.* Minneapolis: University of Minnesota Press.

Stafford, Pauline. 1998. "La mutation familiale: A suitable case for caution." In *The community, the family and the saint: Patterns of power in early medieval Europe,* eds. Joyce Hill and Mary Swan. Turnhout, Belgium: International Medieval Research, 4.

Stearns, Peter N. 2006. *Childhood in world history.* New York: Routledge.

Stingre, Didier. 1991. "La question de l'enfance malheureuse: Son approche hospitalière à Bordeaux du Moyen-Age au xixe siècle." *Bulletin de la société française d'histoire des hôpitaux* 65: 20–25.

Stortz, Martha Ellen. 2001. "'Where or when was your servant innocent?': Augustine on childhood." In *The child in Christian thought,* ed. Marcia J. Bunge. Grand Rapids, MI: Eerdmans.

Stouff, Louis. 1986. *Arles à la fin du Moyen-Age.* 2 vols. Aix-en-Provence: Université de Provence.

Stroppiana, Luigi. 1970. "Spunti di pediatria nel Corpus hippocraticum." *Rivista di Storia della Medicina* 14: 77–95.

Sudhoff, Karl. 1925. *Erstlinge der pädiatrischen Literatur.* Munich: Verlag der Münchner Drucke.

Sudhoff, Karl. 1915. "Nochmals Dr. Cornelius Roelants von Mecheln." *Janus* 20: 443–458.

Suger. [d. 1151] 1992. *The deeds of Louis the Fat.* Translated by Richard Cusimano and John Moorhead. Washington, DC: Catholic University of America Press.

Swanson, Jenny. 1990. "Childhood and childrearing in *ad status* sermons by later thirteenth century friars." *Journal of Medieval History* 16: 309–331.

Taglia, Kathryn Ann. 1998. "The cultural construction of childhood: Baptism, communion and confirmation." In *Women, marriage and family in medieval Christendom,* eds. Constance M. Rousseau and Joel T. Rosenthal. Kalamazoo: Medieval Institute Publications.

Taglia, Kathryn Ann. 2001. "Delivering a Christian identity: Midwives in northern French synodal legislation, 1200–1500." In *Religion and medicine in the Middle Ages,* eds. Peter Biller and Joseph Ziegler. Woodbridge: York Medieval Press.

Temkin, Owsei. 1956. *Soranus' Gynaecology.* Baltimore: Johns Hopkins University Press.

Thomas of Cantimpré. [d. 1272] 1973. *Liber de natura rerum.* Edited by Helmut Boese. Berlin and New York: Walter de Gruyter.

Thompson, Victoria. 2004. *Dying and death in later Anglo-Saxon England.* Woodbridge: Boydell & Brewer.

Thorner, D., et al., eds. 1986. *A. V. Chayanov on the theory of peasant economy.* Madison: University of Wisconsin Press.

Thorpe, L., ed. and trans. 1969. *Einhard and Notker the Stammerer: Two lives of Charlemagne.* Harmondsworth: Penguin.

Thrupp, Sylvia L. 1948. *The merchant class of mediaeval London, 1300–1500.* Chicago: University of Chicago Press.

Tierney, B. 1959. *Medieval poor law: A sketch of canonical theory and its application in England.* Berkeley and Los Angeles: University of California Press.

Tilly, L. A., and J. W. Scott. 1989. *Women, work and family.* Abingdon: Routledge.

Tobin, Frank, ed. 1989. *Henry Suso: The exemplar with two German sermons.* New York: Paulist Press.

To Figueras, L. 1997. *Familia i hereu a la Catalunya Nord-Oriental (segles x-xii).* Barcelona: l'Abadia de Montserrat.

Traina, Cristina L. H. 2001. "A person in the making: Thomas Aquinas on children and childhood." In *The child in Christian thought,* ed. Marcia J. Bunge. Grand Rapids, MI: Eerdmans.

The trial of Joan of Arc. [fifteenth century] 2005. Translated by Daniel Hobbins. Cambridge, MA: Harvard University Press.

Turnau, Irena 1983. The diffusion of knitting in medieval Europe. In *Cloth and clothing in medieval Europe: Essays in memory of Professor E. M. Carus-Wilson,* eds. N. B. Harte, E. M. Carus-Wilson, and Kenneth G. Ponting. London: Heinemann Educational Books.

Van Gennep, Arnold. 1960. *The rites of passage.* Translated by Monika B. Vizedom and Gabrielle L. Caffee. London: Routledge.

Verger, Jacques. 1999. "The universities and scholasticism." In *The new Cambridge medieval history.* Vol. 5, *c. 1198–c. 1300,* ed. D. Abulafia. Cambridge: Cambridge University Press.

Vésteinsson, Orri. 2007. "The Icelandic house." In *The archaeology of medieval Europe.* Vol. 1, *Eighth to twelfth centuries AD,* eds. James Graham-Campbell with Magdalena Valor. Aarhus, Denmark: Aarhus University Press.

Vico, Romana Martorelli. 2002. *Medicina e filosofia: Per una storia dell'embriologia medievale nel xiii e xiv secolo.* Milan: Guerini e Associati.

Vincent of Beauvais. [d. 1264] 1938. *De eruditione filiorum nobilium.* Edited by Arpad Steiner. Cambridge, MA: Medieval Academy of America, 32.

Vincent of Beauvais. [d. 1264] 1964. "Speculum naturale." In *Speculum Quadruplex sive Speculum Maius.* Graz: Akademische Druck- und Verlagsanstalt.

Vincent, Nicholas. 1996. *Peter des Roches: An alien in English politics 1205–1238.* Cambridge: Cambridge University Press.

Vita Liutbirgae Virginis. [ninth century] 1937. Translated by Ottokar Menzel. *Monumenta Germaniae Historica Deutsches Mittelalter Kritische Studientexte* 3. Leipzig: Karl W. Hiersemann.

Voaden, Rosalynn, and Stephanie Volf. 2000. "Visions of my youth: Representations of the childhood of medieval visionaries." *Gender and History* 12: 665–684.

Ward, Jennifer C. 1997. "English noblewomen and the local community in the later Middle Ages." In *Medieval women in their communities,* ed. Diane Watt. Cardiff: University of Wales Press.

Ward, Jennifer C. 2006. *Women in England in the Middle Ages.* London: Hambledon Continuum.

Ward, Jennifer C. 2002. *Women in medieval Europe 1200–1500.* London: Pearson.

Watkins, R. N., trans. 1969. *Leon Battista Alberti, the family in Renaissance Florence.* Columbia: University of South Carolina Press.

Watt, Diane, ed. 1997. *Medieval women in their communities.* Cardiff: University of Wales Press.

Waugh, Scott L. 1988. *The lordship of England: Royal wardships and marriages in English society and politics, 1217–1327.* Princeton, NJ: Princeton University Press.

Webb, Diana M. 1994. "Friends of the family: Some miracles for children by Italian friars." In *The church and childhood,* ed. Diana Wood. Studies in Church History 31. Oxford: Blackwell.

Wensky, Margret. 1982. "Women's guilds in Cologne in the later Middle Ages." *Journal of European Economic History* 11 (3): 631–650.

Wertheimer, Laura. 2006. "Children of disorder: Clerical parentage, illegitimacy, and reform in the Middle Ages." *Journal of the History of Sexuality* 15 (3): 382–407.

Whitelock, Dorothy, ed. 1968. *English historical documents I, c. 500–1042.* London: Eyre and Spottiswoode.

Whitelock, Dorothy, et al., eds. 1981. *Councils and synods with other documents relating to the English church.* 2 vols. Oxford: Clarendon Press.

Wickham, C. 2005. *Framing the early Middle Ages: Europe and the Mediterranean, 400–800.* Oxford: Oxford University Press.

Wilkinson, Louise J. 2003. "The *Rules* of Robert Grosseteste reconsidered: The lady as estate and household manager in thirteenth-century England." In *The medieval household in Christian Europe, c. 850–c. 1550: Managing power, wealth and the body,* eds. Cordelia Beattie et al. Turnhout, Belgium: Brepols.

William of Conches. [1080–ca. 1150]. "De philosophia mundi." *Patrologia Latina* 176 (89).

William of Conches. [1080–ca. 1150] 1997. *Dragmaticon philosophiae.* Edited by I. Ronca. Notre Dame, IN: University of Notre Dame Press.

William of Saliceto. [1280s] 1476. *Summa conservationis et curationis.* Piacenza: J. P. de Ferratis.

Wilson, Adrian. 1980. "The infancy of the history of childhood: An appraisal of Philippe Ariès." *History and Theory* 19 (2): 132–153.

Wilson, Katharina M. 1998. *Hrotsvit of Gandersheim: A florilegium of her works.* Woodbridge: Boydell Press.

Woodbine, George E., ed., and Samuel E. Thorne, trans. 1968. *Bracton de legibus et consuetudinibus Angliae: Bracton on the laws and customs of England.* 4 vols. Cambridge, MA: Belknap Press of Harvard University Press in association with the Selden Society.

Wood-Legh, K. L. 1956. *A small household of the fifteenth century.* Manchester: Manchester University Press.

Woolgar, C. M. 1999. *The great household in late medieval England.* New Haven, CT, and London: Yale University Press.

Woolgar, C. M., D. Serjeantson, and T. Waldron, T., eds. 2006. *Food in medieval England: Diet and nutrition.* Oxford: Oxford University Press.

Wright, Craig M. 1989. *Music and ceremony at Notre Dame de Paris, 500–1550.* Cambridge: Cambridge University Press.

Youngs, Deborah. 2006. *The life cycle in Western Europe, c. 1300–c. 1500.* Manchester: Manchester University Press.

Zika, C. 1988. "Hosts, processions and pilgrimages: Controlling the sacred in fifteenth-century Germany." *Past and Present* 118: 38–43.

CONTRIBUTORS

Sophia Adams lectures in archaeology at Canterbury Christ Church University. Her archaeological career has included academic and commercial work in the United Kingdom, Scandinavia, Mali, and the Caribbean, covering a range of periods from prehistoric to postmedieval. She is the current holder of an Arts and Humanities Research Council collaborative doctorate award based at the British Museum and the University of Leicester, working on a study of late Hallstatt and early-middle La Tène brooches in Britain.

Carol Bargeron is associate professor of history in the Department of Humanities at Central State University in Ohio. She specializes in the intellectual and social history of the Muslim world in the medieval and modern periods. Her work has appeared in *Theology and Science, Medieval Encounters,* and other scholarly publications. She most recently contributed an extended literary biographical essay on the Sudanese Muslim intellectual, Hasan al-Turabi to the *Dictionary of Literary Biography*, vol. 346 (2009), which was devoted to twentieth-century Arab writers. Her current research project focuses on concepts of identity among the Arab young.

Valerie L. Garver is assistant professor of history at Northern Illinois University. In addition to recent articles on Carolingian childhood and women, she is the author of *Women and Aristocratic Culture in the Carolingian World* (Cornell University Press, 2009). Currently, she is working on a book project tentatively entitled *The Meanings and Functions of Textiles in the Carolingian World.*

P. J. P. Goldberg is a reader in medieval history at the University of York. He has published extensively on gender, sexuality, and the family. Most recently, he has published *Communal Discord, Child Abduction and Rape in the Later Middle Ages* (Palgrave, 2008) and has edited *Medieval Domesticity: Home, Housing and Household in Medieval England* (with Maryanne Kowaleski; Cambridge University Press, 2008) and *Richard Scrope: Archbishop, Rebel, Martyr* (Shaun Tyas, 2007).

Richard Huscroft teaches history at Westminster School in London. His principal area of interest is the political and constitutional history of thirteenth-century England. His publications include *Ruling England, 1042–1216* (Pearson Education, 2004), *Expulsion: England's Jewish Solution* (Tempus, 2006), and *The Norman Conquest: A New Introduction* (Longman, 2009).

William F. MacLehose is lecturer in medieval medicine at the Wellcome Trust Centre for the History of Medicine at University College London. His primary research interest lies in the intersections of medicine, religion, and morality in the central Middle Ages. To date, he has focused on the history of embryology, maternity, and child care in the Greco-Arabic tradition of the medieval West. He is the author of *A Tender Age: Cultural Anxieties over the Child in the Twelfth and Thirteenth Centuries* (Columbia University Press, 2008).

Phillipp R. Schofield is professor of medieval history, Aberystwyth University. His research explores the nature of rural society in the high and late Middle Ages, including the use of law and litigation. His publications include *Peasant and Community in Medieval England, 1200–1500* (Palgrave, 2002). He is presently preparing (with C. Briggs of Cambridge University) a volume for the Selden Society on interpersonal action in manorial courts.

Jennifer C. Ward taught medieval and regional history at Goldsmiths College, University of London, for most of her career. Her research has concentrated on women's history in the Middle Ages; her books include *English Noblewomen in the Later Middle Ages* (Longman, 1992), *Women in Medieval Europe 1200–1500* (2002), and *Women in England in the Middle Ages* (Hambledon Continuum, 2006).

Louise J. Wilkinson is a senior lecturer in medieval history at Canterbury Christ Church University. She is the author of *Women in Thirteenth-Century Lincolnshire* (The Royal Historical Society, 2007) and editor, with Liz Oakley-Brown, of *The Rituals and Rhetoric of Queenship: Medieval to Early Modern* (Four Courts Press, 2009). Her research focuses on women and families in the twelfth and thirteenth centuries. She is currently writing a monograph on Eleanor, the sister of King Henry III and wife of Simon de Montfort, earl of Leicester.

Deborah Youngs is a lecturer in medieval history at Swansea University. Her interests lie in the social and cultural history of late medieval Europe with a particular focus on the aging process. She has published *The Life Cycle in Western Europe, c .1300–c. 1500* (Manchester University Press, 2006) and is currently developing a study on medieval adulthood.

INDEX

Printed in Great Britain
by Amazon

86011318R00149